TABLE OF CONTENTS

Top 20 Test Taking Tips

1. Carefully follow all the test registration procedures
2. Know the test directions, duration, topics, question types, how many questions
3. Setup a flexible study schedule at least 3-4 weeks before test day
4. Study during the time of day you are most alert, relaxed, and stress free
5. Maximize your learning style; visual learner use visual study aids, auditory learner use auditory study aids
6. Focus on your weakest knowledge base
7. Find a study partner to review with and help clarify questions
8. Practice, practice, practice
9. Get a good night's sleep; don't try to cram the night before the test
10. Eat a well balanced meal
11. Know the exact physical location of the testing site; drive the route to the site prior to test day
12. Bring a set of ear plugs; the testing center could be noisy
13. Wear comfortable, loose fitting, layered clothing to the testing center; prepare for it to be either cold or hot during the test
14. Bring at least 2 current forms of ID to the testing center
15. Arrive to the test early; be prepared to wait and be patient
16. Eliminate the obviously wrong answer choices, then guess the first remaining choice
17. Pace yourself; don't rush, but keep working and move on if you get stuck
18. Maintain a positive attitude even if the test is going poorly
19. Keep your first answer unless you are positive it is wrong
20. Check your work, don't make a careless mistake

Personal Health and Development

Nutrients

Processing nutrients

Every human body needs the same nutrients to build bones, muscles, and other tissues, and to give it energy. These nutrients are proteins, carbohydrates, fats, vitamins, minerals, and water. Nutrients are converted into whatever the body needs through the process of digestion. During the digestive process, each organ either mechanically or chemically breaks down food into molecular units that are small enough to be absorbed by the cells of the body. There have been thousands of experiments conducted to determine the right amount of nutrients for a particular population. Epidemiological studies are those that focus on the diet of a particular group of people, while metabolic studies are those that consider the processing of a particular nutrient during animal or human metabolism.

Six kinds of nutrients

There are six kinds of nutrients: proteins, carbohydrates, fats, vitamins, minerals, and water. Proteins, known as the building blocks of the body, are used to grow, maintain, and replace the cells of the body. Carbohydrates are the organic compounds that supply the body with glucose. Simple carbohydrates are referred to as sugars, and complex carbohydrates are called starches. Fats provide energy to the body and help to transport certain vitamins. Minerals are any naturally occurring inorganic elements that are needed in very small amounts so that the body can perform some function. Finally, water is perhaps the most overlooked nutrient, but it is crucial for promoting good digestion and for maintaining body fluids and temperature.

United States Department of Agriculture Nutrition

In order to aid Americans in eating a healthy diet, the United States Department of Agriculture has developed a set of Recommended Daily Allowances that indicate how much of a certain food a person should eat every day. They have also issued a number of guidelines to help with dietary choices. For one thing, they encourage people to eat a wide variety of foods, including plenty of fruits, vegetables, and whole grains. Sugar, salt, and alcoholic beverages should be consumed in moderation. A healthy diet will be low in saturated fat and cholesterol, as these increase the risk of heart disease and cancer. Maintaining a healthy weight throughout life reduces the risk of high blood pressure, heart disease, and stroke.

USDA Food Guide Pyramid

In 1992, the USDA introduced the Food Guide Pyramid as a handy illustration of proper dietary guidelines. There are five components to the food pyramid, and the body requires them in varying amounts. The five groups are as follows: bread, cereal, rice and pasta (6-11 servings); vegetables (3-5 servings); fruits (2-4 servings); milk, yogurt, and cheese (2-3); meat, poultry, fish, eggs, dry beans, and nuts (2-3 servings); and fats, oils, and sweets (less than a serving). Foods in one group cannot substitute for those in another. One of the more controversial aspects of the Food Guide Pyramid was its emphasis on minimizing meat consumption; according to the USDA, the maximum daily intake of protein should only be five to seven ounces.

Recommended daily allowances

The USDA recommends that Americans have between six and eleven servings a day of breads, cereal, rice, and pasta. These foods are considered to be fundamental to a healthy diet because they contain plenty of simple and complex carbohydrates, the latter of which contain plenty of vitamins and minerals. Complex carbohydrates ought to represent about half of an individual's daily consumption. A typical serving from this group could be a slice of toast, or a half-cup of pasta or rice. Brown rice and whole-grain breads and pasta are considered to be the best way to get all the nutrients from a serving. One should also ensure that one is getting plenty of fiber by eating whole-grain or fiber-enriched white bread.

The USDA recommends that individuals have between three and five servings of vegetables every day. Vegetables are low in fat and high in fiber, and provide essential vitamins and minerals. Numerous studies have shown a link between vegetables and a diminished risk of almost every kind of cancer. A single serving of a vegetable can be as little as one cup of a raw, leafy vegetable (like spinach or kale), a half-cup of any other vegetable, three-quarters of a cup of vegetable juice, or one potato or ear of corn. It is best to eat a wide variety of vegetables. Crucifers (winter squash, carrots, broccoli, cabbage, etc.) are high in fiber and vitamins, whereas dark green vegetables like collards and mustard greens are a good source of calcium and iron.

The USDA recommends that every person eat between two and four servings of fruit every day. Fruits, along with whole grains and vegetables, are a good source of vitamins, minerals, and fiber. They have also been proven to be a good safeguard against cancer; in fact, people who eat very little produce have been shown to demonstrate twice as much chance of developing cancer. A serving of fruit may be as little as a medium apple, banana, or orange, a half-cup of sliced or canned fruit, or three-quarters of a cup of fresh fruit juice. Since fruits require different digestive acids than most foods, they are most easily digested when they are consumed on an empty stomach or before the rest of a meal.

The USDA recommends that every person have between two and four servings of meat, poultry, fish, dry beans, eggs, and nuts. All of these foods are excellent sources of protein,

which the body needs to build muscle and bone. These foods also have a high supply of phosphorus, zinc, iron, vitamin B-6, and niacin. One serving from this category may consist of as little as two or three ounces of lean meat, fish, or poultry, an egg, or a half cup of dry beans. It is a good idea to eat a wide variety of foods from this category, as many of them are high in fat. Fish, in particular, is a healthy alternative to beef or pork, as it is extremely high in protein and loaded with vitamins and minerals.

The USDA recommends that each individual consumes two or three servings of milk, yogurt, and cheese every day. All milk products are high in calcium, riboflavin, protein, and vitamins A and B-12. One should be careful when selecting foods from this group, as many dairy products are very high in fat. A serving in this category can be an eight ounce glass of milk, a cup of plain yogurt, one and a half ounces of cheese, or one tablespoon of cheese spread. Obviously, it is healthier to have a glass of skim milk than to reach one's daily ration of dairy by eating cheese spread. Cottage cheese is an especially healthy way to get the right amount of calcium without eating too much fat.

The USDA does not recommend a daily serving amount for fats, oils, and sweets; it feels that these foods should be consumed sparingly. Most items that fall into this category have calories but virtually no nutritional value. These foods may be found as additives to other foods (as in the case of jelly or sweeteners) or as foods in their own right (candy and cookies, for example). Sometimes, processed foods contain high amounts of these foods. Ketchup, "low-fat" yogurt, and soft drinks all have outrageous amounts of either sugar or fat. There is no benefit to consuming these foods, and the body may actually be undermined by excessive consumption of them.

Water

Water is probably the most important thing a person can put into his or her body. Water carries nutrients throughout the body and regulates the temperature. Water lubricates joints, aids digestion, and helps speed waste matter out of the body. Losing even five percent of the body's water causes immediate physical symptoms, like dizziness, fatigue, and headache; losing fifteen percent of the body's water can be fatal. Every person loses between 64 and 80 ounces of water a day, which is equal to about nine large glasses of water. Many fruits and vegetables contain helpful water, but people should still be sure to consume a great deal of water throughout the day. People who are active, live at a high altitude, or travel a great deal should be sure to drink even more water.

Fat

Fats are divided into two main categories: saturated and unsaturated. Saturated fats are mostly found in meat, lard, butter, coconut, and palm oil. These are considered by doctors to be the most hazardous to health because they increase the risk of heart disease and certain kinds of cancer. Unsaturated fats include sunflower oil, corn oil, olive oil, and canola oil. These last two are called monounsaturated fats and are particularly good for the body because they lower cholesterol. Most recent research has concluded that the most harmful kinds of fats are trans fats, which are formed when liquid vegetable oil is processed to make table spreads and cooking fats. These fats have been consistently shown to create buildup in arteries which can damage heart health.

Relationship with cholesterol:
Many fats can increase cholesterol, a substance in the body which has consistently been linked with heart disease. Cholesterol has many positive uses in the body, like helping the liver operate and helping to form many hormones, but if it becomes too abundant it can build up in the arteries and impede the flow of blood. Research suggests that saturated fats cause a more significant buildup of cholesterol than unsaturated fats or other foods that contain cholesterol. In order to minimize cholesterol in the diet, individuals should cut back on fats altogether, but should especially try to limit their intake of saturated fats. Monounsaturated fats, like canola and olive oil, are a good, low cholesterol source of fat.

Fiber

Whole grains, fruits, and vegetables are all excellent sources of fiber. Fiber can be either insoluble or soluble. Insoluble fibers (cellulose and lignin, for example) speed digestion and can reduce the risk of colon cancer and heart disease. Wheat and corn bran, leafy vegetables, and fruit and vegetable skins are all great sources of insoluble fiber. Soluble fibers (pectins and gums, for example) lower cholesterol levels and help manage the level of blood sugar. They can be found in the pulp of fruits and vegetables, oats, beans, and barley. Doctors warn that most Americans do not eat nearly enough fiber. However, increasing fiber in your diet should be done gradually, as a sudden increase in fiber can result in bloating, cramps, and diarrhea.

Evaluating foods

There is a great deal of information printed on the Nutrition Facts label on every packaged food.

- Calories describe the amount of energy that can be derived from the food. Specifically, a calorie is defined as the amount of energy needed to raise the temperature of one gram of water by one degree Celsius.
- Serving size, which was often manipulated by food companies to make their products seem healthier, is now strictly regulated by the government. All of the producers of a certain kind of food are required to

use a similar serving size so that it is easier for consumers to compare.

- At the bottom of every food label, the number of calories for every gram of fat, carbohydrates, and protein will be listed.

Daily values
On a food label, the daily values are the amount of each nutrient that a person should consume every day. Most of the daily values, including those for total fat, saturated fat, carbohydrates, fiber, and protein, are set in the assumption of a 2000-calorie diet. The daily values for cholesterol, sodium, vitamins, and minerals are the same for every adult. The percent daily values, then, indicate what percentage of a particular nutrient is found in the food. Obviously, the ideal diet would include 100% of each nutrient. Individuals who consume considerably less or more than 2000 calories a day should adjust their daily values for total fat, saturated fats, and cholesterol accordingly.

There are certain categories that everyone should check when evaluating a food. You should always try to determine the percentage of fat calories in a food. You should avoid fatty foods, particularly those high in saturated fats. Cholesterol is only found in animal products, and many high-fat foods may actually not contain any cholesterol at all. Sugars are not listed on food labels because doctors have yet to agree on a reasonable daily limit. A food is considered high in fiber if it contains five or more grams per serving. A high level of calcium is 200 or more milligrams per serving. It is especially important to check the level of sodium, because most Americans consume far too much. A food is considered a "good" source of a vitamin if it contains 10% of the daily value, and a "high" source if it contains 20% or more.

Vitamins

Vitamins are nutrients that help regulate growth in the body, maintain the quality of tissue, and release the energy from food. Vitamins allow proteins, fats, and carbohydrates to be used by the body. They also aid in the manufacture of blood cells, hormones, and other compounds. Some vitamins do not need to be consumed; vitamin D, for example, is produced by the body after exposure to sunlight, and is then changed into an active form in the liver and kidneys. Most vitamins, though, need to be ingested. Some vitamins, like A, D, E, and K, are fat-soluble and are absorbed through the intestinal membrane. Others, like vitamins B and C, are water-soluble: absorbed directly into the blood stream and evacuated through urine and sweat.

Vitamin supplements
Many Americans take daily vitamin supplements in the hopes of guarding against certain health problems, despite doubts from the scientific community as to the effectiveness of these supplements. Most health professionals insist that the best way to get the right amount of nutrients is to use the Food Guide Pyramid and eat a wide variety of foods. Still, some people may be unable to eat all the foods they need, and so dietary supplements can be to their advantage. Dietary supplements can be particularly useful for getting obscure nutrients, like capsaicin from hot peppers that is known to protect DNA from carcinogens. Dietary supplements can be sold as such as long as they do not make any claims to diagnose, prevent, treat, or cure any disease.

Multivitamin supplements
As long as people don't depend on multivitamins to supply all of their nutrients and justify an unhealthy diet, there is no harm in taking a daily multivitamin. Most of the health dangers associated with vitamin supplements stem from taking huge daily doses of a single vitamin. Indeed, most of the

health benefits provided by vitamins can only be provided by a combination of vitamins, and not by an increase in any one substance. This is particularly true for fat-soluble vitamins, like A and D, which will build up in the intestinal tract if they are taken in excess. Overconsumption of water-soluble vitamins can cause health problems as well, however. Vitamin C, which many people take in isolation during cold and flu season, can cause stomachaches and nausea.

Folic acid

In the last several years, food manufacturers in the United States have begun adding folic acid (folate, a B vitamin) to their product. This is mainly done because a deficiency of folic acid has been linked to birth defects like spinal bifida. In addition, folic acid helps to synthesize hemoglobin, a molecule that carries oxygen in the bloodstream. Folic acid has also been credited with reducing the risk of cervical and other cancers. Many elderly individuals have a low amount of folic acid in their bodies, and scientists believe this may be somewhat responsible for coronary artery disease. Women who are trying to get pregnant should always make sure they are getting enough folic acid in their diet.

Minerals

Minerals are nutrients that help with the growth and maintenance of tissues in the body. They aid in the formation of bones and teeth, in muscle function, and they help the nervous system to transmit information. Major minerals are those of which the body needs about 100 milligrams a day. Sodium, potassium, chloride, calcium, phosphorus, and magnesium are all major minerals. Trace minerals are those of which the body needs 10 milligrams or less a day. Iron, zinc, selenium, molybdenum, iodine, cobalt, copper, manganese, fluoride, and chromium are all examples of trace minerals. Although it is widely acknowledged that the body requires all of these trace minerals, it has not yet been proven that a greater or smaller amount affects the risk of illness.

Calcium

The most prevalent mineral in the body is calcium. Calcium aids in the operation of the brain and heart and helps builds strong bone tissue. It is especially important for pregnant women to have enough calcium, because they will need some to provide to their unborn babies. Calcium has also been shown to prevent colon cancer and control high blood pressure. People in their teens and twenties should be sure to get enough calcium, as a calcium deficiency in these years has been linked to the occurrence of osteoporosis in later life. An individual should be able to get most of his or her calcium from calcium-rich foods, but sometimes a calcium supplement may be necessary. If so, calcium citrate and calcium carbonate are recommended, as supplements from bone meal and dolomite may contain harmful lead.

Iron

Iron is one of the essential components of hemoglobin, the protein that carries oxygen through the bloodstream to all the tissues of the body. Oxygen is essential to the conversion of food into energy, so an iron deficiency can create a lack of body energy known as anemia. Getting enough iron is especially important for women, because their stores of iron are drained by menstruation, pregnancy, and nursing. Indeed, about half of all women of childbearing age receive less than the recommended daily value of iron. If you are suffering from iron deficiency, you will experience, nervousness, chronic fatigue, depression, sleeplessness, and an increased vulnerability to infection.

Antioxidants

Antioxidants are those substances that prevent the negative side effects of oxidation within the body. Three of the most commonly discussed antioxidants are vitamin C, vitamin E, and beta carotene. Besides the unique benefits of each of these nutrients, antioxidants are believed to prevent the damage to the body done by free radicals (oxygen molecules), smog, smoke, and radiation. All of these substances are capable of preventing the cells of the body from properly performing their functions. People who consume a large number of antioxidants exhibit lower rates of heart disease, some cancers, cataracts, and infectious illness. However, it has not been shown that consuming antioxidant supplements necessarily provides a safeguard against disease.

Metabolism

An individual's metabolism is the sum of all of the vital processes that require the energy and nutrients from food. The majority of metabolism is devoted to maintaining basic processes like respiration, heart rate, and blood pressure, and is known as the resting metabolic rate. Individuals will also use up energy digesting food or engaging in any physical activity. Metabolic rate is dependent on both heredity and habits: though some people may have a naturally higher metabolism than others, exercise has been shown to raise the general metabolic rate. Muscle tends to metabolize calories more quickly than fat. When individuals lose a great deal of weight quickly, the body will try to protect itself by lowering the metabolism. When weight is gained, on the other hand, metabolism tends to rise.

Diets

Vegetarianism
There are a number of different diets that fall under the heading of vegetarianism. Lacto-vegetarians eat dairy products as well as fruits, vegetables, and grains. Ovo-lacto-vegetarians add eggs to this diet. The most extreme vegetarians only consume plant foods; these people are known as vegans. For vegetarians, the biggest challenge in eating properly is getting complete proteins; meat, fish, poultry, and eggs all provide the nine essential amino acids, while other proteins like beans or nuts may have a low amount of one or more of these. For this reason, it is important for vegetarians to consume complementary proteins, like beans and rice, or sesame seeds and chickpeas. In general, vegetarians have lower levels of cholesterol and are less likely to be overweight.

Diet foods
Too often, individuals assume that eating foods labeled as fat free, low-calorie, or "light" gives them permission to eat as much as they want. However, many of these so-called diet foods are high in sugar and may be high in calories despite being low in fat. Too much of any food, no matter how healthy, is counterproductive to a diet plan. In particular, artificial sweeteners and fake fats should be consumed in moderation.

Yo-yo syndrome
Another common dieting problem is the yo-yo syndrome, in which the individual repeatedly loses and then regains weight. Studies have shown that continual weight fluctuation can be hazardous to the health. Exercise, however, has been credited with maintaining a healthy metabolism even while dieting. This enables the person to keep weight off once it has been lost.

Extremely low-calorie diets
Although healthy weight loss does entail reducing the number of calories ingested daily, and diet that drastically alters caloric intake should be avoided. Some risky diets suggest consuming less than 800 calories a day, which can be hazardous to health. Losing weight quickly typically means losing muscle weight, and the heart muscle may become so weak that it struggles to support the body. Moreover, low-calorie diets tend to slow down the metabolism, which means that energy will be reduced and the body will struggle to maintain the new weight. If you develop nausea, abdominal pains, sudden hair loss, irregular menstruation, or chronic fatigue, you may have reduced your caloric intake too much; you should immediately resume normal eating habits and see a doctor.

Diet products

Everyone has seen the advertisements for diet pills that promise to reduce weight with minimal effort. As recently as the 1970's, American women were sold so-called diet pills that were nothing but amphetamines. Even today, the diet pill and weight-loss product industry is enormous. However, many of these products pose a risk to health, and may not even effectively reduce weight, as the individuals who take them may feel empowered to eat as much as they like. Liquid diets should also be avoided in most cases. Although today's liquid diets offer a more comprehensive range of proteins, carbohydrates, vitamins, and minerals than those of the past, they should still only be tried under close medical supervision.

Exercise

For most people, the balanced diet depicted in the Food Pyramid will supply all the nutrients the body needs to maintain a program of physical fitness. However, individuals who are seriously testing their endurance by exercising for periods of more than an hour at a time will need to increase their intake of complex carbohydrates, which keep the level of blood sugar stable and increase the amount of available glycogen. Contrary to popular thought, heavy workouts do not require a diet high in protein, and in fact consuming too much protein can put a severe strain on the kidneys and liver. Similarly, most health experts discourage the use of dietary supplements and body-building foods unless under supervision, because these products can easily result in nutritional imbalances.

Psychological health

In order to achieve psychological health, you must have an accurate and favorable impression of yourself. Having healthy self-esteem does not mean overestimating your talents and value; it means feeling good about your role in life and expecting that you will have the personal resources to deal with any adversity. A person who has a reasonable concept of themselves will be able to tolerate the faults of others, because he or she will be cognizant of his or her own faults. Part of establishing a realistic but positive view of the world is accepting that there are many things that you will be unable to change in life, and that rather than making yourself miserable about them you can direct your attention to those things which can be helped.

Personal autonomy

A psychologically healthy person will have developed autonomy, or control over him or herself. Autonomous individuals are those who act as they know they should, rather than as they are told to do or as outside forces influence them to do. Unfortunately, many people put too much emphasis on what other people think of them, and so they ignore their own conscience. If the approval of others is the only thing a person seeks, then he or she will never really be happy, but will continuously, desperately be seeking new ways to receive attention and love from outside. Moreover, this attention and love will never be satisfying because it will not be a response to the person's true nature. By cultivating a healthy self-reliance, you make it possible for other people to love you for who you are.

Adult personality

As individuals enter adolescence, they will begin to develop an adult personality: that is, a set of characteristics, values, and beliefs that is unique to themselves. Early on in life, it is common to base one's identity on one's family, or on figures in society with whom one identifies. After a while, though, these connections will be outgrown and an individual will start the long process of selecting those attributes with which he or she feels most at home. The challenge of developing an integrated identity is both more difficult and more exciting in contemporary America, as there are so many subcultures from which to pick and choose. It is important to note that the process of developing an adult personality is never completed; psychologically healthy individuals will continue to evolve through a lifetime.

Intimacy and purpose
Part of becoming a psychologically healthy adult is developing the capacity for intimate relationships and a sense of vocation in your professional life. Only by establishing a positive, autonomous identity are individuals able to enter into loving relationships. Individuals with an uncertain sense of self will not be able to express themselves fully to another person and therefore will be likely to enter into a series of short-term, unsatisfying relationships. As for work, individuals will not be happy unless they can find a job that fulfills them emotionally and spiritually, as well as financially. During middle and later adulthood, it is very common for people to turn their attention to the next generation; at this point, they will want to feel that their work is making the world a better place for the young people that they love.

Defense mechanisms
Part of life is struggling with the conflict between one's own desires and the desires of other people. In order to avoid the psychological pain of rejection, loss, and conflict, people often resort to so-called "defense mechanisms." These are mental habits that can become so ingrained as to be unconscious. The most common defense mechanisms are projection (blaming one's own mistakes on someone else), repression (refusing to think about a painful subject), regression (acting in immature ways that one has outgrown), denial, daydreaming, idealization (viewing things or people as either all good or all bad), rationalization (inventing a reasonable but false reaction to a painful event), passive-aggressive behavior (expressing anger through subtle mean-spirited behavior), and displacement (shifting negative feelings from one person or thing to another). Not all defense mechanisms are entirely unhealthy; humor, for instance, is often a good way to ease pain.

Self-care

Most individuals, even if they have no medical training, are constantly diagnosing themselves and changing their behavior and dict accordingly. This can include taking aspirin for a headache, taking a nap to combat fatigue, or eating a piece of fruit to stimulate the digestive system. Doctors recommend that individuals perform basic tests (like breast exam, testicular exam, and skin exam) on themselves to determine whether they need formal attention. Other tests, like those for pregnancy or blood pressure, require some diagnostic equipment but can still easily be performed by untrained individuals. The most important skill to have when performing self-care, of course, is to know when to seek a more professional opinion.

Vital signs
In order to effectively look after oneself, it is necessary to know what one's vital signs are and how to measure them. The four most common measures considered to be vital signs are body temperature, blood pressure, pulse rate, and respiration rate. Body temperature can be taken with a thermometer, and should be between 96 and 99.9 degrees Fahrenheit, depending on the time of day and sex (women tend to have slightly higher temperatures). Measuring blood pressure requires some equipment; a normal blood pressure is between 120/70 and 140/90, depending on age and sex. A normal pulse rate is about 72 beats per minute. A normal respiration rate is between15 to 20 breaths a minute.

Basic dental care
In order to maintain good dental health, individuals should brush their teeth every morning and night; bacterial buildup is greatest while a person is sleeping, so it is imperative to clean the teeth soon after waking up. It is a good idea always to use a toothbrush that is certified by the American Dental Association, and that has soft, rounded bristles. It is also essential to floss every day to remove the plaque that a toothbrush can't

reach. Cleaning slowly between teeth removes plaque and food that can be destructive to dental health if they are allowed to accumulate. Every person should if possible see a dentist twice a year for a cleaning and general examination. Many forms of health insurance include provisions for these visits.

Basic dental problems

Since the introduction of fluoridated water and toothpaste, dental health in the United States has improved markedly. There are a few conditions that individuals need to be on the lookout for, however. Gum disease is an inflammation of the gum and the bone that holds teeth in place; it is caused by plaque, a film of bacteria that can accrue on the teeth. The early stage of gum disease is called gingivitis. If gingivitis goes untreated, it can lead to periodontitis, the condition in which infection has spread to the roots of the teeth. Gum disease may be present if an individual bleeds while brushing or flossing, or has red or puffy gums, bad breath, or shifting teeth. Individuals who are developing gum disease should visit a dentist to have their teeth scraped and evaluated.

Hygiene

Besides helping you maintain an attractive appearance, hygiene is essential for keeping you healthy and free of disease. The body is usually covered with a certain amount of bacteria, but if this number is allowed to grow too high you may place yourself at risk for disease. Individuals who fail to regularly wash their hair are more likely to have head lice, and those who fail to properly clean their genital are more likely to contract a urinary infection. Good hygiene can also reduce an individual's contagiousness to others when he or she is sick. Hygiene is especially important when dealing with food: failing to wash everything involved in the preparation of a meal can result in the spread of bacterial infections like E. Coli and hepatitis A.

Personal hygiene practices

There are a few basic hygiene practices that students should be encouraged to perform habitually in order to stay clean and reduce the risk of disease. Everyone should wash his or her hair and body once a day, and should wash his or her hands more frequently than that. Teeth should be brushed between one and three times daily. Always wash hands before eating, avoid spitting or nose-picking, and hold a hand in front of your face when sneezing. Try to avoid coming into contact with any body fluids, and keep clothes and living space clean. Finally, avoid putting your fingers in your mouth, and try not to touch any animals before eating.

Quackery

Quackery is the informal name given to any medical advice or information that is given by someone who is either unqualified or incompetent in that field. There is a long history of quackery in medicine, which the federal government in the United States attempts to curtail through legislation requiring practicing physicians to get licenses and drugs to pass standardized inspections. At present, the majority of products that can be considered quackery by medical science are the so-called "natural" remedies offered by health food stores. Quackery continues to have some standing because of general ignorance about health issues, the placebo effect (in which patients may report positive effects simply because they expect them), and distrust of modern medicine.

Medical advertising

Medicine and pharmaceuticals has become big business in the past few decades, and companies now make lavish expenditures on advertising to try and show their products to the consumer. It is important that consumers, then, be equipped with the skills to interpret and judge medical advertising. First of all, on should isolate the claims made by the advertising; some prescription medications are not allowed by law to declare what they will do, so this may be trickier than it sounds. Next, consider the sources cited by the advertising, if any are cited at all. Are these sources reputable? Advertising can be a positive influence if it helps a consumer learn more about what new products are available; still, all final decisions regarding medication or therapy should be made in consultation with a licensed physician.

Good health care

Individuals can improve the quality of their health care if they abide by a few simple rules. First of all, they should try to remain informed on the health issues that are relevant to their lives. They should also try to find a solid primary care physician that listens to their complaints and concerns. It is never a bad idea to get a second opinion, though, especially for important decisions. It is important to ascertain that medical decisions are made on the basis of scientific evaluation, rather than on the basis if the doctor's opinion. Patients should always be prepared to speak up and ask questions of they are confused or dubious about a diagnosis. Finally, many patients take notes while they are at the doctor, so that they can look up things later or confer with a knowledgeable friend.

Medical history
During a basic medical examination, a doctor should have a summary of your medical history, including any major illnesses or injuries, allergies, and past treatments. Sometimes, a physician may need to know information that the patient considers private, like sexual history. Unless there is a particular reason for withholding such information, patients can be confident that a doctor will not divulge confidential matters. A patient has to be honest if a doctor is to make the appropriate diagnoses and prescriptions. It is also important for the patient to point out the doctor any unusual bumps, rashes, or pains that he or she may be having. If necessary, patients should write out a summary of their current health so that

they will be prepared to give a doctor all the important information.

Basic medical exams
During a basic medical examination, a doctor will typically use a small, concentrated flashlight called an ophthalmoscope to inspect the lens, retina, and blood vessels of the patient's eyes. After this, the doctors should inspect the ears, mouth, tongue, teeth, and gums. The doctor will also palpate the patient's neck, checking to see if the lymph glands are swollen, if there are any lumps in the thyroid gland, and if there are any signs that a stroke might be coming. The doctor will use a stethoscope to listen to the noises made by the heart, making sure that there are no signs of heart murmur or irregular contractions. The stethoscope is also used to listen to the lungs, particularly for the signs of asthma or emphysema. Tapping on the chest and back can indicate the size and condition of the heart and lungs.

During a basic medical examination, a doctor will typically probe the patient's abdomen with his or her fingers, searching for tender spots or irregularities in the liver and other organs. Certain deformities may indicate alcoholism, hepatitis, or a hernia. A doctor may also use a gloved hand to check the rectum for hemorrhoids and other growths. Many male patients will receive rectal exams to check for a swollen prostate gland. During this part of the examination, it is typical for a doctor to check a male patient's testicles and spermatic cords for any abnormalities. A doctor will also check the patient's pulse in several different areas, to ensure that circulation is good. Checking the blood pressure is another routine part of any medical exam.

Female patients are likely to receive a pelvic exam when they make a routine trip to the doctor, especially the gynecologist (for many women, a gynecologist is their primary care physician). During a pelvic exam, the woman reclines with her heels raised in stirrups at the edge of the table. The doctor will then

- 14 -

inspect the labia, clitoris, and vaginal opening. Using a lubricated, gloved finger, the doctor will also examine the vagina, looking for abnormalities in it, as well as in the uterus, fallopian tubes, and ovaries. Most doctors have a nurse in attendance during this procedure, in order to make the patient feel more comfortable. Many women also insist that this procedure be performed by a female doctor.

During the course of a basic medical exam, a doctor will examine the reflexes of the patient. This is done by striking certain places on the body with a rubber hammer and observing the response. Abnormal reflexes may indicate a disorder of the nerves. A doctor will also examine the patient's skin for color, moisture, and elasticity. Abnormalities of the skin may indicate malnutrition, diabetes, or potentially skin cancer. An examination of the hair and nails of the patient can help a doctor determine whether the patient has any blood disorders or other internal problems. Finally, doctors will always check the condition of the patient's ankles, as swollen ankles can be a sign of heart, kidney, or lung disease.

Basic medical tests
There are certain diagnostic tests that a doctor may recommend for a patient during a basic medical examination. A chest X ray is sometimes advised if a doctor thinks the patient may have abnormalities in his or her heart or lungs. Smokers and individuals with a family history of heart disease are often encouraged to get a regular chest X ray. A doctor may also recommend an electrocardiogram, in which the electrical activity of the heart is measured. An electrocardiogram can indicate damage of the heart muscle as well as hardening of the arteries. Many doctors will also perform a routine urinalysis, in which the patient's urine is assessed in a laboratory. If the urine has too much glucose, for instance, it may be an indication of diabetes.

Often, a doctor will recommend that a patient have a blood test as part of a routine examination. A blood sample will be taken and sent to a laboratory for analysis. The analysis generally consists of a basic blood cell count. Having a high number of white blood cells is considered an indication of infection, or possibly leukemia. If there are too few red blood cells, the patient may be suffering from anemia. The various components of blood will also be measured. A high level of glucose indicates diabetes, while excessive amounts of uric acid may mean gout or kidney stones. If there is a high level of cholesterol found in the blood, this may indicate some risk of heart disease.

Alcohol standards

Any liquid that contains sugar and is fermented will produce the colorless liquid known as alcohol. The kind of alcohol found in alcoholic beverages is ethyl alcohol. Since different alcoholic beverages contain different amounts of alcohol, a standard measurement for one drink has been created. In health literature, a single drink may be 12 ounces of beer (assumed to be 5% alcohol), 4 ounces of table wine (12% alcohol), 2.5 ounces of fortified wine (20%), or one ounce of distilled spirits (50% alcohol). Each of these drinks contains approximately half an ounce of ethyl alcohol. The amount of alcohol may also be measured in terms of proof, which is derived by multiplying the percentage of alcohol by 2. Thus, a bottle of whiskey that is 40% alcohol will be marked as 80 proof.

Blood-alcohol concentration
In order to figure out what amount of alcohol a person may consume at a time, it is important to determine their blood-alcohol concentration. BAC is the measure taken by breath or urine samples, including those administered to drivers suspected of being under the influence. According to the Federal Department of Transportation, a person should be considered unfit to drive if he or she has a BAC of 0.08% or higher. This is

approximately the BAC that a 150-pound man will have after consuming three drinks in an hour. A BAC of 0.05% or higher will cause a person to experience many of the problems associated with intoxication; a BAC of 0.2% will probably result in the person losing consciousness; a BAC of 0.3% can result in a coma; and a BAC of 0.4% generally means death.

Response to alcohol
There are a few things that will determine the severity of an individual's response to alcohol. Obviously, the more alcohol that is consumed, the higher the individual's blood-alcohol concentration will be. Also, since the liver can only process half an ounce of alcohol every hour, drinking quickly will result in a higher level of intoxication. More potent forms of alcohol, like liquor and fortified wine, get into the bloodstream more quickly, especially if they are accompanied by carbonated beverages. Heavy individuals tend to get drunk more slowly, as they have an excess of water with which to dilute the incoming alcohol. Women typically can drink less than men, because they have less of the stomach enzyme that neutralizes alcohol. Older individuals tend to have less water, and so are more affected by alcohol. If an individual has an empty stomach, does not regularly consume alcohol, or has taken some prescription medicines, he or she will be more quickly intoxicated.

Recommended levels consumption
Alcohol is not entirely bad for the body; in fact, there is consistent evidence that suggests a single drink every day can reduce an individual's risk of heart disease. This is truer for men than for women. The National Institute of Alcohol and Alcohol Abuse suggests that men should have no more than two drinks every day, and women should have no more than one. This amount should be adjusted depending on an individual's weight, or age. Many individuals, including pregnant women, people with ulcers, people on certain prescription medications, or those operating heavy machinery, shouldn't drink

at all. The health risks associated with alcohol increase in proportion to the amount of alcohol that is consumed.

Alcohol intoxication
The immediate consequence of alcohol consumption is intoxication. Individuals who become intoxicated from alcohol will exhibit negative behavioral and psychological changes, which may include aggressive behavior, inappropriate sexual conduct, mood changes, or impaired judgment. Intoxication is generally manifested in the following: slurred speech, poor coordination, unsteady walking, abnormal eye movements, impaired concentration and memory, and a general stupor. Severe intoxication may cause a loss of concentration, coma, and even death. Intoxicated individuals are also at greater risk of infection, as alcohol suppresses the work of the immune system. Severely intoxicated individuals may be at risk of shock, particularly if they lose consciousness.

Effects of alcohol on the body
From the moment it is consumed, and even before the individual notices any of the psychological effects, alcohol is at work in the human body. It is almost immediately absorbed into the bloodstream through the walls of the stomach and the upper intestine. Typically, it takes about fifteen minutes for the alcohol in a drink to reach the bloodstream, and usually about an hour for the amount of alcohol to reach its peak. Once in the bloodstream, alcohol is carried to the liver, heart, and brain. Although alcohol cannot leave the body until it is metabolized by the liver, it is a diuretic which accelerates the removal of other liquids from the body; thus, alcohol has a dehydrating effect. Alcohol also lowers the temperature of the body.

Effects of alcohol on the digestive system
The first stop for alcohol is the stomach. It is partially broken down there, and the remainder of it is absorbed into the bloodstream through the stomach lining. While in the stomach, alcohol stimulates the

- 16 -

release of certain chemicals that tend to irritate the lining; it is for this reason that heavy drinking often causes nausea, and chronic drinking may contribute to ulcers. The alcohol in the bloodstream moves on to the liver, where for the most part it will be converted into fat. If an individual consumes four or five drinks a day for a few weeks, his or her liver cells will accrue a large amount of fat. Alcohol may also eventually cause white blood cells to attack the liver, which can cause irreparable damage.

Effects of alcohol on the cardiovascular and immune systems

Alcohol is thought to have some positive effects on the cardiovascular system. Light drinkers seem to have healthier hearts, suffer fewer heart attacks, have less cholesterol problems, and be at less of a risk for heart disease. However, excessive drinking will weaken the heart muscle, and alcohol in combination with other drugs (including tobacco and cocaine) is known to have negative effects on the heart. Chronic alcohol use will also inhibit the creation of white blood cells, which help fight infection, and red blood cells, which carry oxygen around the body. If consumed by a person suffering from infection (like a cold or flu), alcohol will suppress the immune system's ability to fight the infection.

Effects of alcohol on the brain

When consumed in low volume, alcohol alters the areas of the brain that influence behavior, so that the individual will feel more relaxed and less inhibited. Of course, this is accompanied by weakened concentration, memory, judgment, and motor control. Heavy drinkers may experience long-term intelligence and memory impairment. Alcohol depresses the central nervous system and slows down the activity of the neurons in the brain. This dulling of mental reactions increases in proportion of alcohol consumed, and can culminate in unconsciousness, coma, or even death. Although one or two drinks may have a pleasant tranquilizing or relaxing

effect, many more can entirely snuff out central nervous system activity.

Effects of alcohol on behavior and judgment

Alcohol has a number of effects on behavior and judgment. For one thing, it is known to impair sensory perceptions: the eye is less able to adjust to bright lights, and the ear has difficulty distinguishing sounds. The senses of smell and taste are also diminished by excessive consumption of alcohol. Alcohol will decrease sensitivity in general, making it possible for individuals to feel comfortable in extreme temperatures that may be hazardous to their health. Intoxication typically causes an impairment of motor skills, meaning that activities performed with the muscles cannot be done with any precision or coordination. Finally, intoxication usually has a negative effect on sexual performance, even though it may increase interest in sexual activity.

Consumption with other drugs

The dangers of alcohol may be magnified greatly if it is consumed in combination with other drugs, whether legal or illegal. Indeed, more than half of the most frequently prescribed drugs contain one or more ingredients that react with alcohol. In most cases, this is because the ingredient affects the same areas of the brain as alcohol, thus increasing the effects on the person. Particularly in cases where alcohol is mixed with an anti-depressant or anti-anxiety medication, the results of this synergistic combination can be fatal. One drug that is thought to have negative consequences when taken with alcohol is aspirin. Although many people take aspirin to alleviate the negative consequences of drinking, research has shown that aspirin may diminish the stomach's ability to process alcohol.

Alcohol-related death

There are a variety of ways in which alcohol can kill those who abuse it. The biggest killer of alcoholics is injury, most of the time auto accidents involving drink driving. In fact, alcohol is involved in at least half of all traffic fatalities (as well as being involved in half of all homicides and a quarter of all suicides). After injury, the second most common cause of death related to alcohol is cirrhosis of the liver and other digestive disease. Health professionals believe that about half of the people admitted into the hospital have a health problem related to alcohol. As one would expect, young drinkers are more likely to die from injury, and older drinkers more likely to succumb to alcohol-related illness.

Reasons for consuming alcohol

Alcohol has been popular throughout history because it depresses the central nervous system and makes people feel more relaxed. People also often drink in celebration, or when meeting with friends, as alcohol tends to reduce inhibitions and male conversation easier. People who drink alcohol often report feeling smarter, sexier, or stronger, even if studies indicate the opposite. Alcohol is also used by many people as a way to escape personal problems or a bad mood. Many people drink because they are swayed by the massive advertising campaigns launched by brewers; indeed, there is often controversy over the effects of alcohol advertising on underage consumers. Finally, many people drink in order to emulate people they admire, whether famous figures, family members, or peers.

Light, infrequent, moderate, and social drinking

Though there are no set standards for the varying degrees of alcohol consumption, there are a few basic patterns of drinking that are agreed upon by health professionals. Light drinking is usually defined as having three or fewer alcoholic beverages every week. Infrequent drinking is having less than one drink a month, but more than one drink in a year. Infrequent drinkers can often be those who rarely drink without consuming four or more drinks in a sitting. A moderate drinker is one who has approximately 12 drinks a week, and whose drinking does not interfere with the other areas of his or her

life. Social drinking is not defined by a particular quantity; rather, it is drinking at a level consistent with one's peer group, whether this level is high or low.

Problem and binge drinking

The individuals who are at great risk of developing health problems from alcohol are those who follow the patterns known as problem drinking and binge drinking. Problem drinking is defined as any amount of drinking that interferes with a major part of the individual's life, whether safety, sleep, energy, family relationships, sexual activity, or health. Although some of the negative consequences associated with problem drinking are immediate (like bad judgment and physical impairment), other effects of consistent alcohol abuse may only be evident over the long term. Binge drinking is defined for a man as having five or more drinks in a sitting (the amount is four for a woman).Binge drinking is most common among young, single men.

Drinking and driving

The most common crime in the United States is drinking and driving. In order to combat this menace to public safety, many communities offer free rides to people who have had too much to drink. Police frequently set up checkpoints along major roads, so that they can check drivers for the signs of intoxication. There has also been a move to increase the legal consequences of a drunk-driving ticket, and many states revoke a license for the first offence. At present, the National Commission Against Drunk Driving defines a drunk driver as one with blood-alcohol content above 0.15%, although most states will take a driver from behind the wheel for a BAC of above0.08%. Most drunk drivers are single men between the ages of 25 and 45.

Alcohol abuse

Alcohol abuse is defined by the American Psychiatric Association as the continued use of alcohol despite an awareness of any social, physical, psychological, or professional problems it is causing. Alcohol abuse can also entail drinking in dangerous ways situations, as for instance before driving a car. An individual who is diagnosed as an alcohol abuser usually has trouble fulfilling one of his or her major roles at work, school, or home, and may have legal problems related to alcohol. He or she may frequently abuse alcohol at inappropriate or dangerous times, like at work or before driving. Also, an individual may be diagnosed as having a problem with alcohol abuse if he or she continues to drink despite persistent relation trouble caused by drinking.

Alcohol dependence

Alcohol dependence is differentiated from alcohol abuse in that it involves the development of a physical craving for alcohol, a gradually increasing tolerance of its effects, and a painful withdrawal if drinking is ceased. Individuals with an alcohol dependency will begin drinking because it produces a feeling of pleasure or a decrease in anxiety. Eventually, though, they will require more alcohol to achieve the desired effect. Individuals with a dependency on alcohol who stop drinking often develop physical problems including sweating, a rapid pulse, insomnia, nausea, anxiety, or temporary hallucinations. Usually, such an individual will continue drinking to avoid these problems, and will find themselves unable to stop their consumption.

Alcoholism

The National Council on Alcoholism and Drug Dependence consider alcoholism as a disease that is influenced by social, environmental, and genetic factors. The common features of alcoholism are the inability to control consumption, continued drinking despite negative consequences, and distorted thinking patterns (like irrational denial). It is important to note that alcoholism is not simply the result of a weak will, but is a physiological state that may require medical treatment to be corrected. Many individuals may have a problem with alcoholism and not realize it if they are still functional in the rest of their life and if they only drink in social situations. Alcoholics tend to be those who, even when they aren't drinking, place an undue amount of psychological emphasis on alcohol.

Causes

Although there is not yet any hard evidence, there is plenty of anecdotal material to suggest that individuals can inherit a predisposition to alcoholism. For instance, the son of an alcoholic white male is four times as likely to develop alcoholism, even if he was adopted by another family at birth. Interestingly, the identical twin of an alcoholic is twice as likely as a fraternal twin to develop some disorder related to alcoholism. Brain scans have shown that the sons of alcoholic fathers have a characteristic pattern of brain wave activity. Still, despite all of this fascinating data, it should be noted that scientists have not yet been able to identify the specific gene that makes an individual more susceptible to alcoholism.

It is quite common for an alcoholic to begin drinking in order to escape personal and psychological problems. Indeed, studies have shown that approximately half of all the individuals who are diagnosed with alcoholism have another mental disorder. Alcohol is frequently linked with both depression and anxiety disorders. Another common cause of alcoholism is having a parent who abuses alcohol. It has been documented that the children of alcoholics are about five times as likely to develop alcoholism themselves. This is perhaps because the children have become used to some of the problems associated with alcoholism, for instance poor academic and social performance, unstable family life, and antisocial tendencies.

Types I and II

Over the past few decades, the health professionals working towards better prevention and treatment for alcoholism have developed a few different classes of the disease. Type I alcoholics are those who begin a pattern of heavy drinking sometime after the age of 25, often in response to some personal misfortune. These individuals are able to refrain from drinking for a long period of time and will feel very conflicted about their drinking problem. Type II alcoholics, on the other hand, usually become dependent on alcohol before the age of 25, and are likely to have a close relative who also has an alcohol problem. These people tend to drink regardless of their personal situation, and experience no feelings of guilt or fear regarding their alcoholism.

Female alcoholism

Even though women are less likely to abuse alcohol than men, many women still drink too much. Furthermore, women tend to drink for different reasons than men. Many women have an increased susceptibility to alcohol written into their genes. Female alcoholics are more likely than male alcoholics to have a parent who drinks heavily, has psychiatric problems, or has attempted suicide. About a quarter of female alcoholics report that they were physically or sexually abused during childhood. Women are more likely than men to be depressed before and during a period of alcoholism. Women who are single, separated, or divorced tend to drink more than married women, though women who cohabitate with a male without being married are the most likely to be problem drinkers. Women tend to drink more when they lose a social role, as when their children grow up and leave, they lose their job, or they are divorced.

Health effects of alcohol on women

Besides the obvious risks of alcohol as regards sexual behavior and driving, women face a number of health consequences for chronic alcoholism. Women take alcohol into the bloodstream more easily than men, and so they are more likely to suffer liver damage from overwhelming amounts of alcohol than are men. Moderate and heavy drinking may also contribute to infertility, menstrual problems, sexual dysfunction, and premenstrual syndrome. If a woman drinks during pregnancy, her child may develop fetal alcohol syndrome: he or she will be born with a small head, abnormal facial features, and possible mental retardation. Other babies of drinking mothers may be underweight or irritable as newborns. Female alcoholics are at greater risk for breast cancer, osteoporosis, and heart disease.

Treatment for female alcoholics

Unfortunately, female alcoholics do not always receive the same quality of care and social support as male alcoholics. Often, this is because of financial limitations, or because women may be consumed with the responsibilities of raising children. Studies have also shown that women are more likely to blame their personal problems on anxiety or depression, whereas men are more ready to admit their drinking problem. Women are more likely to become addicted to prescription medications along with alcohol, or to develop eating disorders and sexual dysfunctions. One of the approaches that many health professionals advocate is to target the causes of female alcoholism, like low self-esteem and depression. Other organizations, like Women for Sobriety, are working to ensure that female alcoholism is recognized as a serious problem that demands attention.

Detoxification

Whenever an individual with an alcohol problem begins treatment, the first step is detoxification, or the gradual removal of alcohol from the system. Most of the time, detoxification does not produce major withdrawal symptoms. However, those who have been drinking heavily for a long period may develop severe symptoms, including seizures and delirium tremens (also known as DTs). Delirium tremens is a condition in which the individual becomes agitated, and may have delusions, a rapid heart beat, sweating, vivid hallucinations, fever, and trembling hands. This condition is most likely to strike those alcoholics who also suffer from malnutrition, depression, or fatigue, and usually ceases after a few alcohol-free days.

Treatment with medication
If alcoholism is caught in its early stages, it is often treated with anti-depressant or anti-anxiety medication. Doctors believe that those drugs which increase the amount of serotonin in the brain may help reduce painful cravings for alcohol. Doctors also recommend that recovering alcoholics take vitamin supplements to remedy the malnutrition that prolonged alcoholism may cause. For especially sever cases, doctors may prescribe Antabuse (the commercial name for the drug disulfiram), which causes an individual to become nauseous or ill when they consume alcohol. Individuals on this medication must also be careful to avoid foods that have been marinated or cooked in alcohol; some sensitive individuals may even have an adverse reaction to the alcohol in shaving lotion while they are on the drug. This drug, though it is effective in forcing an individual to stop drinking, does not treat any of the psychological or social causes of drinking.

Inpatient and outpatient treatment
For a long time, a four-week stay at a psychiatric hospital or residential facility was considered necessary for a recovering alcoholic. This inpatient treatment was usually successful, too: over 70% of those who completed such a treatment were sober for five years afterward, according to one study. Unfortunately, inpatient treatment is expensive, and insurance companies have been increasingly unwilling to pay for it. So, outpatient treatments like group therapy, family therapy, interventions, and organizations like Alcoholics Anonymous have become more popular in recent years. Some studies have indicated that intensive outpatient treatment can be as effective as inpatient care, especially if the individual continues it for at least a year.

Interventions
Brief interventions are short, intense training sessions that teach alcoholics the skills they will need to battle their drinking problem. These programs, which typically last about eight weeks and center on topics like "assertiveness" and "self-esteem," are best suited for individuals who do not have a physical dependence on alcohol.

Moderation training
Moderation training tries to equip drinkers with the skills to manage their drinking, by showing them ways to reduce consumption and avoid problematic situations. This method is somewhat controversial, as some critics assert that the only good choice for chronic abusers of alcohol is abstinence. Advocates of moderation training, however, insist that their programs are targeted at less severe cases, and that they offer more realistic expectations than other programs.

AA
The most famous self-help program for individuals battling a drinking problem is Alcoholics Anonymous. This global organization seeks to force alcoholics to admit their problems and to rely on one another for support in solving them. Every member of AA will have a "sponsor," another member whom they can call upon if they are tempted to drink. AA also features a 12-step program, in which members are forced to take responsibility, to own up to the problems that drinking causes, and to ask God for help. The 12-step model devised by AA has been used in many other self-help organizations. There are other self-help groups, like Rational Recovery, that adhere to a similar philosophy as AA without the emphasis on spirituality.

Recovery
Defeating alcoholism is often the most difficult challenge an individual will face in his or her lifetime. Relapse into drinking is

- 21 -

quite common; some studies estimate that 90% of recovering alcoholics will drink again in their first year after quitting. The people who tend to be successful at abstaining from alcohol are those who have something to lose: that is, parents and people with important jobs. Almost every recovering alcoholic will experience mood swings and an occasional temptation to drink. More and more, relapse prevention is a part of treatment. Relapse prevention involves giving the individual the information and skills to cope with the temptations of alcohol, as well as providing a support network that the individual can rely on in times of stress. Exercise and a general reduction in stress seem to be most helpful in creating a permanent life away from alcohol.

Tobacco and nicotine

Smoking or otherwise ingesting tobacco creates an immediate effect on the body and brain. The primary active ingredient in tobacco is nicotine, a colorless, oily compound. Nicotine can be poisonous if it is ingested in a concentrated amount. Inhaling cigarette smoke into the lungs causes about 90% of the nicotine to be absorbed into the body. Nicotine stimulates the cerebral cortex, enhancing mood and alertness. It also can act as a sedative if it is taken in large doses. Nicotine triggers the production of adrenaline, increasing the blood pressure and speeding up the heart rate. Nicotine also decreases hunger, dulls the taste buds, and prevents the creation of urine. The FDA has classified nicotine as a dangerous and addictive drug. It is known to contribute to heart and respiratory disease.

Tar and carbon monoxide
When it is burning, tobacco creates tar and carbon monoxide. Tar is a sticky, dark fluid made up of several hundred chemicals. Some of these chemicals are poisonous, and some are carcinogens. When tobacco smoke is inhaled, tar tends to settle in the bronchial tubes of the lungs, where it will damage the mucus and cilia that are charged with escorting harmful products out of the respiratory system. The smoke from burning tobacco also produces an amount of carbon monoxide about 400 times the amount considered safe by industry. Carbon monoxide is very bad for health: it prevents hemoglobin from carrying oxygen through the blood, impairs the nervous system, and is thought to be partly responsible for many heart attacks and strokes.

Heart disease
Despite the attention given to lung cancer, the leading cause of smoking-related death is actually heart disease. Smoking doubles the risk of heart attack, and smokers are much less likely to recover from an attack. Smoking is considered to be more damaging to heart health than high blood pressure and high cholesterol, though it is even more dangerous when it is combined with one or both of those. Smoking is known to cause the condition cardiomyopathy, or the weakening of the heart's pumping action. Most doctors assume that it is either the tar or the nicotine in tobacco that creates this condition. Although some heart problems, like arteriosclerosis (hardening of the arteries), persist, smokers can immediately improve the health of their heart by quitting, no matter how long they have smoked.

Stroke
Although tobacco use is not usually associated with the risk of stroke, there is clear scientific evidence that links a long-term smoking habit with an increased risk of a debilitating or fatal stroke. Indeed, even when other risk factors are taken into consideration smoking doubles the risk of stroke in men and women. Individuals suffering from hypertension (high blood pressure) exhibit the greatest benefits from quitting. Smoking seems to raise the risk of stroke by weakening the heart muscle, which in turn makes it more difficult for the body to clear blockages in the arteries that can eventually decrease the amount of blood to the brain. Individuals who quit smoking will reduce their risk of stroke, but it will never be

quite as low as those who never took up the habit.

Cancer

The risk of cancer rises in proportion to the amount that an individual smokes, the age at which they started smoking, and the length of time they have had the habit. Individuals who smoke two or more packs a day develop lung cancer between 15 and 25 times as often as non-smokers, though, interestingly, precancerous lung tissue will repair itself if the individual should quit smoking. Former smokers who have abstained for fifteen years get lung cancer only slightly more often than those who never smoker. The chemicals in cigarette smoke activate an enzyme that in turn produces carcinogens, making the development of cancer more likely. Depressed smokers are more likely to develop lung cancer, possibly because depression diminishes the effectiveness of the immune system.

Respiratory disease

One of the more immediate areas where smoking damages health is respiratory function. Even very new smokers can develop the breathlessness, cough, and excessive phlegm associated with heavy smoking. Smoking is known to contribute to instances of chronic obstructive lung disease, or COLD, a designation which includes both bronchitis and emphysema. These conditions are typically caused by a persistent inability to inhale enough air, which results in the destruction of air sacs and a strain on the heart. Chronic bronchitis is the condition in which the production of mucus increases and the bronchial tubes become inflamed, both of which help to narrow the air passages. In short, smoking is the most dangerous form of air pollution.

Miscellaneous health problems

There are seemingly countless ways in which smoking can damage health. Smokers are far more likely to develop gum disease or to lose teeth. Even when a smoker practices good oral hygiene, he or she can still suffer from damage to the bones that support teeth. A smoking habit is known to contribute to the formation of mouth and stomach ulcers, and cirrhosis of the liver. Smoking is blamed for a worsening in allergic reactions, diabetes, and hypertension. It is not uncommon for a man who smokes more than ten cigarettes a day to become temporarily impotent. Overall, cigarette smokers tend to miss about one-third more days from work and school than do non-smokers, primarily from respiratory illness. And, of course, there is always the danger of fires that begin when lit cigarettes are left unattended.

More medication

On the whole, smokers tend to require more prescription and over-the-counter medication than non-smokers. Often, this medication is required to alleviate the health problems caused by smoking. Unfortunately, there is substantial evidence to suggest that nicotine accelerates the process through which drugs are processed and removed from the body, so these medications may not be able to perform their functions adequately. In particular, this problem seems to affect anti-anxiety drugs, painkillers, tricyclic anti-depressants, anti-asthmatic drugs, and beta blockers. Smokers who are on any of these medications should confer with their doctor to determine whether the prescription needs to be adjusted.

Reasons for smoking

One of the most important factors associated with smoking appears to be education; for instance, about 90% of white males with less than a high school education are current or former smokers. Most scientists also believe that heredity plays a part in the development of a smoking habit. Studies have shown that identical twins (who have the same genes) are more likely to have similar smoking habits than fraternal twins. Young smokers are also very likely to have a parent, especially a mother, who smokes. Many youths will begin smoking as a form of rebellion, or simply to see if they like it. Unfortunately, young smokers rarely acknowledge the tremendous addictive power of cigarettes; most of them state that they are able to quit at any time, yet few actually do.

Many misguided individuals will take up smoking because they think it will help them lose weight. Indeed, the accelerated metabolism caused by nicotine does mean that smokers tend to burn about a hundred more calories every day than non-smokers. Though most who quit smoking will put on a little weight, their increased ability to exercise should enable them to get back in shape. Advertising is another culprit in persuading individuals to take up smoking. Many critics of tobacco advertising claim that it targets young people, women, and minorities. For this reason and because of the harmful effects of tobacco, the government has placed restrictions on advertising. Finally, many individuals smoke to relieve the stress of their lives. Unfortunately, using tobacco as a medication to reduce stress only increases the chance of becoming dependent on it quickly.

Psychological addiction

Tobacco creates in the user certain psychological changes that may become addictive over time. For instance, nicotine is known to stimulate the part of the brain that generates feelings of satisfaction or well-being. Nicotine is also known to temporarily enhance memory, the performance of repetitive tasks, and the tolerance of pain. It is also credited with reducing hunger and anxiety. Individuals suffering from depression may also seek relief through tobacco. Studies have consistently shown that depressed individuals are far more likely than others to develop a smoking habit. Even more troubling, the effects of depression make it much more difficult to quit smoking, so the interdependent relation between tobacco use and depression is likely to continue for a long time.

Physical addiction

Nicotine is consistently shown to be far more addictive than alcohol; whereas only one in ten users of alcohol will eventually become alcoholics, approximately eight of ten heavy smokers will attempt and fail to quit. The method that nicotine uses is similar to that of other addictive substances: it creates an immediate positive feeling when taken; it will cause painful withdrawal symptoms if it is not taken; and it stimulates powerful cravings in the user even after it is removed from the system. Nicotine addiction can become so string that a heavy smoker will experience withdrawal symptoms a mere two hours after smoking. Persistent tobacco use will also lead to an increased tolerance for nicotine, and so the user will have to consume more and more to achieve the pleasure or avoid the pain.

Women

Sadly, the number of women smokers seems to be rising in both wealthy and developing countries. For this reason, lung cancer has surpassed breast cancer as a killer of women. There are also health dangers from smoking that are unique to women. For one thing, smoking damages a woman's reproductive system, so that many women smokers will become infertile or will begin menopause earlier than they should. Female smokers are also more likely to develop osteoporosis. Smoking during pregnancy increases the risk of miscarriage, internal bleeding, premature delivery, and certain birth defects. There is substantial evidence, however, to suggest that quitting smoking at any point during a pregnancy will decrease the health risks for the mother and child alike.

Smokeless tobacco

As smoking becomes less and less acceptable in public places, sales of smokeless tobacco products are on the rise. The category smokeless tobacco includes snuff (a powdered tobacco that can be either sniffed or sucked) and chewing tobacco. With these products, nicotine is absorbed by the mucous membranes of the nose or mouth. Although smoking is considered to be a greater health

- 24 -

risk, smokeless tobacco products still create a dependence on nicotine and are known to contribute to the formation of cancer. Snuff, in particular, is very high in nicotine and quadruples the user's risk of mouth cancer. Users of smokeless tobacco also can suffer from bad breath, discolored teeth, cavities, and gum disease.

Types of smoke
Mainstream smoke is that smoke which is taken directly into the lungs by the smoker; sidestream smoke (otherwise known as second-hand smoke) is the smoke inhaled by everyone in the presence of a smoker. The smoking of a cigarette typically entails about eight or nine inhalations of mainstream smoke, each lasting for a few seconds. Sidestream smoke is actually different in composition from mainstream smoke: it has twice as much tar and nicotine, and five times as much carbon monoxide. Indeed, about 3000 people develop lung cancer each year as a result of second-hand smoke. In terms of causing cancer, sidestream smoke is thought to be more dangerous than radon gas and most of the pollutants limited by federal law.

Families of smokers
Even if they are not smokers themselves, the people who live with smokers are at an increased risk of developing serious health disorders. Secondhand smoke is known to contribute to asthma and bronchitis in children, as well as increasing the risk of sudden infant death syndrome. The spouses of smokers are about 30% more likely to develop lung cancer than are other non-smokers. Similarly, children that grow up in homes where one or both parents smoke are several times more likely to develop lung cancer, heart disease, and stroke. Finally, opinion polls have discovered that most children object to their parents' smoking, worry about the health dangers posed to themselves by second-hand smoke, and dislike the odor of smoke in their hair and clothing.

Quitting tobacco
It is extremely difficult to quit smoking by oneself, though many people try. Some doctors think that a nicotine addiction is the most difficult addiction to break. Most smokers will have to try several times before they are able to quit successfully. When smokers try to quit all by themselves, they usually begin by throwing away all of their cigarettes, by cutting down on their intake, or by switching to a less potent brand. Successful quitters are usually those who develop some other hobby, often physical exercise, to take the place of smoking. It is also a good idea to explore various means of relaxation apart from tobacco, so that kicking the habit will not be an extremely stressful event.

Studies have consistently shown that individuals who join some kind of support group have a much higher chance of permanently ending a smoking addiction. Every year, the American Cancer Society puts on about 1500 clinics in which individuals get the training and the encouragement they need to quit smoking. The American Lung Association also organizes group therapy sessions for those who hope to quit, and they emphasize cooperation and group interdependence as a tool for avoiding tobacco. It is also common for businesses to sponsor smoking cessation programs for their employees (particularly if they think smoking habits are costing their business money). Some program use aversion therapy, in which some kind of negative experience (like an electric shock or bad taste) is given to the user every time he or she lights up, in the hopes of persuading him or her from starting again.

Nicotine gum
Nicotine gum, usually sold under the name Nicorette, is a chewing gum that gradually releases nicotine. This nicotine is absorbed through the mucous membranes of the mouth and, although it is not significant enough to produce the pleasant effects of a cigarette, will minimize the symptoms of withdrawal

from smoking. This product is fairly expensive (a month's supply goes for about $45) and has a somewhat bitter taste. Nicotine gum is not meant to become a long-term habit in its own right, and because it contains nicotine it has many of the damaging effects on health as smoking. Pregnant women or individuals with heart disease would not use nicotine gum. Individuals who use nicotine gum should gradually reduce their consumption until they are entirely free of the nicotine addiction.

Nicotine patches
Nicotine patches, formally know as nicotine transdermal delivery systems, are affixed to the skin and slowly provide a low level of nicotine to the body. Typically, patches are worn for between 6 and 16 weeks. Although the patch is known to minimize withdrawal symptoms, it has been most successful only with those individuals who are highly motivated to quit, are enrolled in some kind of counseling program, and were smoking more than a pack of cigarettes every day. Doctors caution those who use the patch that, although it can help diminish the physical dependency on nicotine, it does not reduce the psychological addiction. Pregnant women and individuals with heart disease should not use the patch, and under no circumstances should any individual wear more than one patch at a time.

Hypnosis and acupuncture
Many individuals who have tried unsuccessfully to quit smoking in the past will explore hypnosis and acupuncture therapy. When hypnosis is used, the individual is put into a mild trance state and given suggestions that will hopefully persuade them to quit smoking. Hypnosis may not affect the physical dependence on nicotine, but it can create a good attitude for quitting successfully. When acupuncture therapy is given, the individual has a circular needle or staple inserted into the flap in front of his or

her ear hole. This therapy is meant to stimulate the production of calming chemicals in the brain, and those who are given the therapy are encouraged to gently move the needle or staple when they feel a temptation to smoke.

Drug abuse

A drug is any chemical substance that changes the way a person acts or feels. Drugs may affect a person's mental, physical, and emotional state. Though many drugs are taken to improve the condition of the body, or to remedy personal problems, drugs can also undermine health by distorting a person's mind and weakening a person's body. According to the World Health Organization, drug abuse is any excessive drug use that is not approved by the medical profession. The use of some drugs in any quantity is considered abuse; other drugs must be taken in large quantities before they are considered to have been abused. There are health risks involved with the use of any drug, legal or illegal, insofar as they introduce a foreign substance into the balanced system of physical health.

Administering drugs
Drugs can e introduced to the body through a host of different means. The most common way of taking a drug is by swallowing it in solid, liquid, or plasma form. This method is a bit slower than placing a drug directly into the bloodstream via injection. Drugs may also be inhaled; inhalants that are placed in a plastic bag and breathed are said to be huffed. There are also a few different types of injection: intravenous injections are made directly into a vein; intramuscular injections are made into muscle tissue; and subcutaneous injections are made below the skin. Of these, intravenous injections act the fastest, while the effects of a subcutaneous injection may not be felt for ten minutes or more.

Variables affecting drug use

The particular effects experienced by a drug user depend on a few different variables: dosage, individual characteristics, and setting. For most drugs, an increase in dosage will intensify the effects of the drug. There may also be a change in the effect experienced from a drug at low dosage than from that same drug at a higher dosage. Every person will respond differently to a drug as well, depending on their psychological and physical state. The enzymes in the bloodstream play a major role in reducing drug levels in the blood, so an individual's drug experience will largely depend on the quality and quantity of his or her enzymes. Many people report a change in the effects of a drug related to their setting; a stressful situation, for instance, may cause the effects of some drugs to be more intense.

Drug toxicity

The toxicity level of a drug is the amount of it that when taken will be poisonous to the body. A drug taken at a toxic level will cause either temporary or permanent damage to the body. Indeed, the enzymes in the liver that are responsible for breaking down drugs are called detoxification enzymes. Drugs may act locally, generally, or selectively. A drug acts locally when it only affects a specific area of the body. A drug acts generally when it affects an entire system of the body. A barbiturate, for instance, has a deadening effect on the entire nervous system. A drug acts selectively when it has a much greater effect on one organ or system than any other. Some anesthetics, for instance, isolate a particular part of the body to be numbed.

Drug interactions

There are four main ways in which drugs can interact. In an additive interaction, the cumulative effect of all the drugs taken is simply the sum total of the individual effects of each drug. In a synergistic interaction, however, the cumulative effect of all the drugs taken is greater than the effects of each individual drug. An example of a synergistic interaction is when barbiturates are mixed with alcohol, resulting in a greatly magnified depressant effect. A drug interaction is referred to as potentiating when one drug increases the effect of another. Alcohol, for example, has a potentiating effect on some cold medicines. Drugs are said to be antagonistic when they either neutralize or stifle the effects of one another.

Over-the counter drugs

In the United States, there are more than half a million health products that can be purchased without the approval of a doctor. Many of these products (aspirin, for example) can have serious side effects. Some drugs that could formerly only be obtained with a doctor's permission are now available for immediate purchase, though consumers should be aware of their possible dangers. Nasal sprays, for instance, can have the opposite effect than they intend if they are used too often. Laxatives can also do permanent damage to the body if they are taken too regularly. Eye drops may eventually make eyes redder if they are used habitually. Lastly, over-the-counter sleep aids have not yet been adequately researched, and some doctors suspect they may have negative consequences for mental health.

Prescription drugs

Every year, the Food and Drug Administration of the United States grants permission for the production of about twenty new prescription drugs. Though these drugs can be very beneficial, they are frequently misused. The most common mistakes associated with prescription drug use are overdosing, underdosing, leaving information off of prescriptions, ordering the wrong dosage form (liquid instead of solid, for instance), and neglecting to recognize an allergic reaction to some drug. Failure to properly take a prescription medication can lead to recurrent infections, medical complications, and even death. Some patients endanger their own health by failing to adhere to the dosage schedule, or be neglecting to tell their doctor about side effects.

Physical side effects

There is no prescription drug which does not cause some side effects, even if these go unnoticed by the patient. It is very common to have an allergic reaction to a drug. The most common allergic reactions are to penicillin and other antibiotics. These allergic responses may entail nausea, hives, a drop in blood pressure, constriction of the breathing passages, and even collapse. Patients who suffer an extreme reaction may require an immediate shot of adrenaline to maintain their vital processes. With other drugs, complications can include heart problems, blood disorders, birth defects, blindness, and memory problems. It is for this reason that prescription drugs should only be taken under the close supervision of a doctor.

Psychological side effects

Sometimes, it is more difficult for patients to notice the psychological effects of a prescription medication than the physical side effects. The drugs most likely to cause noticeable psychological problems are those for depression, high blood pressure, epilepsy, asthma, insomnia, and arthritis. Doctors assert that psychological problems associate with drugs are more likely to affect people as they get older, especially if they are taking a large number of medications. Many of these drugs either induce depression by slowing the blood pressure, or induce anxiety by overstimulating the nervous system. The best way to manage to psychological side effects of a prescription drug is to learn as much as possible about the drug and closely monitor yourself in consultation with a doctor.

Generic drugs

When doctors refer to the generic name of a drug, they mean the chemical name. A particular drug may be sold under a variety of different brand names, which may cost a great deal more than the generic form of the drug. Most of the time, there is no substantial difference between the brand-name version of a drug and the generic, so many patients save a bit of money by using the latter. In order to get the best value out of prescription medications, one should confer with one's doctor about one's diet and activity level, to ensure that the prescribed dosage is appropriate. It is also important to learn how to store particular prescriptions, so that they do not diminish in effectiveness or become contaminated.

Caffeine

Caffeine is the most commonly used mind-altering (psychotropic) drug in the world. It is a stimulant, so it relieves drowsiness and aids in the performance of repetitive tasks. There is some anecdotal evidence to suggest that caffeine improves physical performance and endurance. On the other hand, overconsumption of caffeine can lead to anxiety, dizziness, insomnia, upset stomach, and addiction. Caffeine does enter the tissues of a growing fetus, although there is no evidence to suggest that it causes birth defects. Extremely high doses of caffeine can result in seizure and respiratory failure. Withdrawal from caffeine can be a painful process, and should be done gradually.

Substance abuse

In recent years, medical professionals have shifted from viewing drug addiction as a sign of immorality to seeing it as a legitimate physiological disorder, which can be treated by medicine and psychological therapy. Scientists believe that prolonged use of drugs can cause chemical changes in the brain that create addiction, and can endure for the entirety of the person's life. The most common traits of chemical dependency are loss of control over dosage and frequency of use, and continued use despite harmful consequences. Unfortunately, one of the other common characteristics of drug addiction is the refusal to admit that it exists. Many doctors believe that only by removing the stigma of drug addiction will it be possible to treat all those who need help.

Psychological and physical dependence

A psychological dependence on drugs may begin as a craving for the pleasurable feelings or relief from anxiety that the drug provides. However, this craving can soon turn into a dependency on the drug in order to perform normal mental operations. A physical dependency, on the other hand, is said to occur when the individual requires increasing amounts of the drug to get the desired effect. Many drugs, like marijuana or hallucinogens, do not cause withdrawal symptoms; others, like heroin or cocaine, may be extremely painful to stop using. Individuals with a severe chemical dependency will eventually use a drug like this simply to avoid experiencing the effects of withdrawal. Typically, an individual with a severe dependency will try to stop many times without success.

Variables of drug abuse

In clinical terms, intoxication is the behavioral, psychological, and physiological changes that occur in a drug user. In the beginning stages of drug addiction, the goal is usually intoxication. Later in the addiction process, however, the goal of use tends to be avoiding withdrawal symptoms. Withdrawal is any physiological distress that occurs because a drug is not taken. Many drug abusers take several different drugs, though they may prefer only one; this condition is known as polyabuse. Studies have also shown that there is a significant overlap between people with chemical dependencies and people with psychological disorders. This overlap is known as comorbidity, and in part accounts for the profound problems that many drug abusers face in trying to escape their addictions.

Biology of drug addiction

Scientists have recently made great progress in understanding the biology of addiction by observing that many abused substances (alcohol, marijuana, and cocaine, for instance) trigger the release of dopamine in the brain. Dopamine is a neurochemical associated with the feeling of satisfaction and pleasure. Not only do many addictive substances raise the level of dopamine in the brain, they also alter the pathways through which dopamine is released and accessed in the brain, so that it becomes possible for the user to enjoy these feelings only when the particular substance is used. There is also evidence to suggest that individual born with especially low levels of dopamine may be more susceptible to drug addiction.

Non-biological addiction

Some individuals are at a higher risk of addiction because they lack self-control, have no moral opposition to drugs, have low self-esteem, or are depressed. Research has also shown that individuals who live in isolation or in poverty are more likely to become addicted to drugs. People who associate with drug users are more likely to become users themselves. Drugs that produce a short-lived but intense state of intoxication (cocaine, for instance) are more likely to be addictive, as are those that have especially painful withdrawal symptoms. Most of the people who will experiment with drugs do so during adolescence. Although many have suggested that drugs like alcohol, tobacco, and marijuana lead to use of harder drugs, most research on this subject has been inconclusive.

Chronic drug use

The effects of habitual drug use can be either chronic (resulting from long-term use) or acute (resulting from a single dose). Acute effects are usually determined by the particular drug; first-time users of stimulants, for instance, may be overcome with a powerful sense of anger. The effects of chronic drug use are more predictable. Over a long period of time, consistent drug users may feel tired, lose weight, have a nagging cough, or develop overall body aches. Drug abusers often suffer from blackouts, and may undergo psychological turmoil and bouts of paranoia. Typically, the stress involved with supporting and maintaining a habit increases over time, and this stress adds to the damage done by the drug itself.

- 29 -

Amphetamines

For a long time, amphetamines were prescribed to control weight gain. Now, however, doctors have decided that these powerful stimulants can be extremely addictive and dangerous to health. Some common names of amphetamines are Benzedrine, Dexedrine, Methedrine. Other substances that are related to amphetamines include Ritalin, Cylert, and Preludin. Amphetamines are usually taken orally, though they may also be snorted, smoked, or injected. Some forms of methamphetamine are extremely addictive and can have effects lasting from between twelve to fourteen hours. These products all trigger the release of adrenaline, which stimulates the central nervous system and raises the heart rate.

Amphetamines make the user very alert and full of energy. Users typically report a feeling of well-being and confidence, and a sense that they are thinking very clearly, even though research does not indicate that this is so. Amphetamine users are very talkative and animated, to the point of being uncomfortably restless. Large dosages will produce confusion, incoherent speech, anxiety, and even heart palpitations. In the short-term, amphetamine use can cause heart trouble, a loss of coordination, anger, nausea, or chills. Over the long term, it may cause malnutrition, skin disorders, insomnia, depression, vitamin deficiencies, and brain damage affecting the areas controlling speech. Withdrawing from amphetamines can also be a very difficult and painful process.

Cannabis

Cannabis, also known as marijuana, pot or hashish, is a commonly abused drug. When taken, it relaxes the mind and body, affects the mood, and heightens sensory perceptions. Cannabis use speeds up the heart rate, dries out the mouth and throat, impairs the ability to react to external stimuli and causes lethargy. In large doses, cannabis may cause hallucinations and panic attacks. Long-term users of cannabis exhibit decreased motivation and laziness. The general risks of prolonged cannabis use are a psychological dependence, impaired memory and cognitive abilities, increased blood pressure, lung cancer, emphysema, impaired coordination, and diminished fertility.

Cocaine and crack

Cocaine and its deadly derivative, crack, are among the most addictive and deadly substances that are commonly abused. When they are taken, whether through inhalation or intravenous injection, they accelerate the mental and physical processes, and create in the mind of the user a feeling of invulnerability and high energy. They may cause health problems in the short term ranging from headaches and shaking to seizures, collapse, and death. Over the long term, cocaine and crack users usually have impaired sexual function, blood pressure problems, heart trouble, brain hemorrhaging, hepatitis, and malnutrition. Users of these drugs are also more likely to contract the HIV virus. Cocaine users become paranoid, angry, and suspicious.

Hallucinogens

Hallucinogens are those substances, like LSD, mescaline, and psilocybin, which create profound changes in the mind's ability to function. When taken, hallucinogens will produce visions and temporary feelings of satisfaction and euphoria. They may also lead to an increased heart rate, blood pressure, and body temperature. They are associated with headaches, nausea, sweating, trembling, heart palpitations, and poor coordination. More serious, perhaps, is the possibility of having an extremely traumatic psychological experience while under the influence of one of these drugs. Many individuals report long-term, possibly permanent side effects from hallucinogens. These side effects may include depression, flashbacks, and delusions.

Inhalants

Inhalants are those drugs which are taken into the body through huffing or vigorous inhalation. They typically produce momentary hallucinations and a feeling of well-being. The effects of inhalants typically only last for a period of seconds. Inhalants have been blamed for dizziness, involuntary eye movements, nausea, lethargy, poor coordination, impaired motor skills, nosebleeds, loss of appetite, aggressiveness, and an increased risk of accident and injury. Furthermore, the chronic use of inhalants may lead to hepatitis, kidney failure, respiratory trouble, irregular heartbeat, bone problems, and heart failure. It is quite possible to die the first time you ever try an inhalant.

Opioids
The opioid family of narcotics (opium, morphine, heroin) relaxes the central nervous system and provides a temporary relief to physical pain. They also produce a short-term sense of mental well-being and satisfaction. They have serious health consequences, however. Opioids are blamed for restlessness, nausea, weight loss, loss of sex drive, slurred speech, sweating, drowsiness, and impaired judgment, attention, and memory. Over time, many individuals will become extremely addicted to opioids, and will suffer from malnutrition, an impaired immune system, infections of the heart and lungs, hepatitis, tetanus, depression, skin abscesses, and even the HIV virus. It is also possible to overdose on these drugs and lapse into a coma or die.

Phencyclidine
Phencyclidine (PCP), otherwise known as PCP or angel dust, is one of the more dangerous drugs that are commonly abused. When it is taken, it immediately produces a profound change in perceptions, including hallucinations and delusions of personal strength. Individuals on PCP may incorrectly believe that they are invulnerable. Besides the obvious risks associated with this psychological condition, PCP users will experience flushing, an increase in heart rate, diminished sensitivity to pain, impaired coordination and speech, and possibly be put into a stupor. The use of PCP can cause a psychosis, will increase the risk of danger to

the user and those around the user, and can cause immediate coma and death.

Barbiturates
Barbiturates are those drugs that slow down the central nervous system and, in the beginning stages of use, reduce physical and mental tension. Barbiturates are also known to decrease alertness and to induce drowsiness. Besides the obvious risks barbiturates pose to a driver, there is also the danger of slowed breathing, weak heartbeat, disrupted sleep, impaired vision, confusion, chronic lethargy, and irritability. Over a long period of time, many abusers of barbiturates will become dependent on the drug, and may become virtually comatose. Indeed, excessively large doses of barbiturates can immediately result in coma, stupor, or death. There are tremendously painful withdrawal symptoms associated with barbiturates.

Ecstasy
The complex chemical MDMA, popularly known as Ecstasy, has emerged as one of the most common and dangerous drugs of the past decade. Originally developed as a solution to social anxiety and depression, Ecstasy has become popular among young people, who report that it causes a feeling of happiness and euphoria. Users of the drug, however, also report some troubling side effects. Ecstasy has been linked with insomnia, nausea, fatigue, and problems with concentrating. It is particularly dangerous to take the drug in a chaotic and hot environment, like a dance club, because it is liable to dehydrate the user to a dangerous degree. There have been scores of deaths blamed on Ecstasy, most of the time because the user raised their body temperature to around 110 degrees.

Treatment of drug dependence

For most drug users, the most difficult part of the recovery process is admitting that they have a problem. Sometimes, it is necessary for friends and family to intervene in order to get the user to realize the dangers of his or her behavior. Once this is accomplished, treatment can take place in an outpatient facility, a residential facility, or a hospital. Many individuals receive both physical and psychological therapy to help them break the addiction in its every form. For drugs that have painful withdrawal effects, it is recommended that the user be supervised closely by a professional. One of the key parts of any rehabilitation effort is continued contact with the patient after the period of therapy, as most addicts will relapse into their former behaviors after release.

Twelve-step programs
Though it was first introduced by Alcoholics Anonymous, the twelve-step method of recovery has become the model for rehabilitation in over 200 organizations. The basic tenet of a twelve-step program is that the user is powerless to control his or her own addiction. In order to be a part of the program, the individual must want to quit. Then, he or she will get in touch with a group and attend meetings. One of the fundamental parts of the twelve-step program is the cooperation among members; when one feels tempted to relapse into the former behavior, he or she is supposed to call on other members for support. Individuals are ultimately responsible for themselves, however, and are not required to pay dues or to attend any meeting if they do not desire.

Relapse prevention
Most substance abusers will relapse several times after kicking the habit. This is important for both the user and the user's support group to know, so that they do not become too frustrated at any setbacks on the road to recovery. Some therapists even say that these relapses can strengthen self-understanding and make it more likely that future relapses can be avoided. Over time, abusers should be able to recognize the stimuli that tend to make them use, and they should learn to avoid these people, places, and situations. It is also important to make the distinction between a minor and a major relapse; often, it is a huge victory for a

recovering addict to keep a minor relapse from turning into a major one.

Physical education classes

Safety training
The point of any safety training for physical education classes is to reduce injury among students and staff. According to recent figures, the most injuries are associated with football, baseball, basketball, gymnastics, and skiing, respectively. It is important that teachers do not assume that students will know which safety precautions they need to make. On the contrary, teachers should make a point of stating all the necessary safety requirements for ach activity, and posting a list of safety guidelines where every student can read it. Moreover, teachers should receive regular safety instruction from knowledgeable professionals. Finally, teachers should always be aware of any medical issues relevant to particular students, in the event of an emergency.

Avoiding injuries
In order to avoid unnecessary injuries in class, physical education teachers can follow a few simple guidelines. First, they should conduct safety orientations with students any time they are to begin a new activity or begin using a new piece of equipment. When students are to be spread out over a wide area, it is a good idea to designate a couple of students as safety monitors, to ensure that play remains safe and civil. Teachers should always check to make sure playing fields are free of debris and athletic equipment is in good working order; this includes keeping an inventory of physical education equipment. If an injury should occur, detailed records of it should be kept so that, later, teachers can consider how similar injuries may be avoided in the future.

Safety committees
As part of a comprehensive program to ensure safety in physical education classes, a committee should be formed to provide a forum for people who want to discuss issues

of safety. This committee should meet regularly to propose and ratify safety initiatives, debate the inclusion of new activities, and consider any injuries that have recently occurred. Such a committee should include school administrators, teachers, school nurses, parents, and students. It is especially important for school administrators to be a part of the committee, as they be held legally liable for any accidents that occur in class. Students are also a crucial part of this committee, as they are the most likely group to observe new threats to safety.

Warming up and cooling down
There are important reasons for warming up before and cooling down after exercise. For one thing, performance is always enhanced by warming up. Muscles tend to work more effectively when their temperature has been slightly raised; they are also more resistant to strains and tears at a higher temperature. Warming up directs the blood to working muscles, and gives the heart time to adjust to the increased demands of the muscles. Warming up also stimulates the secretion of synovial fluid into the joints, which makes them less likely to suffer wear and tear. Warming up should include slow stretching and low-impact cardiovascular exercise. Cooling down is important for easing the body's transition to a normal resting condition. By stretching and slowly decreasing cardiovascular workload, the heart is aided in its readjustment.

Assessing personal fitness
Personal fitness is particular to the individual: some people may be considered fit when they can run for a mile without stopping, while others may be athletic enough to accomplish that feat without really being in shape. Most people will acquire a sense of their own fitness only after spending a great deal of time exercising, setting fitness goals, and working to achieve them. However, those who want more objective data on their physical condition may submit to testing at a sports medicine laboratory. There, they will have their muscular and cardiovascular endurance measured on a treadmill, their body fat measured in a submersion tank, and their flexibility tested through a variety of trials.

Physical Best
Physical Best is a package of health education materials compiled by the American Fitness Alliance. The resources of Physical Best are designed to be implemented by physical education teachers, and include guidebooks, suggested activities, and videos. The goal of all the materials provided by Physical Best is to maximize the time spent on task, allow students to receive individual feedback on their performance, keep instruction time to a minimum, and encourage effective class management. There are a variety of activities, both competitive and non-competitive, vigorous and more relaxed, that will be suitable for any class. The Physical best guides also offer easy ways to assess student fitness and motivate students to better health behaviors.

President's Challenge
The Active Lifestyle Program of the President's Challenge is designed to encourage a healthy amount of physical exercise for young adults. This program is slightly less rigorous than the Presidential Champions Program. For this program, the goal is to exercise for an hour a day (thirty minutes for adults) at least five days a week, for six weeks. Any activity is acceptable, as long as it uses large muscle groups and provides a good cardio-vascular workout. The President's Challenge website recommends tennis, basketball, hiking, or even doing chores vigorously. The President's Challenge provides an activity log for keeping track of progress, and will send an award to those who complete the program. According to the President's Challenge website, teens should walk a certain number of steps every day: 11,000 or more for girls, and 13,000 or more for boys.

The Presidential Champions Program in the President's Challenge is designed to be a

- 33 -

rigorous development of physical fitness. In this program, points are earned based on the amount of calories that are consumed by each activity, with a maximum of 750 points a day. There are a number of different activities that earn points, from aerobics to racquetball to martial arts. In the Advanced Performance portion of the Presidential Champions program, individuals can earn Bronze Stars by acquiring 40,000 points. The website asserts that individuals who run approximately 40 miles a week should be able to earn a Bronze Star in a little over ten weeks. As with the other programs in the President's Challenge, an activity log is provided complementary so that you can track your progress.

Fitnessgram

Fitnessgram is a software package designed to effectively assess student fitness. Besides showing students there current level of fitness, it shows them specific areas where theyc an improve, and charts their progress. Fitnessgram declares that it can give a more helpful assessment of fitness because it compares student scores to carefully-researched standards; because it focuses on fitness as it relates to health, rather than as it relates to sports performance; and because it goes beyond assessment to recommend activities for students based on their performance. Fitnessgram also declares that students will enjoy the interactive nature of the software, wherein they can explore their own fitness and monitor their own progress.

Basic first-aid

Since it is necessary to act fast when an emergency happens, it is a good idea to think ahead and have a plan in place. If you are in a public place, you may want to begin by shouting for help, to see if a doctor is available. Someone should immediately dial 911. Do not attempt any resuscitation techniques unless you are trained. If you have a car and it is appropriate, you should immediately take the victim to the nearest hospital. Furthermore, every home should have some basic first-aid supplies. A good first-aid kit will include bandages, sterile gauze pads, scissors, adhesive tape, calamine lotion, cotton balls, thermometer, ipecac syrup (to induce vomiting), a sharp needle, and safety pins.

Treating an open wound

When treating an open wound, first apply direct pressure to the wounded area, covering it entirely. This should be done with sterile gauze or a sanitary pad; ice or cold water in the pad can help slow bleeding. Apply steady pressure for between five and fifteen minutes. If possible, elevate the wound above the heart, as this can help to slow bleeding. If after fifteen minutes the bleeding has stopped, the victim may need to see a doctor for further treatment. This is also the case if stitches will be require to keep the wound closed, if the victim has not had a tetanus shot within the last ten years, or if the injury appears serious and shown no sign of decreasing in blood loss.

Treating internal bleeding

If you suspect that a person is bleeding internally (for instance, if they cough or vomit up blood, or if they pass blood in their waste matter), do not allow that person to take any fluids or medication, because these could get in the way if surgery is necessary. Lay the victim flat and cover him or her with a light blanket, then seek medical attention immediately.

Treating a bloody nose

If a person is experiencing a bloody nose, have them sit down, leaning slightly forward. The victim should spit out any blood in his or her nose or mouth. Apply light but steady pressure to the area for about ten minutes, and then if the bleeding continues, pack the nose with gauze. If there is foreign object lodged in the nose, do not attempt to remove it.

Treating breathing problems

If an unconscious victim is either not breathing or shows no signs of breath, lay him on his back on the ground. Loosen any clothing that may be constricting some part of the body. Immediately check the air passages for any foreign objects, and then open the air passage by tilting the head back and lifting the chin up. Pinch the nostrils shut with thumb and index finger, then deliver two deep breaths directly into the victim's mouth. Each of these breaths should last from one to ten seconds. After each, look at the victim's chest to see of it rises. Repeat this process once every five seconds, until medical help arrives. If your breaths do not seem to raise the victim's chest, tilt the head back further and check for signs of choking.

Treating a broken bone
If you think someone may have broken a bone, restrict him or her from moving unless there is some immediate danger. First, ensure that the individual is breathing normally. If the person is bleeding, apply pressure to the wound before assessing the potentially broken bone. Never try to push a broken bone back into place, especially if it is protruding from the skin. If possible, applying a moist compress to any exposed bone can prevent drying that may make it more difficult for the bone to heal. Never try to straighten a fracture, and never allow the victim of a broken bone to walk. Any unstable fractures should be placed in a splint to prevent painful motions.

Treating burns
If a person has been burned by fire, cool the burned area with water as soon as possible. This will help to stop the burn process. Next, remove the victim's garments and jewelry, and cover the victim with clean sheets or towels. Once the victim is secure, call for emergency medical assistance. If burns have been caused by chemicals, wash the affected area immediately with cool water. Affected areas should be washed for at least twenty minutes. When the eyes are burned by chemicals, the victim will require immediate medical attention even after the eyes have been washed with cool water for twenty minutes.

Treating a conscious choking victim
Never slap an individual's back if he or she appears to be choking; this can make the situation worse. If the victim is conscious but cannot cough, speak, or breathe, perform the Heimlich maneuver. First, stand behind the victim, wrapping your arms around his or her waist. Make a fist with one hand and place the fist just above the victim's navel. Grab the fist with your other hand and pull upward sharply, trying not to exert too much pressure against the rib cage with your forearms. Repeat this procedure until the victim is either no longer choking or has lost consciousness. This procedure can be performed on oneself, either with one's fist or by pressing sharply against some stationary object, like the back of a chair.

Treating an unconscious choking victim
If a person is choking and has lost consciousness, first lie him or her on the ground and perform mouth-to mouth resuscitation. If this does not seem to work, give the person a few abdominal thrusts, as in the Heimlich maneuver. Repeat this from six to ten times if necessary. Next, try to clear the victim's airway: tilt his or her head back, use your thumb to depress his or her tongue, and gently sweep a hooked finger through the back of the throat to remove any objects. Repeat the sequence of abdominal thrusts, probing of the mouth, and mouth-to-mouth resuscitation as many times as necessary. If the victim suddenly is revived but nothing has come out of his or her mouth, go to the hospital. Hard matter can damage the internal organs as it passes through the body.

Treating a drowning victim
A person who has drowned can die four to six minutes after they have stopped breathing. First, get the victim out of the water immediately. Place the victim on his or her back and, if he or she is not breathing, immediately begin performing mouth-to-mouth resuscitation. Continue this treatment either until the victim begins breathing normally or help arrives. It should be noted that it can take as long as two hours for a

- 35 -

drowning victim to regain independent breathing. Never leave a victim of drowning alone. Once the victim has begun breathing normally, simply wait nearby until professional help arrives. Resuscitation efforts can be suspended if the individual begins coughing.

Treating a victim of electrical shock
If you believe a person has been rendered unconscious by an electrical shock, approach them cautiously. You should always make sure that the source of the electricity has been turned off. If the victim's breathing has stopped or is weak, immediately begin mouth-to-mouth resuscitation. Even if the victim should regain consciousness, it is a good idea to call for emergency medical assistance. While you are waiting for help to arrive, cover the victim with a blanket or coat, and have them lie flat with legs slightly raised. Support the victim's head with a pillow, but do not give the victim anything to eat or drink. Never put butter, a burn spray, or any other household remedy on an electrical burn, even those that appear minor.

Treating the victim of a heart attack
An individual may be suffering from a heart attack if he or she has an intense clenching pain in the chest, has shortness of breath, sweats heavily, is nauseous, has an irregular pulse, has pale or bluish skin, and is beset by severe anxiety. If you believe someone may be having a heart attack, immediately call for medical assistance. Have the person sit up, and loosen any tight clothing. Try to keep the person comfortably warm. If the person is on medication for angina pectoris, help him or her take it. If the person is unconscious and you are trained to perform CPR, then do so after checking for a pulse at the wrist or neck. If there is no pulse, perform CPR along with mouth-to-mouth resuscitation. Even if you are untrained, performing chest compressions until help arrives is recommended for victims of a heart attack.

Treating a victim of poisoning

If you feel an individual has been poisoned, you should be prepared to call 911 and the Poison Control Center and tell them the kind and quantity of poison that has been ingested, as well as the symptoms. Do not administer any medications unless you are instructed to do so by a professional. If a poisoned child is conscious, give him or her a little bit of water to dilute the poison. If a victim of poisoning is unconscious, make sure that he or she is breathing and, if not, perform mouth-to-mouth resuscitation. If he or she is vomiting, make sure they do not choke. Even though vomiting is the easiest way to remove poisons from the body, never try to induce vomiting when an individual has swallowed acid or an alkaline substance.

Life guarding certification

The American Red Cross offers a comprehensive training program for individuals seeking to become lifeguards. The program includes training on basic surveillance skills, water and land rescue, first aid and CPR, and the responsibilities of the professional lifeguard, which include encouraging public safety and handling unruly swimmers. Many lifeguard will also benefit from becoming certified to use an automated external defibrillator (AED), and being trained to prevent disease transmission. Individuals must be at least fifteen years old to receive certification as a trained lifeguard. Many of the skills learned during lifeguard training can be used in emergency situations away from the water.

Physical educators

Liability
Because they supervise students during the performance of sometimes-dangerous activities, physical educators should be aware of the legal codes that affect their profession. Most cases in which physical educators are held responsible for the injury of a student hinge on the idea of liability. For a physical education teacher, the law asserts that he or she is liable, or responsible, for maintaining

- 36 -

certain standards of safety on the job. If a student is injured and the physical education teacher is found to have failed to provide the basic level of training and supervision for that activity, he or she is said to be negligent. Negligence on the part of a physical educator is considered to be a tort, a crime committed by one person against another.

Negligence

In order to prove that a physical educator has been negligent, the court must consider a few different points. First, the court must decide what constitutes the duty of the school and the teacher; has the conduct of the teacher made it impossible for this duty to be fulfilled? The court must also determine that an injury has in fact occurred. In order to be charged with negligence, an actual injury must have occurred at a time when the teacher should have been in a position to prevent it. The court must also establish that the injury was a direct result of the failure of the teacher to perform his or her duty. Finally, the court will have to establish that the injury suffered by the student could have been reasonably anticipated by a teacher.

Types of negligence

There are a few different types of negligence with which a physical educator may be charged. Malfeasance occurs when the teacher has committed some act which is against the law. Misfeasance, on the other hand, occurs when the teacher obeys the law but does not do so well enough to prevent injury. Nonfeasance occurs when a teacher has failed to perform some act which could have prevented injury to a student. Contributory negligence occurs when the injured student is in part to blame for his or her injury. Finally, comparative (or shared) negligence is said to have occurred when both the injured student and the teacher are to blame. In this case, the student can only receive compensation from the teacher if he or she can prove that the teacher is more to blame.

Physical education equipment

In order to avoid being found liable for any injuries suffered by students with the school's physical education equipment, teachers should be sure to observe a few basic rules of caution concerning the equipment. First, teachers should constantly monitor school equipment to ensure that it is functioning properly and is not a danger to students. Broken or damaged equipment should be immediately removed and/or replaced. The grass on school playing fields should be kept short and free of debris, and the floors of the gymnasium should be dry enough for students to run without slipping. Teachers should always bear in mind the legal concept of "attractive nuisance": that is, teachers are responsible for removing any piece of equipment which could be dangerous and which will probably be intriguing to students.

Avoiding injury

In order to minimize the situations in which they can potentially be said to have been negligent, physical educators should observe a few basic rules when supervising physical activities. For one thing, teachers should avoid creating mismatches in competitive events; students on both sides are at greater risk of injury when they compete with someone of vastly different skill level. For any activities which can reasonably be considered dangerous, students should have to fill out a waiver absolving the school of all responsibility for injuries sustained in the normal course of play. Students may also need to be subjected to medical examinations if there is a possibility that a health issue may put them at a greater risk of injury during an activity. Finally, it is essential that students warm up properly before physical activities, as this greatly reduces the risk of injury.

Minimizing the effects of a lawsuit

No matter how responsible and cautious they are, many physical educators will be charged with negligence for a student injury at some point in their career. In order to avoid having their professional life seriously damaged by such allegations, teachers should make sure that they have liability insurance. This is

- 37 -

typically provided by the school district. Oftentimes, a good liability insurance policy allows the teacher to settle cases out of court. Teachers should also be sure to keep good records of any accidents, as these will be important to a legal defense. Finally, teachers should create and maintain a comprehensive checklist of safety and emergency care guidelines, so that they will be prepared in the event of any injury and can demonstrate an intention to protect students.

Disease and Health-Risk Prevention

Aging

Aging skin

As you get older, you can expect that your skin will become less resilient and will stretch more easily. Of particular danger to aging skin is exposure to ultraviolet radiation from the sun. Over a long period of exposure, the skin will develop wrinkles and areas of spotty pigmentation. These effects can be avoided by wearing hats, gloves, and sunglasses, and by wearing sunscreen on any exposed parts of the body. Human skin typically becomes drier as it ages, so it is increasingly important to keep it moisturized with lotions or oils. Overusing soaps and antiperspirants can contribute to the dryness of skin. Also, the sweat and oil glands of the skin will naturally diminish in function as you age.

Body fat and hair

Most individuals increase in body fat as they get older, although they also diminish in overall body size because of a reduction in muscle mass and body water content. Regular exercise, including weight training, can help to forestall these changes in body composition. Oftentimes, the higher levels of body fat in older individuals create a higher risk of disease, so it is important to monitor your weight throughout your life. The natural graying of the hair as you age is the result of the deaths of the cells that produce pigment at the base of the follicle. Individual hair shafts are thickest at age 20, and gradually shrink after that. Most individuals have hair as fine as they did as an infant once they reach the age of seventy.

Hearing

For most people, it becomes progressively more difficult to distinguish high-pitched and hissing noises. Indeed, hearing loss is currently ranked as the fourth most-common chronic physical disability in the United States. Even though hearing may diminish early in life, most people don't notice hearing loss until it has progressed beyond repair. In order to guard against future hearing loss, you should avoid exposing yourself to loud noises. Recent research has also suggested that a high-fat diet may contribute to hearing loss later in life by clogging the blood vessels that nourish hearing organs. Individuals should wear earplugs or protective ear guards when confronting loud music or machinery.

Eyesight

Most people in their forties will develop presbyopia, a reduced ability to focus on nearby objects. Presbyopia is caused by the slowing of the expansions and contractions of the lens. This often makes it more difficult for people to read by a dim light, or to drive at night. Aging individuals also are prone to cataracts, a clouding of the lens caused by natural oxidation of the eye. Most individuals who suffer from minor cataracts do not know it, and therefore aging individuals should undergo regular eye examinations to determine whether they may continue driving. It is also quite common for individuals to adjust to changes in light more slowly and to have inferior depth perception as they age.

Taste, smell, and teeth

As individuals age, their senses of taste and smell will tend to deteriorate. Approximately two-thirds of the taste buds in the mouth will die by the age of seventy, along with many of the smell receptors in the nose. The ability to smell is often diminished by a long-term exposure to smoke or smog. Many of the medication prescribed to elderly individuals interfere with the sense of taste. Thanks to fluorinated water and advances in dentistry, it is quite possible to have the same teeth for a lifetime. Indeed, most dental problems later in life are caused by abuse, neglect, and disease rather than aging. Crunchy foods seem to do a good job of keeping the teeth and gums in shape. Periodontitis, one common cause of tooth loss, is due to an excess of plaque, and can be avoided with proper dental hygiene.

Bones

Throughout life, bones are constantly regenerating themselves in a process known as remodeling. Once a person reaches his or her mid-thirties, he or she is absorbing more old bone than he or she is creating, so bone mass decreases. This is especially problematic for women, who tend to have less dense bones than men. Bone loss for women accelerates after menopause, and about a quarter of all women will develop osteoporosis, a condition in which bones become weaker, more porous, and more vulnerable to fracture. This condition is especially common in women above the age of 60. In order to reduce the risk of osteoporosis, women should ensure that their diet is rich in calcium, and that they regularly participate in vigorous exercise.

Muscles

The muscles of the human body tend to decrease in size and strength with age, although this process can be slowed with regular exercise. The deterioration of muscle is in large part due to the body's decreased ability to synthesize protein. The lack of protein causes muscles to atrophy and lose their ability to contract. Fat and collagen tend to accumulate in the muscles as they age. Muscles also become more vulnerable to strains and cramps. Muscle strength usually declines after the age of forty, with men losing up to 20% of their strength by the age of sixty, and women often losing more. Weakening back muscles (along with deterioration of the spinal discs) account for the loss of height in aging individuals.

Heart

Even though the resting heart rate stays approximately the same throughout life, the amount of blood pumped with each heart beat will decrease as a person ages. This is most apparent during exercise, as the heart takes a longer time to reach a high rate, as well as to return to its resting rate. Most of

the serious heart defects that are traditionally associated with aging, such as strokes and heart attacks, are caused by arteriosclerosis and high blood pressure rather than simple deterioration from age. Heart health can be maintained through a healthy diet and regular exercise. Many older individuals benefit from taking a bit of aspirin every day after about the age of forty.

Lungs and the immune system

Interestingly, the human respiratory system actually seems to become stronger with age. All of the myriad infections to which the body is exposed tend to increase the immunity, and so people tend to be somewhat resilient against colds and flu by the time they reach middle age. Also, unless an individual is out of shape or smokes, he or she should not lose any of his or her lung capacity. As for the immune system, it need not necessarily deteriorate of a person remains in shape and eats right. The only inevitable decline in the immune system that can be credited to age is a slight atrophy of the thymus gland. As people get older, they tend to be at an increased risk of cancer and infectious disease, although they are also more capable of accepting an organ transplant. Of course, being in good shape increases an individual's chances of recovering from illness at any age.

Brain

Once you reach the age of fifty, only about half as much blood is reaching your brain as did when you were ten. When you reach the age of 85, your brain will have lost between 10 and 20% of its mass. Most of this weight is lost through the atrophy of nerve cells, particularly in the cerebral cortex. Although this would seem to diminish mental function, there is evidence that the brain continues to create new dendrites (that is, connections between neurons) around the nerve cells that remain. Often, individuals notice a change in their sleeping patterns as they age. In most cases, the deepest part of sleep is briefer in old age, thus accounting for the reputation of old people as light sleepers.

Sex organs

There is no reason why people cannot continue to enjoy a satisfying sex life as they age. Although there is a natural slowing of the arousal response as people age, there is no evidence that women will lose the capacity for orgasm, or men for erection and ejaculation. Women typically stop menstruating at around the age of fifty, and may experience some adverse effects of this hormonal change. Many women offset the negative effects of menstruation by receiving estrogen supplements. For men, aging typically means that it will be more difficult to develop and maintain an erection. Also, men may have some problems urinating if the prostate gland becomes enlarged. Enlargement of the prostate can usually be treated without diminishing sexual function.

Social changes

As an individual ages, he or she will have to embrace new social roles and relationships. Many people have a hard time adjusting to the abundant free time they have after retirement. It is also common for people to feel a bit depressed and listless, as they struggle to determine what will be the motivating force in their lives. Individuals should make a conscious effort to develop hobbies and interests as they age. Many married couples will have to adjust to spending more time together, and may have to "rediscover" one another after their children leave the home. Finally, for many people retirement entails a new economic arrangement. Since retired individuals typically have a smaller income, they need to be cognizant of their financial situation and make the proper arrangements.

Dementia

Only about 7% of the population will develop dementia, a severe deterioration of mental function. One of the most common symptoms of dementia is a chronic inability to assess one's present situation; for this reason, demented individuals often seem confused and disoriented. As dementia progresses, memory loss can become quite severe.

Fortunately, many if the causes of dementia (for instance dehydration, depression, alcoholism, and problems with prescription medication) can be treated. Individuals suffering from dementia will need more time to understand things that are said to them, and may need guidance in moving from one place to another. Demented individuals may also have a compulsion to reminisce about the past, although this is not necessarily a bad thing.

Alzheimer's disease

Alzheimer's disease is a fatal brain disorder that results in the destruction of nerve cells. As nerve cells are destroyed, the brain becomes unable to produce the neurotransmitter acetylcholine, and it becomes very difficult for the different parts of the brain to communicate. At first, Alzheimer's is manifested as forgetfulness and an inability to concentrate. Eventually, it will evolve into severe memory loss, depression, anxiety, and finally the total deterioration of basic physical processes. There is no clear picture of how Alzheimer's develops, although it generally develops in the elderly and appears to be at least partially hereditary. Although there are some prescription drugs that are effective at slowing the memory loss caused by Alzheimer's, there is no permanent treatment yet available.

Caring for the elderly

Family involvement

In most families, one of the grown children of an elderly individual will assume a care-giving role. Oftentimes, this entails bringing the parent into their home, arranging for alternative housing, or establishing care for the parent in the parent's own home. This situation has become increasingly common as the average life expectancy has risen over the past few decades. Caring for an aging parent is extremely hard work, and so one should avail oneself of all community resources and be sure to follow the advice of health professionals. One of the most important things a family can do as some of its members age is to honestly and openly confront the challenge, acknowledging the help that will be needed and making plans to arrange the appropriate care.

Community resources
Most communities have established some resources for aging individuals. There are often senior citizens' centers or adult day-care centers, where elderly individuals can get meals and meet both with health professionals and with people of their own age. Many communities provide visiting nurses and homemakers, to ensure that the elderly are being given enough care and that their homes do not fall into disrepair. Oftentimes, a community will have a service that delivers inexpensive or free meals to the elderly. Some communities offer inexpensive legal aid to aging individuals who need it, and others have hospitals where the elderly can go during the day to receive physical therapy and free medical advice.

Death

5 varieties of death
As technology has made it possible for individuals who have in many senses died to be kept technically alive, health professionals have had to create a more complex set of definitions for death. Death is now considered as appearing in five varieties: functional, cellular, cardiac, brain, and spiritual. Functional death is when heart beat and respiration have ceased. Cellular death has occurred when the cells of the body have begun dying after the heart stops supplying them with oxygen and nutrients. Cardiac death is when the heart has stopped beating. Brain death is the termination of brain activity, in which there are no electrical impulses in the brain, and no reflexes. According to many religions, spiritual death is the moment at which the soul leaves the body.

Emotional responses
The great commentator on death Elisabeth Kubler-Ross has identified five stages of personal reaction to death. The first stage is denial, in which the person rejects the idea of death; this period is somewhat necessary so that the individual can overcome the initial shock of the news. The next stage is anger, in which the individual is resentful that he or she should have to die, rather than somebody else. In the next stage, the individual tries to bargain his or her way out of the predicament. In the fourth stage, depression, the individual finally begins to absorb the inevitability of his or her death, and is profoundly saddened. In the fifth and last stage, the individual accepts the inevitability of death and is neither sad nor fearful.

Grief
Sadly, many people spend the last portion of their life battling grief and depression. Most people will experience a number of losses as they grow older, their family and friends die, their health declines, and they can no longer do many of the things they enjoy. There is no immediate cure for this kind of psychological pain; in fact, doctors say that it will usually take about two years to recover from the loss of a loved one. Older people who seem to have lost their pleasure in life should be encouraged to seek therapeutic help. Many individuals find solace in discussing their problems with others, and some prescription medications appear to be able to mitigate the pain of loss.

Ethics of death
There is always a great deal of controversy surrounding individuals who lapse into a long-term coma or persistent vegetative state. There is a slight difference between the two conditions: an individual in a coma is entirely unconscious, with no memory or feelings, whereas an individual in a persistent vegetative state is awake but unaware of anything that is going on around him or her. For a long time, doctors would not allow the removal of a feeding tube, respirator, or water from an individual who was not brain-

dead. In the 1970's, though, the courts allowed the removal of a ventilator from a comatose individual. The question of when or if to remove artificial means of life remains extremely contentious.

Advance directives

In order to ease the process of death, many individuals compose in advance directions for their medical treatment if they should suffer a serious injury or illness. Sometimes, an individual will specify a health-care proxy, someone who is authorized to make medical decisions for them if they are unconscious or unable to act in their own behalf. Other individuals may compose what is known as a do-no-resuscitate order, in which they state that they do not want to be revived and kept alive by artificial means. An elderly or ill individual may also grant power of attorney to another person, thus giving that person the authority to make financial decisions on his or her behalf in the event of injury or illness.

Living wills

Living wills are a kind of advance directive wherein people may specify that they do not wish to be kept alive by artificial means, or that they would like every possible effort to be made to revive them. Most states recognize living wills as legally binding and have developed special forms for their composition. In a holographic will, the individual specifies how he or she would like his or her property divided after death. Individuals who die intestate (that is, without a will) will have their property divided by the state. Many states will recognize a holographic will even if it is composed informally. A typical will includes an executor, lists the property to be divided, selects a guardian for any children, and specifies funeral arrangements.

Hospice

Hospices are health-care facilities or agencies that seek to provide care for individuals in their final days. Individuals who receive hospice care may do so at a hospice facility proper, or in their own homes. In any case, the hospice strives to make the setting as comfortable and peaceful as possible. Hospice teams usually consist of nurse, physicians, chaplains, and social workers. They provide a combination of medical and emotional care not only for the fading individual, but for the friends and family at his or her bedside. Hospice facilities are able to provide the round-the-clock care that allows the loved ones of the patient to spend his or her last hours communing, rather than taking care of practical concerns.

Physician-assisted suicide

Despite the end of Dr. Jack Kevorkian's controversial career, there remains a great deal of argument over whether physicians should be allowed to assist the suicides of patients with terminal illness. Many doctors, with the approval of the patients' family and friends, will not pursue any extreme measures to preserve life; this is known as passive euthanasia. In other situations, though, the patient may ask that a doctor help him or her to commit suicide, if the pain of a terminal illness has become too much to bear. This practice is currently illegal in the United States, although it has been practiced for many years in the Netherlands. The American Medical Association openly states that it finds the practice of euthanasia to be unethical.

Overpopulation

Though global population growth seems to be stabilizing, some scientists are still concerned that the number of people on the earth will soon outstrip the resources needed to support them. In order to keep population growth in check, many health organizations are actively promoting birth control in developing countries. Experts estimate that if every country is well-equipped with contraceptives, the population could be about 2 billion people smaller in 2100 than they expect. It is also important that women in developing countries be given good access to education; women with good jobs are likely to have fewer and healthier babies. Finally, men should also be encourage to take equal responsibility for their children; men who have to take care of their kids are less likely to have too many.

Pollution

Many people wouldn't consider pollution a personal health issue, but polluted air and water can affect every aspect of a person's life. Scientists define pollution as any change in the air, soil, or water that impairs its ability to host life. Most pollution is the byproduct of human acts. Environmental agents that change the DNA of living cells are called mutagens, and they can lead to the development of cancer. Pollutants that can pass through the placenta of a woman and cause damage to an unborn child are called teratogens. Some of the common health problems associated with pollution are nasal discharge, eye irritation, constricted air passages, birth defects, nausea, coughing, and cancer.

Climate change

One of the areas of environmental concern that could have the most effect on personal health is global warming. Most scientists agree that the massive burning of fossil fuels such as oil and gas are creating a buildup of carbon dioxide, methane, and nitrous dioxide in the atmosphere. This is known as the greenhouse effect, and is credited already with causing shifts in the global climate. If glaciers continue to melt and raise the seal level worldwide, there could be major problems for man and the many species on which we depend. Along with the problems stemming from global warming are those cause by damage to the earth's ozone layer. Scientists believe that the ozone layer, which helps protect life on earth from the damaging radiation of the sun, has been seriously compromised by the release of man-made chemicals called chlorofluorocarbons.

Smog

Smog is the informal name given to the combination of smoke, gases, and fog that accumulates in major industrial or metropolitan areas. Most smog is created by motor vehicles, wood-burning stoves, industrial factories, and electric utilities plants. Gray smog, which is mainly sulfur dioxide, is common in the eastern U.S. because of the high concentration of industry. This kind of smog acts like cigarette smoke on the lungs, impairing the ability of the cilia to expel particulates. Brown smog comes from automobiles and is mainly composed of nitrogen dioxide. Ozone, one of the other components of brown smog, can impair the immune system. Automobiles are also known to produce carbon monoxide, which diminishes the ability of the red blood cells to carry oxygen.

Water supply

Even though Americans have generally been able to rely on the water supply, in recent years some concerns have been raised about the prevalence of potentially dangerous chemicals in the water supply. Fluoride, which has greatly improved teeth in America since it was added to the water supply, may be damaging to bone strength if it is consumed in great volume. Chlorine, which is often added to water to kill bacteria, may increase the risk of bladder cancer. One of the most dangerous chemicals that can affect water is lead, which is known to leach from pipes and enter the drinking supply. High amounts of lead in the body can cause serious damage to the brain and heart.

Pesticides

More and more, food buyers are taking an interest in the number of pesticides that are used on the products they buy. Of course, it should be noted that not all pesticides are bad; many plants and animals produce their own pesticides, which have always been consumed by humans. There are dangers

- 44 -

associated with some commercial pesticides, however. Organic foods are those that have been produced without help from commercial chemicals at any stage. The requirements for a certain product to be certified organic may vary from state to state. Some states require that no chemicals have been used on the product, whereas others are willing to certify a product as organic as long as it has no chemical residues. There is as yet uncertain evidence that organic products provide major health advantages.

Irradiation and genetically-engineered foods: Irradiation is the process whereby foods are exposed to radiation in order to prolong their shelf life. Irradiation does not make food radioactive. Irradiation effectively kills all the microorganisms in a food, so that it can be canned and stored for an extended period without degradation. At this point, there is no conclusive research to suggest that irradiated foods are a health risk. In fact, the FDA has recently approved the use of irradiation on red meat to eliminate the bacteria that cause food poisoning. Another controversial area in food production is genetic engineering. Genetically-engineered foods are modified specifically to add or remove certain traits. There is a great deal of debate as to whether it is ethical and safe for scientists to change the basic genetics of the food we eat.

Medical assistance

Primary, secondary , and tertiary care
Individuals seeking medical assistance have a number of options from which to choose. Primary care, otherwise known as ambulatory or outpatient care, is generally provided by a primary care physician in an office, an emergency room, or a clinic. Secondary care is generally provided by the specialists or subspecialists in a hospital. Secondary care may be provided in an inpatient or outpatient setting. Tertiary care includes the most major procedures, like open-heart surgery, kidney dialysis, and organ transplants. Tertiary care is generally conducted at regional specialty hospitals and at university-affiliated hospitals, where specialists in the particular disease or treatment are situated.

Outpatient treatment centers
Many procedures that at one time required overnight hospitalization can now be performed at outpatient centers. Outpatient centers can be freestanding and self-sustaining, or they can be affiliated with a larger medical center. Outpatient centers have become the preferred place to get a tonsillectomy, cataract removal, breast biopsy, vasectomy, or plastic surgery procedure. Because they have much lower overhead costs, outpatient facilities are able to provide services for a fraction of the cost for a similar procedure at a hospital. For this reason, insurance companies encourage their clients to have minor surgery performed at one of these centers. A popular spin-off of the outpatient treatment center is the freestanding emergency center, where people can receive treatment for minor illness or injury in a short amount of time.

Hospitals
There are a few different kinds of hospitals. Private (or community) hospitals are those that have between 50 and 400 beds and provide more personalized care than do public hospitals. Private hospitals may be run either for profit or as a non-profit business. In public hospitals, the care is administered by the health service of the city, county, military, or Veterans Administration. Whereas the quality of care in a private hospital is determined by the skill of the doctors, the quality of care in a public hospital is more dependent on the general state of the institution that runs it. In the United States, there are approximately 300 hospitals that are directly affiliated with university medical schools. These hospitals often offer the most advanced treatments, because the doctors there are required to stay abreast of all developments in their respective fields.

Evaluating a hospital

If you have the time, it is a good idea to compare various hospitals before determining where to receive treatment. One easy way to find out about a hospital is to simply ask your doctor which hospital he or she recommends, and why. Another way to evaluate hospitals is to inquire about the ratio of nurses to patients; many hospitals that are trying to cut costs will provide an inadequate number of nurses. If you are having a rare procedure performed, you may want to ask whether a hospital has performed that procedure recently, and what success rate the hospital has had. If it is possible to do so, you should tour the various hospitals, checking to ensure that they are clean and orderly, and that the staff is courteous.

Inpatient and emergency services

The most expensive form of health care is inpatient health care at a hospital. Because it is so expensive, many insurance companies require conclusive proof that inpatient treatment is necessary before they will pay for it. Patients should be on the lookout for insurance companies that pay for treatment on the basis if diagnostic-related groups (DRGs): this means that the insurance company pays a flat fee for a certain kind of procedure, and so the hospital can make money if they can provide the service at a cheaper cost. Emergency room visits can also be very expensive, and should only be made when absolutely necessary. Most of the time, patients who are not in dire need of help will wait for a long time and will be presented with a large bill, which may not be covered by their health insurance.

Home health care

As it becomes less financially viable to remain in a hospital for a long period of time, more individuals are receiving treatment while they recuperate and rest at home. Many treatments which could once only be performed in hospitals (for instance kidney dialysis, chemotherapy, and traction) can now be administered in a residence. Doctors are even beginning to make house calls again.

Most of the time, the people who oversee the release of hospital patients (known in the industry as discharge planners) will arrange a program of home health care for those who need it. Also, individuals who desire home health care can contact the local health care professionals to ask if that service is provided. Most insurance policies will cover a reasonable amount of home health care.

Health insurance

For a long time, most Americans relied on traditional indemnity insurance policies to pay most of their major medical expenses. In this system, a policyholder would pay a percentage of the hospitalization costs as well as a deductible, a minimum that must be paid by the individual before the insurance company begins contributing. This system gave patients the freedom to choose their own doctors and hospitals, but sometimes didn't cover routine checkups or screenings. Also, individuals who already had some medical condition at the time the policy was acquired would not be able to get any money for the treatment of that condition. Because of these factors, there has been a shift from indemnity coverage to managed care.

Managed-care plans

Most people today have left behind indemnity insurance in favor of a managed-care plan, which tend to cost less but provide less flexibility. Networks of hospitals, doctors, and other health care providers come together and agree to charge a standard rate for the customers of a managed-care organization. In order to get treated, a person in a managed-care plan often must follow detailed procedures and fill out a great deal of paperwork. Managed-care plans consider many treatments unnecessary and refuse to pay for them. Also, patients may have to pay themselves for a visit to a doctor not part of the network. Many people have criticized managed-care plans for undertreating their patients, and being swamped in bureaucratic battles.

PPOs

In a preferred provider organization, a group of physicians and hospitals sign an agreement with some group (a union, for instance, or an insurance company) whose members will then receive discounted medical treatment. The members of a PPO typically have to pay a 10% co-payment to see any doctor within the network, and a higher co-payment should they wish to see some other doctor. Members of a PPO usually have to get approval before they can undergo any expensive procedures. One particular type of PPO is a point-of-service plan, in which members can use doctors outside the network but have to pay the difference between that doctor's rate and the discounted rate of doctors within the network.

HMOs

Health maintenance organizations, commonly known as HMOs, are managed-care plans in which a member makes a standard monthly payment for basic medical services. More than a quarter of the United States population receives health care as a member of an HMO. The expense of an HMO is generally small, with members not having to pay a deductible or a large co-payment. The main criticism of HMOs is that they limit the consumer to a small network of doctors and hospitals. In answer to this criticism, open-ended HMO plans have been introduced which allow the consumer to receive treatment at a facility and from a doctor of their choice. These plans are slightly more expensive, however.

Physicians

Training

In the United States, it takes at least three years of premedical studies (with an emphasis on physics, biology, and chemistry) followed by four (occasionally 3 or 5) years of medical school before a person can become a physician. The first two years are devoted to basic subjects: anatomy, embryology, pharmacology, and others. In the last two years, aspiring physicians work in cooperation with practicing physicians in hospitals. After this, they must pass a series of national board examinations and complete a one-year internship in a hospital. Finally, they will have to finish a period of residency, in which they will become trained and certified in a particular field. Residency can last anywhere from two to five years.

Certification

The majority of certified physicians are either specialists or subspecialists: that is, they focus almost exclusively on one part of the body, system of organs, type of disease, or type of treatment. For a long time, these specialists were better paid and more esteemed in the medical community. However, recent changes in the structure of health care in the United States have put more emphasis on the work of so-called primary care physicians: family practitioners and pediatricians, for instance. These physicians typically provide routine checkups, treatment of common ailments, and basic medication. Primary care physicians now are more responsible for determining whether a patient needs to seek the aid of a specialist.

Other healthcare providers

Nurses

In order to become a registered nurse, individuals must undergo a rigorous training and graduate from a school of nursing that is approved by the state. Registered nurses may have a bachelor's or associate degree, and they can opt to specialize in certain areas, like intensive care or midwifery. If they receive extra training they may become nurse practitioners, at which point they can run a community clinic or even go into private practice. A licensed practical nurse, also known as a licensed vocational nurse, is licensed by the state and can work alongside either a registered nurse or a physician. Nursing aides and orderlies are those individuals who help nurses to perform their duties, usually by providing comfort directly to the patient.

Dentists

In order to become a dentist, an individual must complete a bachelor's degree with an emphasis in biology and chemistry, and then graduate from dental school. Dental school is a four-year venture; the first two years focus on general science, and the second two are composed of clinical work having to do with dentistry. After this program is finished, the individual will be either a Doctor of Dental Surgery (DDS) or Doctor of Medical Dentistry (DMD). At this point, a prospective dentist will have to pass a written and clinical examination to receive a license to practice. Successful candidates can either become specialists in some area of dentistry or begin a general practice. One of the most common dental specialties is orthodontics, the straightening of the teeth.

Chiropractors

The study of chiropractics suggests that most human ailments are caused by a misalignment of the bones. Chiropractors are especially attentive to the vertebrae in the back, as they believe damage to the nerve tissue in the back can create problems in other parts of the body. In order to become a chiropractor, an individual must complete two years of college-level training, and then spend four years in a special school for chiropractors. Chiropractors are known for advocating preventive care and wellness training rather than surgery or medication. Although X rays are often used in making chiropractic diagnoses, most chiropractic treatment relies simply on the manipulation of bones. Chiropractors must be licensed by the state in which they practice.

Psychiatrists and psychologists

Many people confuse the two most common types of mental health professionals, psychiatrists and psychologists. A psychiatrist has a degree in medicine and has received specialized training in treating mental illness. They are allowed to prescribe medication and make other medical decisions. Many psychiatrists specialize in treating a particular age or condition.

Psychologists, on the other hand, have completed a graduate program in mental functioning, but they cannot prescribe medicine. In order to practice, they have to be licensed by some state board. Many psychologists have received a doctorate or even post-doctoral training in a particular area of treatment. Many psychologists specialize in working with children or families.

Allied-health professionals

The field of allied-health professionals includes all those people who work in tandem with doctors and nurses to provide health care. Many of these individuals have specialized in a particular area. Optometrists, for instance, are trained to diagnose visual abnormalities and prescribe corrective lenses, though they cannot prescribe medication. Podiatrists are specially trained to help individuals with foot problems. Respiratory therapists treat breathing disorders. Pharmacists are licensed to dispense medications when a doctor writes a prescription. Occupational therapists help disabled individuals make the best of their situation. Paramedics provide emergency care. Radiological technicians prepare patients for X rays and take and develop X rays. Speech pathologists measure hearing ability and help individuals overcome trouble with speaking.

Infections

Vectors of infection

The major vectors, or means of transmission, of infection are through animals or insects, other people, food, water, and air. Many people catch infections from their house pets or livestock, or through common insects. The housefly, for instance, has been shown to spread dysentery, diarrhea, and typhoid fever. People also transmit pathogens to one another by sneezing, kissing, and touching one another. Most bacterial infections are transmitted through food, especially food that has been undercooked or not been washed. Some of the food-borne pathogens can be

- 48 -

quite deadly. It is less common in the United States than elsewhere for pathogens to be carried by the water supply; however, water found in outdoor bodies is likely to be a carrier of many pathogens.

Stages of infection
In the case of a virus, infection begins when the viral cells enter the body and penetrate the wall of a cell. During this first period, known as the incubation period, the pathogen multiplies while the host is unaware, because he or she has not yet begun to experience any symptoms. Once the body begins to fight the infection in earnest, the prodromal stage has begun. Dying cells release chemicals to stall the invasion; other chemicals speed more blood to the infected area. At this point, the individual is very contagious and is experiencing some symptoms. After a while, the body's forces will gain the advantage, and the recovery period begins. Though it may eliminate all the traces of the infection, the body is not able to become permanently immune to many viruses.

Groups at high risk
As one would expect, infectious viruses pose the greatest danger to those individuals who are already weakened or in poor health. For instance, children are especially vulnerable to viruses; typically, almost half the population of children will contract a virus that is circulating a particular community. The elderly are also likely to suffer from infectious disease, because even though they are usually less likely to contract a virus, they will undergo more damage to their health when they do. Individuals who are regularly ill or are taking medications to suppress the immune system are more likely to contract a disease. Likewise, smokers and individuals who live in poorly-ventilated buildings are more susceptible to the transmission of infectious disease.

Emergence and recurrence
Emerging diseases are those that have only recently been recognized, are increasing in humans, or are likely to spread to new geographical areas in the near future. The most pervasive emerging disease is the HIV virus, which is believed to have originated in central Africa. Diseases may also re-emerge later in a slightly mutated form that is resistant to the previous methods of treatment. Viruses and bacteria are capable of endless alterations, and even a simple change may enable them to become stronger or more deadly. Another reason why emerging and recurring disease is a growing problem in the world is the infiltration of civilization into previously uninhabited territories; people are encountering millions of microbes that have never been seen before.

Common illnesses

Common cold
The common cold is one of the peskiest and irritating viruses, though it is rarely a great risk to long-term health. One reason the cold is so difficult to fight is that there are over 200 varieties of the virus, so the body is never able to develop a comprehensive immunity. The cold virus is typically spread through the air or through contact. There is no completely effective medical treatment, either. Indeed, doctors warn that taking aspirin and Tylenol may actually suppress the antibodies that the body needs to fight the infection, and may therefore contribute to some symptoms. There is also no conclusive evidence to support taking vitamin C in large doses. Antihistamines, which many people credit with relieving the symptoms of the common cold, may make the user drowsy.

Influenza
The influenza virus is somewhat similar to the viruses of the common cold, but it tends to have more severe and prolonged symptoms. The flu virus is extremely contagious, particularly during its incubation period. There are both A and B varieties of influenza; influenza A is generally considered the most dangerous. Doctors increasingly recommend getting an annual immunization against the flu. This must be done every year because the flu virus changes and becomes

- 49 -

resistant to the antibodies of the past. The only individuals who are cautioned against being immunized are those with an allergy to eggs. Doctors are optimistic that the future will bring not only better vaccinations but a permanent cure for both influenza and the common cold.

Mononucleosis

Mononucleosis is a viral disease most commonly found among people between the ages of 15 and 24. It is spread by kissing or other close contact. The symptoms of mononucleosis include a sore throat, headache, fever, nausea, and, most characteristically, prolonged periods of weakness. These symptoms may last a month or more. There is no great long-term risk to health from mononucleosis, although trying to exercise vigorously may cause the spleen to rupture. It is also possible for the liver to become inflamed, though this is rare. At present, there is no good treatment for mononucleosis; individuals who suspect that they have it should see their doctor for a blood test.

Hepatitis

There are 5 varieties of hepatitis (A, B, C, Delta, and E), a virus that causes the liver to become inflamed. Many people will die each year as a result of this infection. The symptoms of hepatitis include headaches, fever, fatigue, nausea, and vomiting. The liver will enlarge and become sensitive to the touch, and the person's skin may develop the yellowish tinge of jaundice. The best way to treat hepatitis is to get plenty of rest and to avoid alcohol and drugs that will put the liver to work. In order to avoid contracting hepatitis in the first place, one should practice good hygiene and avoid using illegal drugs or engaging in risky sex. There are available vaccinations for hepatitis A and B. Hepatitis B is responsible for most of the hepatitis-related deaths.

Pneumonia

Pneumonia can be caused by bacteria, virus, or by foreign particles in the air. When it is contracted, fluid fills the intricate network of spongy tissue in the lungs. When it is contracted in its bacterial form, the symptoms are shortness of breath, fever, and general weakness. Symptoms related to every variety include coughing, high fever, chills, and abundant phlegm. Antibiotics can be used to treat bacterial pneumonia if they are administered quickly enough. Individuals who have had pneumonia in the past are advised to get a vaccination for it, especially if they are over the age of fifty. Pneumonia may develop very slowly, or it may occur so fast that it greatly endangers health.

Tuberculosis

At one time, tuberculosis was the leading cause of death in the United States. Indeed, it is so common that even today one-third of the world's population is infected with the disease, although not all of these people will develop the active form of the disease. TB is extremely contagious, and when it does emerge it typically does so on a large scale, often contaminating entire populations in a brief period. The symptoms most commonly associated with TB are fatigue, chills, loss of appetite, coughing, and night sweats. Although most TB patients recover fully after about six months, it is best to take steps to avoid the disease. If you think you may be infected, you should see your doctor immediately and ask for a TB test.

Group A and Group B Strep infection

Although a sore throat is a common symptom of a winter cold, if the symptom is actually the result of group A streptococcus bacteria it can be much more serious. Strep bacteria will eventually travel to the kidneys, liver, and heart if they are not treated promptly with antibiotics. Once there, they will cause rheumatic fever, an inflammation of the heart that can lead to joint pain and an irregular heartbeat. There are tests currently available that can diagnose strep throat in moments. Group B streptococcus, on the other hand, only affects pregnant women and their newly-born children. Very young women and those with poor health are the most likely victims of this disease, which causes scores of infant deaths each year. Doctors recommend being screened for group B strep while pregnant.

Lyme disease

Lyme disease is a bacterial infection spread by ticks. The most common symptoms of the infection are joint inflammation, heart arrhythmia, severe headaches, and memory lapses. In pregnant women, Lyme disease may cause birth defects and miscarriages. For obvious reasons, hunters, campers, and people who spend a great deal of time in the outdoors are the most likely to contract Lyme disease. It is important, therefore, to always check yourself for ticks, which may be very tiny, every time you have been in a wooded area. Most people that are infected will notice some skin lesions, often a red blotch around the area of the bite. If you spot a tick already on your body, remove it quickly with a pair of tweezers, making sure that the head does not stay embedded below the skin.

Vaginal infections

There are three main types of vaginal infection: trichmoniasis, candidiasis, and bacterial vaginosis. Trichmoniasis is suffered when protozoa in the vagina multiply quickly, creating burning, itching, and painful discharge. Males may carry this infection without displaying any of the symptoms. The infection known as candidiasis begins when a normal yeast found in the vagina becomes too abundant, causing burning, itching, and a whitish discharge. There are numerous over-the-counter treatments for this infection. Bacterial vaginosis occurs when the microorganisms that live in the vagina are altered, the result being a whitish-gray discharge and a fishy aroma. This infection most often affects women who have numerous sexual partners.

Urinary tract infections

The urethra, bladder, and kidney are all subject to urinary tract infection. More women develop UTI than do men, probably because a woman's shorter urethra makes it easier for bacteria to enter the bladder and kidneys. The health complaints associated with urinary tract infections are burning, painful urination, chills, fever, fatigue, and blood in the urine. The individuals at the greatest risk are those who are pregnant, ride a bicycle frequently, have an irritated or enlarged urethra or bladder, or have an enlarged prostate. Many young women who have sex frequently and use a diaphragm have recurring problems with urinary tract infection. In many cases antibiotics have had success in treating these infections if they are administered promptly.

HIV

Although the number of people suffering from HIV (human immunodeficiency virus) or AIDS has declined in the United States in recent years, there is still a tremendous health risk associated with the virus. Although the disease was once linked with homosexual males, the highest rates of growth are currently among heterosexuals in developing countries. HIV is generally spread through vaginal sexual contact, although it is also possible to spread the disease through anal or oral sex if either partner loses some blood during the operation. It is also commonly spread among drug users through the sharing of contaminated needles. Other, rarer ways of contracting HIV are through blood transfusions, blood products, and organ transplants

HIV infection

When doctors refer to an HIV infection, they mean the array of health problems that are caused by the virus upon its entrance into the bloodstream. Although it is technically possible for the body to fight off an HIV infection, in almost every case the virus quickly destroys the cell-mediated immune system, and makes the individual extremely vulnerable to cancers and other infections. Once the immune system recognizes the presence of HIV, it usually mass-produces cells to fight the virus, but these are quickly overwhelmed by the rapid multiplication of viral cells. Immediately after contracting the disease, the victim will often have flu-like symptoms and fatigue. After this period, though, it is possible that no more signs of disease will be experienced for several weeks to a year.

AIDS

Individuals who have previously been diagnosed with HIV may be diagnosed with AIDS if they develop a severe or debilitating illness or if their immune system has become extremely impaired. AIDS victims may suffer from persistent bouts of pneumonia, fever, or diarrhea. they may also begin to experience neurological problems, like dementia and impaired motor skills. It is important to note that people do not actually die from the AIDS virus; rather, they succumb to another infection after AIDS has weakened their immune system. The most common secondary infections a re pneumonia, tuberculosis, and thrush; secondary cancers commonly associated with AIDS include Kaposi's sarcoma and cervical cancer.

Reducing your risk

The best way to protect yourself from HIV is to practice abstinence and avoid sharing needles. Individuals should also know a few other basic facts about transmission. For instance, casual contact with another person does not carry the risk of catching HIV; since the virus only lives in breast milk, blood, semen, and vaginal fluid, it cannot be exchanged by incidental, friendly contact. It is impossible to tell from looking at a person whether they have HIV. Individuals are at a greater risk of HIV if they already have a sexual infection. Teenage girls may be at more risk of contracting HIV through sexual contact because the immature cervix is more prone to infection. There are no reported cases of HIV transmission during kissing.

HIV testing

Most of the time, HIV tests do not search for the virus itself, but rather for the antibodies created to fight it. However, because the immune system may take three to six months before responding to the presence of the virus, these tests are not always accurate. The two most common kinds of HIV test are the ELISA test, which measures the level of certain antibodies created to fight HIV, and the Western blot test, which is more expensive and accurate, and is usually performed to confirm the results of an ELISA test. There are even home testing kits available now, in which the patient pricks his or her own finger and sends it off to a laboratory. Doctors recommend HIV testing for anyone who has had sex with a homosexual or bisexual male, anyone who ahs shared needles, anyone who received a blood transfusion between the years 19878 and 1985, and anyone who has had sex with a person who fulfills one of the other requirements.

Latest treatments

Scientists have made some real progress in learning how to fight HIV and AIDS. Recently, they have had success with protease inhibitor drugs, which boost the level of protective T cells and reduce the quantity of HIV in the blood stream. Though this treatment may be hard on the patient, if it can be endured it usually causes a severe reduction in the symptoms associated with HIV. The new treatments for this disease are extremely expensive, however, and are not yet available in the developing countries where they are need ed most. Some individuals, moreover, will not receive any befit from the "cocktail" of drugs. The search is ongoing for a total cure for the virus, with scientists spending a great deal of time focusing on those individuals who seem to be able to live long lives with HIV.

Sexually transmitted diseases

Sexually transmitted diseases, otherwise known as venereal diseases, are among the top ten most frequently reported diseases in the United States. although any sexually active individual is eligible to contract an STD, the most frequently infected populations are young adults and homosexual males; even unborn children can catch an STD from their mother, however. Although STDs are currently at their highest-ever rate in the United States, they are even more prevalent in developing countries because of inadequate health care, poor access to treatment, and low-grade prevention measures. All of the STD pathogens like the warm, viscous surfaces of the body, and are repelled by light, cold, and dryness. It is quite possible to have more than one STD at a time.

STDs and young people
According to the Center for Disease Control, young people are the most likely to contract an STD. In fact, some studies have indicated that about half of all people will contract a sexually transmitted disease by the time they are thirty. Women are much more likely than men to catch such a disease as a result of heterosexual intercourse. There are a few reasons why young people may be at greater risk. For one thing, they often have a feeling of invulnerability that persuades them to behave thoughtlessly. They are also more likely to have multiple partners, which places them at a greater risk. Young people are less prone to use condoms. Finally, young people are more frequent users of drugs and alcohol, which tend to lead to foolish sexual behavior.

Chlamydia
Though it is less commonly discussed than other disease, chlamydia is the most frequently trnsmitted sexual disease in the United States. This infection is more common in young women, and especially in African-Americans. The population at the greatest risk of contracting chlamydia is people under 25 who have more than one sexual partner within a two-month period, especially women who use birth control pills or other non-barrier contraceptives. The symptoms of chlamydia are vaginal or urethral irritation, itching, painful urination, and a slight discharge. Chlamydia may have serious consequences for unborn children if the mother becomes infected during pregnancy. There are several prescription drugs that have had success battling this disease.

Pelvic inflammatory disease
Although pelvic inflammatory disease (PID) is not actually a sexually transmitted disease, it is typically caused by complications due to an STD. PID is simply an infection of a woman's fallopian tubes or uterus. It can lead to scarring and obstruction of the fallopian tubes that is so severe that it can harm fertility, sometimes permanently. Some evidence suggests that smoking may contribute to PID, although some bacteria from an STD must also be present. Chlamydia and gonorrhea are the most frequent culprits for PID. Unfortunately, PID may go unrecognized until scarring has reached a significant level. Some women may experience slight abdominal pain or discharge. Treatment usually entails hospitalization and antibiotics.

Gonorrhea
Sexual contact, including oral sex, is the most common means of transmission for gonorrhea, also known as the "clap." For a male, the symptoms of gonorrhea are obvious and painful: yellow-white discharge from the penis and burning urination. For many women, though, the disease may arrive without any noticeable symptoms. The bacteria that cause gonorrhea can live inside a woman's reproductive organs for years, continuing to infect the woman's sexual partners. If left untreated, the disease can spread throughout the body and cause heart problems and infertility. There has recently been developed a blood test for gonorrhea, although the best way of checking for it remains analyzing a culture taken from the male's urethra or the female's cervix. Specific antibiotics are generally used to treat this painful disease.

Nongonococcal urethritis
Nongonococcal urethritis refers to any inflammation of the urethra that is not the result of an infection of gonorrhea. NGU is the most common STD among males, though it can also be spread by fungi and bacteria entering the body, or by an allergy to soaps or contraceptive products. The symptoms are

- 53 -

typically similar to those of gonorrhea, including discharge from the penis and mild burning during urination. Although these symptoms may vanish after two or three weeks, the infection will remain and can travel throughout the body, and lead to further illness. There is a well-established test for NGU, and the quick administration of a prescription medication typically eliminates the problem in a short time.

Syphilis
Syphilis is a bacteria-based disease that prospers in the warm and moist tissues of the reproductive system. Syphilis can enter the body through any break in the skin, after which it makes its way into the bloodstream. There are a couple clear stages in a syphilis infection. During primary syphilis, a lesion will develop on the body, usually about the size of a dime. This lesion appears at the precise location where the bacteria entered the body. In secondary syphilis, the victim may develop a rash, whitish patches on the mouth or throat, a fever, or large sores on the mouth and genitals. These symptoms can last for several months. In latent syphilis, there are no symptoms, even though the bacteria are attacking the organs of the body. After a couple years of harboring the infection, the victim is usually not contagious.

Herpes
Herpes is the name for a collection of similar, common viral infections. usually, herpes simplex 1 causes cold sores and blisters around the mouth, while herpes simplex 2 causes similar blisters in the genital area. The virus is transmitted by contact with the infected areas. Open herpes sores are highly contagious. Herpes never fully goes away, but will return from time to time throughout the life of the host. It is especially likely to recur during times of stress or during pregnancy. Over time, these attacks will usually diminish in frequency. Herpes can be treated with a number of prescription medications, and the symptoms can be mitigated with cold compresses and ice packs. Scientists are currently working on a vaccine to protect people from herpes infection.

Human papilloma virus
The human papilloma virus, which is known to cause genital warts, is the most common viral STD. HPV is typically transmitted through vaginal, anal, or oral sex. Over half of the people infected with this virus will never display any symptoms. The rest will develop genital warts in the period between three weeks and eighteen months after contact. HPV is known to cause urinary obstruction and bleeding, and in women may contribute to cervical cancer. There is at present no way to fully eliminate HPV, though some intensive treatments have been known to discourage recurrence. There is however, an effective test to determine whether an individual has HPV, even when it is latent.

Chancroids
Chancroids are soft, painful scars that are the result of a bacterial infection contracted during sexual contact. Although many chancroids will heal by themselves, others may spread to the nearby lymph glands and have a devastating effect on the tissue in the area. Many doctors believe that chancroids increase an individual's vulnerability to the HIV virus. Typically, a chancroid is treated with antibiotics. individuals should also try to reduce the risk of chancroids by keeping their genitals clean. If a chancroid develops, the victim should immediately see a doctor. It is also a good idea to determine where the chancroid was acquired, and to warn that person about the risk of infection.

Pubic lice and scabies
Pubic lice and scabies are usually, though not always, transmitted during sexual contact. Pubic lice are tiny creatures that live in the hairy areas of the body, generally around the genitals. They cause intense itching, and the resultant scratching may result n sores and scabs. Lice lay tiny eggs, called nits, which are attached to the base of the hair follicle. scabies, on the other hand, are caused by a tiny mite that crawls under the skin and lays

eggs. As these eggs develop, they cause severe itching and pain. Both of these infestations can be treated with a medicated shampoo, though this may not always eradicate unhatched eggs. It is important to immediately dry-clean all sheets and clothing after an outbreak of pubic lice or scabies.

Cardiovascular health

Smoking

By now, most Americans should know that smoking poses a great danger to the health of the human heart. Indeed, every year smoking is blamed for over 250,000 deaths from cardiovascular disease. Smokers are more likely to have heart attacks, they are more likely to get clogged arteries, and they are more likely to have reduced levels of beneficial blood fats. Specifically, nicotine has been shown to over stimulate the heart, and the carbon monoxide in cigarette smoke has been shown to reduce the supply of oxygen in the blood. Tars and other tobacco residues build up in the lungs, making it increasingly easy for cholesterol to mount. Finally, smoking has been clearly linked with an increase in blood clotting, which not only cause pain, but can lead to strokes and heart attacks.

High blood pressure

An individual's blood pressure is created by the contractions of the heart as it pumps blood, and the resistance of the walls of the veins and arteries through which the blood flows. So, when blood pressure is measured, a reading is given for the contraction of the heart (systolic blood pressure) as well as the period of release (diastolic blood pressure). Blood pressure is highest during the systolic period and lowest during the diastolic period. High blood pressure (hypertension) exists when the artery walls become constricted and pressure is raised to a dangerous level. A person with high blood pressure often will have a strong and stiff heart, which will make it difficult for the heart to adequately fill with blood in each beat. This problem can eventually lead to cardiovascular disease.

Blood fats

Cholesterol is found in foods and made by the body. A high level of cho0lesterol indicates a high buildup of plaque on the arterial walls, and can increase the likelihood of a heart attack. Triglycerides flow through the blood after a meal, and are highest when an individual's diet is high in calories, sugar, alcohol, and starches. An abnormal amount of triglycerides has been linked with heart disease, especially in women. Lipoproteins are composed of protein and fat. High-density lipoproteins, composed mostly of protein, get rid of excess cholesterol; low-density lipoproteins line the arteries with excess cholesterol. Young people and athletes are more likely to have a high level of helpful, high-density lipoproteins.

Other cardiovascular concerns

Diabetes mellitus is an endocrine disorder that increases the risk of arteriosclerosis and hypertension. Exercise, medication, and an appropriate diet can minimize the risks of diabetes if it is caught early. Doctors have also asserted that losing weight can help an individual avoid heart trouble. Excess pounds put a strain on the heart, and so it not surprising that obese men and women have increased risk of cardiovascular disease. There are also a number of psychological factors that are though to contribute to heart disease. Stress, anger, and hostility have all been linked with heart trouble. Scientists believe that these negative emotions send adrenaline into the bloodstream, where it triggers the release of fat and the buildup of cholesterol on the arterial walls. There are also some studies to indicate that depression may contribute to cardiovascular problems.

Uncontrollable factors

Unfortunately, there are a few characteristics associated with a greater risk of heart disease that are beyond the control of any individual. Many problematic traits can be inherited, so individuals whose families have a history of heart trouble are more at risk. African-Americans are twice as likely as whites to develop high blood pressure. Age is also a factor in heart disease; most of the people who die for cardiovascular reasons are over the age of 65. Men have a greater risk of heart trouble than women, perhaps because estrogen helps to produce beneficial high-density proteins. Interestingly, bald men under the age of 55 are more likely to have a heart attack than men of a similar age but with a full head of hair.

Angina pectoris

When the heart experiences a sudden, temporary drop in the flow of oxygen to the heart tissue, it is called angina pectoris. This condition is usually accompanied by discomfort in the chest. Individuals are at a greater risk of angina when they place great demands on their heart, for instance when they are under stress or exercising. If angina becomes severe and persistent, the individual should see medical treatment, as he or she may be at greater risk of a heart attack. Many people, however, have been known to suffer from angina pectoris for years without ever having any further heart trouble. When angina is diagnosed, doctors typically prescribe beta blockers, calcium channel blockers, or nitrates.

Coronary artery spasms

Occasionally, the arteries surrounding the heart will contract for no apparent reason, reducing or even cutting off entirely the flow of blood. These kinds of spasms can cause angina as well as heart attacks, and can even be fatal themselves. Coronary artery spasms may be caused by the clumping of platelets, which will cause the blood vessels to become narrower. Smoking is also linked with this heart problem, and may smokers who quit notice an immediate relief from their coronary pain. There is also a great deal of speculation that stress plays a significant role in causing this heart condition. Finally, doctors have observed that if too much calcium flows into the heart tissue, a spasm may result. This level calcium, however, is not dependent on diet.

Myocardial infarction

The clinical name for a heart attack is myocardial infarction. If the myocardial cells, which surround the heart and cause it to contract, do not get enough oxygen, they may begin to die. This happens when the arteries that supply the myocardium are blocked by plaque or a clot. Even though heart attacks are commonly thought of as sudden events, they are actually a long time in coming. The common signs of heart attack are anxiety, shortness of breath, dizziness, a squeezing pain in the center of the chest, and pain that extends out to the shoulder, arm, jaw, or neck. The period immediately after the beginning of these symptoms is the most important, though many victims try to ignore the signs. If an individual receives treatment immediately for a heart attack, he or she is much more likely to survive this very deadly ordeal.

Heart rate abnormalities

The human heart has an electrical system that regulates the speed of its contractions. There are a few common conditions that affect the speed and regularity of these beats. Tachycardia is a condition in which the heart beats very quickly, over 100 beats per minute. Bradycardia, on the other hand, is when the heart betas under 60 times per minute. This may not necessarily be a health problem; on the contrary, in some individuals it is a sign of excellent fitness. When atrial fibrillation occurs, electrical impulses spread throughout the heart, even as the ventricles continue to beat. This causes an irregular heartbeat, or arrhythmia. Many people who have trouble with abnormal heartbeat are aided by the use of a pacemaker, a battery-powered system that delivers precisely regulated shocks to the heart.

Congestive heart failure

If the heart is not pumping blood at a certain level, fluid will begin to build up in the lungs, hands, and feet. As the fluid builds up in the lungs, it may become difficult to breathe, and the individual is said to be suffering from pulmonary congestion and heart failure. In the other afflicted parts of the body, the fluid will soak through the capillary walls and cause swelling, particularly in the legs and ankles. The clinical term for this swelling is edema. This set of problems, known collectively as congestive heart failure, typically occur when an individual has suffered a myocardial infarction, although they may also occur because of rheumatic fever, birth defects, or hypertension. The only way to treat a congestive heart failure is to lower the intake of salt, take drugs to remove the excess fluid, and to reduce the workload on the heart.

Rheumatic fever
Rheumatic fever most commonly afflicts individuals between the ages of five and fifteen. The symptoms of rheumatic fever are swollen, achy joints, rashes on the skin, and frequent heart damage. Rheumatic fever is always preceded by strep throat. Indeed, a new strain of the streptococcus bacteria has enabled rheumatic fever to make a comeback in recent years, after many scientists thought it was gone for good. It is for this reason that it is essential that individuals recognize the symptoms of strep and seek immediate treatment. If a treatment including antibiotics is not commenced very soon after the infection, the individual runs the risk of developing rheumatic fever and suffering permanent scars on the heart valves.

Congenital heart defects
Congenital heart defects are those which an individual has from birth. Sadly, about eight of every thousand children born in America will have some congenital heart defect. These can come in a number of different forms. Most commonly, an individual will have a hole in the ventricular septum, the wall that separates the two lower chambers of the heart. It is also possible to be born with a hole in the atrial septum, which divides the upper chambers. Occasionally, the arteries that are charged with delivering blood to the body and lungs will be attached at the wrong places, and thus will not do their job as they should. Babies that are born with this

problem often have a bluish tinge because their bodies are not receiving sufficient oxygen.

Avoiding heart problems
Heart disease is one of the more sinister health problems, in that it can creep up on a person with little or no warning. Many autopsies on young children have revealed a shocking level of heart disease. It is a good idea to have both blood pressure and cholesterol level checked in order to be aware of heart condition. It is also important to exercise regularly, as this will keep the heart healthy and reduce the risk of heart attack. Limiting fat and cholesterol intake has been prove3n to help heart health. On the other hand, doctors recommend that individuals eat foods that are high in antioxidants and folic acid, as these substances have been associated with good heart health.

Diagnostic tests
There are currently a number of medical tests that can measure the strength and health of the human heart. An electrocardiogram, also known as an EKG or ECG, is the most common way to measure heart health. An EKG takes a reading of the electrical activity in the heart, and can tell if one part of the heart is receiving insufficient oxygen when under stress. Thallium scintigraphy is another way to detect heart disease. In this procedure, radioactive isotopes are injected into the bloodstream and then observed as they travel through the body, their behavior can tell doctors a great deal about the heart's function. Finally, coronary angiography is a test in which a long tube is placed in the blood vessels of the heart, where it releases a small amount of radioactive material. By observing this material's progress through the body, doctors can determine whether any arteries are blocked.

Treatment with medications
Most of the time, doctors use diuretics, beta blockers, calcium channel blockers, and angiotensin converting enzyme inhibitors to treat individuals with heart trouble. These

last drugs, known in the filed as ACE inhibitors, prevent the release of a hormone that contributes to high blood pressure. Beta blockers are drugs that alter the nervous system such that the heart no longer requires as much blood. Calcium channel blockers slow the flow of calcium ions into the heart, as scientists believe that excess amounts of calcium can cause the heart to violently contract, blocking arterial passages. Many of these heart medications are accompanied by some side effects, like lethargy and chest pain, and they may all be dangerous if they are not taken under close medical supervision.

Surgery

One of the most common surgical procedures performed on the human heart is the coronary bypass. IN this procedure, an artery is taken from the leg of the patient and grafted onto a coronary artery that is blocked. Blood can then travel around the blocked area and reach its destination. These surgeries are performed often, but do not always have the desired effect, and may affect mental functioning. Percutaneous transluminal coronary angioplasty (PTCA), also known as balloon angioplasty, is the most frequently performed heart surgery. It is done to open arteries that have been narrowed by plaque buildup; doctors insert a catheter with a tiny balloon affixed, and then they inflate the balloon temporarily in the narrowed area.

Mechanical aids

There are a few ways that doctors may try to bring external aid to a person whose heart is beyond the point of repair. In extreme cases, doctors may opt to perform a heart transplant. Although the survival rate in these operations has increased dramatically over the past decade, it is still a very risky operation. Individuals waiting for a donor heart may use a left-ventricular-assist device, which aids the ability of the heart to pump blood. Occasionally, doctors are forced to use artificial hearts, particularly when a desperate patient cannot find an immediate heart donor. Most of the recipients of artificial hearts will develop life-threatening complications within a short period of time.

Cancer

Cancer is simply the uncontrolled growth and spread throughout the body of abnormal cells. Cancer cells, unlike the regular cells of the body, do not follow the instructions encoded in the body's DNA. Instead, these cells reproduce themselves quickly, creating neoplasms, or tumors. A tumor may be either benign, which it is not considered dangerous, or malignant (cancerous). Unless they are somehow stopped, cancer cells will continue to grow, crowding out normal cells in a process called infiltration. Cancer cells can also metastasize, or spread to the other parts of the body by entering the bloodstream or lymphatic system. The gradual overtaking of the body by these cancer cells will eventually make it impossible for human life to be sustained.

Kinds of cancer

Every cancer has some characteristics in common, but may be more or less treatable depending on its particular nature. The most common forms of cancer are carcinoma, sarcoma, leukemia, and lymphoma. Carcinoma is the most common kind of cancer; it originates in the cells that line the internal organs and the outside of the body. Sarcomas are those cancers that develop in the connective and supportive tissues of the body, namely bones, muscles, and blood vessels. Leukemias are cancers that originate in the blood-creating parts of the body: the spleen, bone marrow, and the lymph nodes). Lymphomas are cancers that originate in the cells of the lymph system, which is supposed to filter out impurities.

Development

For a long time, researchers have puzzled over how normal cells can turn into cancer cells. A great deal has been learned about this process by studying oncogenes, the genes that normally control growth but have begun behaving abnormally. For unknown reasons, the DNA in these genes actually becomes altered. Cancer can also result when cells fail to effectively deploy their tumor-suppressing genes, which should stop excessive growth. Genetic and environmental factors can also contribute to the appearance of cancer. Some individuals inherit genes which are more likely to develop into certain kinds of cancer, and other individuals may increase their chances of developing cancer by consuming a high-fat diet or exposing themselves to harmful radiation.

Inherited risk

Doctors suspect that about one in ten cancers are due to heredity. Unfortunately, most people still do not realize that genetics can play a role in the development of the disease. Sometimes, a specific cancer-causing gene is passed down from generation to generation. The most frequent locations of these inherited cancers are the breast, brain, blood, muscles, bones, and adrenal gland. Typically, inherited cancers will strike earlier than other forms of the disease, and will often occur more than once in the same person. Genes are also usually responsible for any manifestation of cancer that seems gender-inappropriate: for instance, breast cancer in a man. Doctors say that anyone with a close relative who has had cancer is three times as likely to get the same kind of cancer.

Viruses and the environment

There are a few different non-cancerous viruses that may contribute to the formation of cancer cells in human beings. In particular, certain viruses have been shown to lead to the creation of leukemia and lymphoma, as well as liver and cervical cancer. The HIV virus, of course, is known to lead to Kaposi's sarcoma, as well as certain leukemias and lymphomas. The human papilloma virus can contribute to an outbreak of cervical or penis cancer. Environmental factors may also cause cancer. Many substances, like nickel, asbestos, chromate, or vinyl chloride are proven to be carcinogens. It is also well established that large doses of radiation are very likely to cause cancer, even that kind of electromagnetic radiation produced by electric blankets.

Diet

The easiest thing any individual can do to decrease his or her likelihood of contracting cancer is to eat more fruits and vegetables. Although the best idea is to eat a wide variety of produce, doctors have noted clear benefits In crucifers (broccoli, cauliflower, cabbage, etc.) and other foods that contain a high amount of antioxidants. Although diet supplements may help you to get some of these beneficial nutrients, doctors still recommend eating the fruits and vegetables themselves to get the most value. Individuals can also reduce their risk of cancer by decreasing their consumption of fatty foods. A low-fat diet has been shown to reduce the incidence of colon, ovarian, and pancreatic cancers. It is a good idea to eat unprocessed food as much as possible.

Tobacco and other carcinogens

By now, most Americans should be aware that cigarette smoking increases the risk of developing cancer more than any other single behavior. Not only do cigarettes lead to lung cancer, but also to cancer of the mouth, pharynx, larynx, esophagus, pancreas, and bladder. The risk is not limited to cigarettes, either: pipes, smokeless tobacco, and cigars all carry similar risks. Second-hand smoke has a similar effect; scientists have shown that individuals who are exposed to environmental smoke for more than three hours a day are three times as likely to develop cancer. Besides tobacco, other acknowledged carcinogens are asbestos, dark hair dye, nickel, and vinyl chloride. Individuals should always try to make sure their living and working spaces are well ventilated to reduce the amount of harmful substances in the air.

Skin cancer

Most cases of skin cancer are the result of overexposure to direct sunlight, especially the B range of ultraviolet light. It is also possible fro tanning salons to produce this harmful

- 59 -

radiation. The two most common kinds of skin cancer are basal-cell and squamous-cell. Basal-cell cancer involves the base of the epidermis, which is the outermost layer of skin; squamous-cell cancer affects the cells in the epidermis itself. Both of these cancers can be treated with surgery if they are caught early. Malignant melanoma is the deadliest form of skin cancer, and is known to especially target individuals with blond or red hair, freckles on the upper back, and rough red bumps on the skin (known as actinic keratoses). Individuals who spend a great deal of time in the sun should have their skin checked regularly by a dermatologist.

Breast cancer
Though it is possible for men to develop breast cancer, it is still a disease that primarily affects women. Women are considered to be particularly at risk if they are over the age of 50, have a family history of the disease, have no children, have experienced late menopause, or are obese. In order to guard against this threat, women are advised to perform regular self-examinations for lumps or alterations in their breasts, as well as to receive frequent mammograms (a diagnostic X-ray of the breast). If these procedures discover an abnormal growth, a biopsy will be performed to determine its character. Doctors may then opt to perform a lumpectomy (removal of tumor and surrounding tissue), quadrantectomy (removal of larger area around breast), or mastectomy (removal of the entire breast).

Cervical and ovarian cancers
Women are considered to be prone to cervical cancer if they had intercourse at an early age, have had multiple sex partners, have genital herpes, or have been exposed to environmental smoke. The standard test for cervical cancer is the Pap smear. Women are advised to have one of these performed regularly, as well as to watch out for irregular vaginal discharge or bleeding. Women are considered to be at risk of ovarian cancer if they have a family history of the disease, are infertile, or are obese. Unfortunately, some women may not develop any signs of this disease until it is quite advanced; at that point, they will develop irregular bleeding, digestive or urinary trouble, bloating, and weight gain. Doctors recommend an annual pelvic and rectal exam to help guard against ovarian cancer.

Colon and rectal cancers
Individuals are considered to be at a high risk of developing colon or rectal cancer if they have a personal history of the disease or if they have polyps (growths) in the colon or rectum. Typically, an individual who has one of these cancers will notice bleeding from the rectum, bloody stool, or a general change in their bowel habits. Since these cancers primarily affect people who are above the age of fifty, doctors recommend that every individual of the appropriate age have an annual exam to check for blood in the feces, as well as a digital rectal exam. This is especially important for women, as they are more likely than men to develop these kinds of cancer. When an individual is diagnosed with colon or rectal cancer, the treatment usually includes surgery, radiation therapy, or chemotherapy.

Prostate cancer
Prostate cancer is the most common form of cancer in men besides skin cancer. Doctors assert that a man is at a higher risk of prostate cancer as he ages, if he has a family history of the disease, if he has been exposed to large amounts of cadmium, if he has had a large number of sexual partners, or if he has had several sexually transmitted diseases. A high intake of saturated fats is also thought to contribute to prostate cancer. In recent years, doctors have been able to create a test that measures the level of prostate-specific antigen, the substance created by the body to fight prostate cancer. This has made it easy to diagnose the disease, so long as men go in for a regular exam. All men are advised to get an annual prostate exam.

Testicular cancer

Testicular cancer is not especially common, but it can be quite dangerous, particularly because it most often affects seemingly healthy men between the ages of 18 and 35. Men are at a greater risk if they have an undescended testicle. Testicular cancer usually is accompanied by a swelling or tenderness in one of the testes, so men who experience this condition should seek medical attention immediately. Although it may be necessary to remove a testicle that becomes cancerous, this will not impede a man's sexual function or potency. Testosterone injections may be required if both testicles are removed. If testicular cancer is diagnosed early on, it is very unlikely that the individual will suffer any long-term health problems.

Leukemia, lung cancer, oral cancer

Leukemia is a cancer of the blood that frequently targets individuals with Down syndrome or who have been exposed to large amounts of radiation. Leukemia may be difficult to diagnose, as its early symptoms are very similar to those of the flu. Lung cancer is caused primarily by cigarette smoking, although it can also be attributed to inhalation of asbestos or exposure to radiation. Like leukemia, lung cancer is tough to spot early; a persistent cough and bloody mucus are common warning signs. Oral cancer is most frequently associated with the use of smokeless tobacco or pipes, though it can also develop as a result of alcoholism. If an individual has a persistent mouth sore, a reddish or whitish patch in the mouth, or difficulty chewing or swallowing, he or she should be immediately tested for oral cancer.

Warning signs

There are a few physical symptoms that may indicate cancer. Any change in bowel or bladder habits, or an unusual bleeding or discharge may indicate cancer. Sores that refuse to heal, an obvious change in a wart or mole, or a thickening lump somewhere on the body may also indicate cancer is present. Continual indigestion, trouble swallowing, and a nagging cough may also be a cause for concern. Thankfully, the survival rate for individuals diagnosed with cancer has risen considerably in recent years. Even though media attention has scared the public about the danger of getting cancer from cell phones, microwaves, and dyes, doctors say that they are getting better at detecting and treating cancer all the time.

Chemoprevention

In the past decade, scientists have begun experimenting with ways to diminish the effects of cancer by introducing certain substances, most of them isolated from food, into the body as the disease develops. In order to accomplish this, scientists try to determine which foods are consumed more often by people with a low instance of cancer; they then isolate certain compounds in these foods and give them to cancer victims in the hopes of slowing or reversing the spread of disease. At present, the results of chemoprevention are inconclusive. Although some dietary supplements seem to reduce the risk of cancer in populations that have a generally poor diet, there is yet to be substantial evidence that the introduction of a certain compound has a clear effect on cancer cells.

Cancer therapies

The most common ways of treating cancer are surgery, radiation therapy, chemotherapy, an immunotherapy. When surgery is performed, it is usually to remove the tumor as well as the cells that surround it. This approach is most successful when it is applied to small, contained cancers. Radiation therapy entails exposing the body to powerful radiation, which will destroy cancer cells. It is often administered along with chemotherapy, in which powerful drugs are injected into the body in the hopes of stalling the development of cancer. Immunotherapy tries to rally the body's immune system to fight the cancer. This is often done by injecting antibodies and helpful proteins into the bloodstream.

In extremely severe cases of cancer, a doctor may elect to submit the patient to extremely high doses of radiation and chemotherapy. This, however, is likely to destroy the bone-marrow cells, so the patient will need to receive a transplant of healthy bone marrow, often from a carefully selected donor. This treatment has a mixed rate of success, but it seems to be particularly effective when it is possible to inject quantities of the patient's own bone marrow that were taken before the radiation and chemotherapy. There are at present a number of different experimental techniques that doctors are exploring in cancer treatment. One of these is gene therapy, in which healthy genes are injected into a cancer patient in an effort to resist the overwhelming cancer.

Tay-Sachs disease

Tay-Sachs disease is a rare genetic disease. It is caused by a mutation in one of the genes that makes it impossible for the body to produce an enzyme used by nerves to metabolize fat. The absence of this enzyme means that the central nervous system will gradually degenerate. When it occurs in infants, Tay-Sachs causes mental deterioration, blindness, paralysis, epilepsy, and finally death. Children born with this severe form of the disease usually die between the ages of three and five. It is also possible to have a less-severe form of Tay-Sachs in which the body can produce a small amount of the enzyme; individuals with this form of Tay-Sachs may live to adulthood. There is no treatment for Tay-Sachs.

Sickle cell anemia

Sickle cell anemia is a genetic disease that almost exclusively affects Africans or people of African heritage. The disease gets its name from the odd, sickle-shaped red blood cells that appear in those who have it. An abnormal form of hemoglobin, the protein in red blood cells that allows them to carry oxygen, somehow distorts the red blood cells. These blood cells are then more prone to

being destroyed, and when enough of them are destroyed the result is anemia. In order for an individual to contract sickle cell anemia, both of his or her parents must be carriers of the sickle cell trait. There is no permanent cure for sickle cell anemia, although advances in treatment have made it possible for patients to survive well into adulthood.

Cystic fibrosis

Cystic fibrosis is a genetic disease that primarily affects children. It is basically a disorder of the exocrine glands: a genetic abnormality makes it impossible for chloride to be evacuated from the cells of the body's organs, and this leads to the retention of water in all the organs. Since no water is exiting the organs, the normal secretions of the various organs are much thicker than usual, and the various gland ducts become blocked. The symptoms of cystic fibrosis are malnutrition, diarrhea, respiratory infection, liver disease, diabetes, and distended abdomen. There is no permanent solution to cystic fibrosis, although a change in diet has been known to improve health. Most of those who suffer from this disease do not live past the age of thirty.

Down syndrome

Down syndrome is a common genetic disease caused by the presence of an extra 21st chromosome. The results of Down syndrome are mental retardation, a characteristic face, and other malformations. Many of those who suffer from Down syndrome also have heart problems and are at a greater risk for leukemia. The mental handicaps associated with Down syndrome may not be evident at birth, but are usually recognizable by infancy. Individuals with Down syndrome typically have a round face, low nose, a ring of small spots around the iris, and flat tops of the ears. There is no cure for Down syndrome and, although individuals with this disease can live long and productive lives, most will never be able to live independently.

Mental disorder and mental illness

The American Psychiatric Association defines mental disorder as any behavioral or psychological syndrome that increases the individual's risk of injury or loss of freedom, creates distress for the individual, or impairs some other area of functioning. In other words, a mental disorder is a condition that works against the individual's chances of having a productive, pleasant life. Mental illness is more severe, and is defined by the APA as a mental, behavioral, or emotional disorder that can be diagnosed by a doctor and interferes with the one or more of the individual's activities in life. These activities may include things as simple as dressing, eating, or working.

Anxiety disorders

Phobias
The most common kind of anxiety disorder is a phobia, an irrational and intense fear of some object or situation. About one in ten adults will develop some kind of intense phobia at some point in his or her life. Although many prescription medications have been used to treat phobias, none seem to be very effective unless they are taken along with behavior therapy, in which the individual is subjected to gradually increasing levels of the feared object or situation. Medical hypnosis therapy has also proved effective in combating phobias. An individual may have developed a phobia if he or she recognizes that the fear is excessive or irrational, and is unable to function because of fear.

Panic attacks and disorders
Panic attacks are massive feelings of anxiety, often accompanied by hyperventilation, racing pulse, and dizziness. The victim of a panic attack may become numb in some of their extremities, and will usually feel a string sense of impending doom. Most of these attacks climax after about ten minutes. If an individual has frequent panic attacks, he or she may be said to have panic disorder.

About one-third of all individuals will experience a panic attack before the age of 35. There are two common treatments for panic disorder: cognitive-behavioral therapy, in which the individual learns specific strategies for dealing with a panic attack; and anti-anxiety medication, which only seems to work well when it is combined with behavioral therapy.

Obsessive-compulsive disorder
One extreme kind of anxiety disorder is obsessive-compulsive disorder, in which the individual is plagued by a recurring thought that they cannot escape, and may display repetitive, rigidly formalized behavior. Individuals who suffer from OCD are most often plagued by thoughts of violence, contamination (for instance, being concerned that they are infected), or doubt. The most common compulsions among individuals with OCD are hand washing, cleaning, counting, or checking locks. Individuals suffering from OCD probably recognize that their behavior is irrational but feel powerless to stop it. OCD will eventually get in the way of the person's functioning in other areas of life, and will require treatment. Though OCD is thought to have biological origins, it can be treated with a combination of medication and behavioral therapy.

Major depression

A major depression is an overwhelming feeling of sadness that extends over a long period of time. Though about one in ten Americans will experience a major depression in any given year, only about one in every three of these will seek treatment. Most cases of depression can be helped with psychotherapy, medication, or both. An individual may be depressed of he or she feels sad or discouraged for a long period, lacks energy, has difficulty concentrating, continually thinks of death or suicide, withdraws from his or her social life, has no interest in sex, or has a major change in his or her eating or sleeping habits. Some individuals who do not respond to therapy or

- 63 -

medication may receive electroconvulsive therapy, the administration of electrical current through electrodes placed on the scalp.

Manic depression

Individuals suffering from manic depression (bipolar disorder) will have violent mood swings, ranging from unbridled euphoria to crushing despair. An individual with this form of mental illness may also have wild, uncontrollable thoughts, unrealistic self-confidence, difficulty concentrating, delusions, hallucinations, and odd changes in behavior. During a "high," such an individual may make unrealistic and grandiose plans, or take dangerous risks. During a "low" period, the same individual will feel hopeless, and may contemplate suicide. Manic depression, otherwise known as bipolar disorder, is a very serious disorder that requires immediate medical treatment. Anti-convulsants and lithium carbonate are the most common drugs prescribed to treat this illness.

Suicide

Although suicide is not considered in itself to be a psychiatric disorder, it is the unfortunate result of many of these conditions. Every year about 30,000 Americans will take their own lives, and about ten times this number will make a serious attempt. The rate of suicide among citizens between the ages of 15 and 24 has tripled over the past thirty years. Men are about three times as likely to commit suicide as women, though women make the attempt far more often. The majority of suicides, especially those committed by young people, involve firearms. Suicide is more common among whites, though it appears to be rising quickly among African-American males. Health professionals believe that as many as 80% of those who are at risk of suicide can be helped with immediate therapy.

Risk factors
There are a number of factors that can contribute to make an individual consider taking his or her own life. About 95% of those who commit suicide have some form of mental illness, most commonly depression or alcoholism. Individuals who for whatever reason have lost hope that their life will improve are at a high risk of suicide. There appears to be some hereditary influence, as well: about one in four who tries suicide has a family member who has killed him or herself. Autopsies have shown that suicidal individuals often have a low level of the neurotransmitter serotonin. Finally, it is well documented that individuals who have easy access to firearms are far more likely to commit suicide.

Teenage depression
The proportion of teenagers who are clinically depressed and potentially suicidal has risen dramatically over the past few decades. Unfortunately, teenagers are often withdrawn or aloof, so it can be difficult to discover their emotional state. Some of the warning signs that a teenager may be depressed include irritability, sudden weight change, change in sleep patterns, fatigue, restlessness, and a loss of interest in previously-enjoyed activities. Teenagers with depressed parents do appear more likely to become depressed themselves. Teenagers who have recently endured some family trauma, like the divorce or death of a parent, should be specifically monitored for the signs of depression.

ADHD

Attention deficit/ hyperactivity disorder is the diagnosis given to a range of conditions in which the individual has a hard time controlling motion or sustaining attention. Although ADHD is typically thought of as a disorder that affects children, new research suggests that it is not outgrown, and that adults may be just as likely to suffer from it. Individuals suffering from ADHD are impulsive, constantly in motion, and easily

- 64 -

distracted. They may feel perpetually restless, may be unusually forgetful, and are likely to be socially immature. Although there is no specific test to determine whether someone has ADHD, most doctors are trained to recognize the condition. Most of those who suffer from ADHD are benefited by behavioral therapy and medication.

Schizophrenia

Schizophrenia, one of the most crippling forms of mental illness, exists when an individual loses the unity of his or her mind, and suffers impaired function in almost every mental area. An individual suffering from schizophrenia may see or hear things that do not exist, may believe that an external force is putting thoughts into their head or controlling their behavior, or may suffer delusions about their identity. Many schizophrenics will develop severe anxieties and will become obsessive about protecting themselves. For most individuals, antipsychotic drugs can help to restore mental control and minimize delusional episodes. However, these drugs can cause a person to become apathetic, and many impoverished individuals will lack the resources to receive treatment at all.

Types of therapy

Psychotherapy
Psychotherapy refers to a broad spectrum of counseling techniques based on conversation between a trained professional and an individual seeking help. Most mental health professionals are trained in a few different psychotherapeutic styles, and can tailor their approach to the patient. Progress in psychotherapy can at times be difficult to measure, and insurance companies have grown increasingly unwilling to foot the bills for long treatments. For this reason, many individuals seek psychotherapy for a specific problem, or in order to correct a specific feeling or behavior. Most people find that the process of talking and listening is therapeutic in itself, and can allow them to discover

solutions to their problems that were unavailable through reflection.

Psychodynamic psychotherapy
Most practicing psychotherapists take a dynamic view of mental health; that is, they believe that the individual's unconscious life and experiences during his or her formative years have a tremendous influence on his or her adult behavior. Psychodynamic treatment is often quite brief, and usually is aimed at stopping a particular behavior. Scientific evidence has emerged that suggests that psychodynamic psychotherapy can actually rewire the brain in a matter of weeks, so that the target behavior or feeling becomes habitual. This kind of therapy is often the best option for otherwise high-functioning adults who have experienced a recurring problem or trouble in a particular situation.

Interpersonal therapy
Interpersonal therapy was originally developed by doctors performing research on the treatment of major depression. They discovered that many patients were aided by developing an empathetic relationship with a therapist. IPT does not attempt to treat the origins of a psychological disorder; rather, it helps the individual to improve his or her ability to get along with others. This treatment has been most effective for individuals suffering from major depression, difficulties forming lasting relationships, dysthymia (mild depression), or bulimia. Most IPT treatments last from between 12 and 16 weeks. In them, the therapist usually talks a great deal more than he or she would in psychodynamic psychotherapy.

Cognitive-behavioral therapy
Cognitive-behavioral therapy is designed to help individuals break out of bad or disordered habits of thought or behavior. In cognitive therapy, the therapist helps the individual identify his or her central beliefs, recognize potentially negative thought patterns, and learn new ways of thinking and approaching problems. Cognitive therapy has most clearly benefited individuals suffering

from major depression or anxiety disorders. Behavior therapy follows a similar course, except that it aims to replace problematic behaviors rather than thoughts. Many therapists believe that changing a person's behavior will naturally change his or her thoughts or emotions. Behavior therapy seems to work best when a patient is crippled by a specific habit, for instance alcoholism, drug abuse, or a phobia.

Psychiatric drug therapy
Psychiatric drugs are those that affect the chemistry of the brain and relive the symptoms of mental disorder and illness. In recent years, research has produced a generation of extremely safe and effective psychiatric drugs, which can help individuals with problems ranging from minor depression to schizophrenia. One of the most common types of drug is serotonin-boosting medication, which can be used to treat obsessive-compulsive disorder, attention deficit disorder, and depression. Patients should know, however, that it often takes several weeks for psychiatric medications to begin showing results. Also, they may have serious side effects and may continue to be operative after the individual has stopped taking them.

Many doctors complain that patients have become too reliant on the "quick fix" promised by psychiatric drugs, and are unwilling to take the behavioral steps necessary to permanently improve their condition. Moreover, many patients fail to get valuable information about the drugs that have been prescribed to them. For instance, a patient should always know why a particular medication is prescribed rather than another, and what specific symptoms the medication is designed to treat. A patient should be aware of the potential side effects of any medication, and should know how long it will take for the drug to take effect. As with any medication, a patient should know whether it has dangerous effects when mixed with alcohol or another drug, and he or she should have a clear understanding of how long the drug will have to be taken.

Family and Social Relationships

Diversity

The United States is the most diverse nation in the world. Unfortunately, all of the racial and ethnic groups in America do not have equal access to health education and care. Most minorities rate their health services as inferior to those received by whites. This problem is partly due to racism, and partly due to economics: because the United States government does not provide universal health care to all of its citizens, the wealthy tend to receive the most attention and are the best informed on health issues. Also, some of the cultural groups in the United States do not view Western medicine favorably, and so they are less likely to seek health information or treatment. Individuals who do not speak English are also likely to have problems getting health advice and care.

Health risk
Studies have consistently indicated that some racial or ethnic groups are at particular risk for certain illnesses. For instance, African-Americans tend to have higher blood pressure than whites, and are more likely to have glaucoma, lupus, kidney failure, and liver disease. Native Americans are much more likely than any other group to have diabetes; in fact, among the Pima Indians almost half of the population has this serious condition. Males from Southeast Asia are known to have a higher rate of lung and liver cancer, and Hawaiian women are more likely to develop breast cancer. All of this data indicates that health care professionals need to be educating themselves on the various risks associated with each group so that they can give each patient the appropriate treatment.

Improving minority health education
According to a report published by the National Institute of Health, minorities in the United States face a shorter life expectancy because it is more difficult for them to get health information and treatment. Of course, poverty rather than race may be the prime determinant for the quality of care that an individual receives. To remedy this situation, the NIH has established an office to allocate funds for minority health education. One example of this group's work is a series of public service announcements on hypertension aimed at African-Americans. Studies performed by the NIH indicate that the increased awareness of the risk of high blood pressure has already diminished that danger of this condition among African-Americans.

Teaching a multicultural class
One of the great aspects of teaching in most American classrooms is the diversity of the student population. This diversity can be a great advantage to a class, though it can also be an obstacle if it is not handled properly. Too many teachers take the easy way out and make their instructional methods the same for all students, when it would be to their benefit to modify their methods to best suit the student. Research has found that teachers are most successful when they focus on academic achievement, and allow their students to maintain their cultural differences. The best teachers are also those that attempt to cultivate in their students a fair-minded view of diversity; that is, a pride in their own culture and respect for the cultures of others.

Early sexual development

There are only a few basic physiological differences between males and females. Males have the ability to make sperm and to contribute the y-chromosome that enables a female to give birth to a male. Only females are born with sex cells, menstruate, give birth, and are capable of breast-feeding. In the embryonic stage, males and females have similar sex organs. After a few weeks of development, though, the gonads differentiate into either testes or ovaries. This differentiation depends on the genetic instructions given by the sex chromosomes. If a y-chromosome is present in the embryo, it will develop into a male; if there is no y-chromosome, the embryo will develop as a female. All future differentiation will be motivated by the gonads, not the chromosomes.

Hormone system

Hormones are the chemicals that motivate the body to do certain things. They are produced in the organs that make up the endocrine system. With the exception of the sex organs, males and females have identical endocrine systems. The actions of the hormones are determined by the hypothalamus, an area of the brain about the size of a pea. The hypothalamus sends messages to the pituitary gland, which is directly beneath it. The pituitary gland turns on and off the various glands that produce hormones. Hormones, once released, are carried to their targets by the blood stream, at which point they motivate cells and organs to action. Hormones can influence the way a person looks, feels, behaves, or matures.

Basic sex hormones

The sex hormones that are most important to women are called estrogen and progesterone and are produced in the ovaries. In males, the primary sex hormone is testosterone, which is produced by the adrenal glands and testes. Both men and women do, however, have small amounts of the opposite hormone. Indeed, men need estrogen to have effective sperm. Sex hormones are at work very early in the development of the embryo. When testes are formed, they begin releasing testosterone, which causes the formation of the other male reproductive parts, like the penis. If no testosterone is present, the embryo will develop female genitals. This is true of both natural females and males with malfunctioning testes.

At the onset of puberty, the pituitary gland begins to release the hormones that further differentiate between the sexes. Specifically, the pituitary gland releases gonadotropins, which stimulate the gonads to generate the appropriate sex hormones. As these gonadotropins do their work, the secondary sex characteristics are developed. In females, larger amounts of estrogen cause the breasts to enlarge, the hips to widen, and for fat to be deposited on the hips and buttocks. It also causes her external genitals to enlarge, and initiates the processes of ovulation and menstruation. For males, large amounts of testosterone cause the voice to deepen, the penis to become thicker and longer, muscles to grow stronger, and hair to develop in new places.

Gender

Many people confuse sex and gender. Whereas a person's sex is strictly dependent on his or her sex chromosomes, hormone balance, and genital anatomy, gender refers to the psychological and social parts of being a male or female. Every individual has a sexual identity that is out of his or her control. To a certain degree, gender is also out of the individual's control, as it is a result of the way the individual is raised and how society treats that individual. Still, many people make conscious decisions to alter their gender identity. Some people simply feel more comfortable a gender other than the one they have been raised in, and they may alter their dress, appearance, and behavior to suit their new gender identity.

Gender differences

It is well documented by science that men and women not only have differences in appearance, but actually think and sense in different ways. In most cases, women have stronger senses of hearing, smell, and taste, while men tend to have better vision. Males tend to be stronger, though females often have better fine motor skills. Brain scans have displayed significant differences in the areas of the brain that are more active in

- 68 -

males and females. Of course, there is no telling whether these differences are entirely physiological, or whether upbringing and environment contribute. Most scientists believe that a combination of nature and nurture create the differences between the sexes.

Sexual stereotypes
Although there are clear physiological reasons underlying the various sexual stereotypes, more and more men and women are affirming their personal ability to decide how their sex determines their station in life. Many people are opting for careers which were formerly reserved for the opposite sex; for instance, more men are becoming nurses and secretaries, and more women feel comfortable becoming truck drivers, engineers, and pilots. Many people are adopting androgyny, or the combination of male and female characteristics, as their ideal. They insist that it is more appropriate to let the specifics of particular situation or role determine one's behavior, rather than relying on stale ideas of what it means to be masculine or feminine.

Female anatomy

On a woman, the mons pubis is the round, meaty area located above the pubic bone. The outer lips surrounding the vagina are known as the labia majora. These cover the softer inner lips known as the labia minora. At the upper intersection of the labia minora is a small flap of skin covering the clitoris, which is a small, extremely sensitive erectile organ. Directly below the clitoris is the urethral opening, where urine exits the body. Below the urethral opening is a larger orifice, the vagina. The vagina is the canal leading to all the major reproductive organs in the female body. Below the vagina lies the perineum, which is simply the area between the vagina and the anus. The anus is the opening that leads to the rectum and large intestine.

All of the major reproductive organs in the female body are accessed through the vagina. At the very back end of the vagina lies the cervix: the gateway to the uterus, or womb. The walls of the uterus are composed of a layer of tissue known as the endometrium. On either side of the uterus are the ovaries. Ovaries are about the size of an almond and are composed of egg cells called ova. These eggs are moved from the ovaries to the uterus through the fallopian tubes, canals that extend out and back from the upper uterus. Fallopian tubes have ends that resemble waving fingers. When an egg is released by an ovary, these fingers catch it and direct it into the mouth of the fallopian tube.

Menstrual cycle:
The hormones released by the female body trigger the ovaries to grow a few immature eggs. Typically, only one ovum is developed during each monthly cycle. The growth pf this hormone signals the body to produce more estrogen, which in turn produces more of the hormones responsible for menstruation. In the middle of the cycle, the egg cells are released. This is called ovulation. At this point, the body goes through many of the changes that would support a fertilized egg: the endometrium thickens and becomes richer in nourishing blood, and more estrogen and progesterone are produced. Assuming the egg remains unfertilized, the hormone levels will eventually drop and the uterine lining will be shed, resulting in some bleeding.

PMS
Women who suffer from premenstrual syndrome may endure physical and emotional unrest for a period of up to two weeks, or from the period of ovulation to the beginning of menstruation. These ailments are thought to be caused by hormone imbalances created by the menstrual cycle. Most commonly, PMS is manifested as anxiety, mood changes, hot flashes, dizziness, heart palpitations, changes in appetite, irritability, fatigue, and insomnia. The treatment for PMS depends on the particular

symptoms exhibited by the woman. Relaxation therapy has been effective in combating many of the anxiety issues associated with PMS. Some women benefit from treatments that adjust their sleep cycle. Other, more severe cases may call for the use of antidepressants.

Menstrual problems
Premenstrual dysphoric disorder is not related to PMS. It occurs during the last week of menstruation, and typically involves depression and anxiety. Menstrual cramps (referred to as dysmenorrhea in the medical community) occur in approximately half of all menstruating women. These may be caused by uterine muscles that contract to frequently or violently, depriving the uterus of necessary oxygen. Exercise has been shown to reduce cramps. Amenorrhea, the condition in which a woman stops menstruating, can occur if a woman exercises too much, undergoes a rapid weight change, or has a hormonal disorder. If it is prolonged, amenorrhea can lead to loss of bone density and, obviously, the inability to bear children.

Minimizing menstrual problems
Although some menstrual problems may be inevitable because of the hormone imbalances created, women can still take a few easy steps to minimize discomfort during this process. For one thing, women should continue to exercise; research has shown that physically active women have fewer problems during menstruation. Women can also help themselves by eating regularly and nutritiously, as the body may not be as good at regulating glucose levels during this period. Salt tends to exaggerate bloating problems, and should be avoided along with caffeine. A woman's sensitivity to alcohol may increase during this period, so it is best not to drink too much. Smoking and sweets can also lead to greater menstrual problems.

Toxic shock syndrome
Toxic shock syndrome is a rare but potentially deadly infection that affects women und the age of thirty who use tampons. The symptoms of TSS are a high fever, a rash (especially on the fingers and toes), dizziness, extremely low blood sugar, and abnormalities in several organ systems. In order to reduce the risk of TSS, women may want to opt for sanitary napkins instead of tampons. Of particular hazard are super-absorbent brands of tampon, so women should use caution when choosing a tampon. When tampons are being used, they should be changed three or four times a day. It is a good idea to use sanitary napkins at night, or for at least part of every day during menstruation. When TSS is diagnosed, doctors usually treat it with antibiotics and intensive supportive care.

Perimenopause and menopause
As a woman gets older, her menstrual cycle becomes more erratic and eventually stops altogether. The period from the first irregular cycle to the last menstruation is known as perimenopause. Once a woman has not menstruated for a full year, she is said to have entered menopause. Although many women make this transition with ease, others are seriously affected. The main cause of menopausal troubles is the decline in estrogen level, which can lead to mouth and gum problems, dry or sensitive skin, hot flashes, fatigue, acne, and even hair loss. Shriveling of the clitoris, vulva, and vaginal lining may make intercourse painful. Some doctors have had success in easing women into menopause by giving them replacement hormones.

Male anatomy

The external parts of the male sexual anatomy are the penis and scrotum, the scrotum being the sac that holds the testes. The testes manufacture sperm and testosterone. Sperm are the male reproductive cells. All of the sperm that are not yet mature are stored in the epididymis, a series of tubes next to each teste. The penis itself holds three hollow cylinders: the two corpora cavernosa and the corpora spongiosum. The corpora spongiosum surrounds the urethra, which is the canal through which semen and urine travel. Semen is made up of several substances, mainly water, and is the liquid in which sperm cells are carried out of the body during ejaculation.

The production of seminal fluid requires the work of several different structures. The two tubes that carry the sperm from the epididymis into the urethra are called the vas deferens. The fluid will also pass through the seminal vesicles on its travels, so doctors refer to the seminal vesicles and the vas deferens as the ejaculatory ducts. Some of the seminal fluid will be produced by the prostate gland and secreted into the urethra during ejaculation. The Cowper's glands, also, links up with the urethra and is activated during arousal and ejaculation. The Cowper's gland secretes a small amount of fluid at the beginning of arousal; this fluid is not semen itself, though it may contain sperm.

Circumcision

When male children are born, they have a bit of skin covering the end of their penis. For over half of the boys in the United States, this foreskin will be cut off in a process known as circumcision. Circumcision is prescribed by both the Jewish and Muslim religions, though many others opt for it as well. Medical proponents of circumcision claim that it reduces the dangers posed by a buildup of oils or secretions under the foreskin. Indeed, studies have shown that uncircumcised males are more likely to develop urinary tract infections. However, those who oppose circumcision claim it is unnecessary, painful, and that the procedure creates a risk of infection. There is no clear consensus on the impact of circumcision on sexual performance and satisfaction.

Sexuality

Childhood sexuality

It seems odd and even perverse to refer to sexuality in childhood, but many of the foundations for later sexual experience are laid in the early years of an individual's life. For infants, the mouth is the main area for sensual pleasure. By the age of 3 or 4, most children become interested in the differences between males and females, and may start to develop vaguely romantic feelings towards another person. It is very important for parents to discuss these topics with their children, so that the children will have a framework of understanding for these complex and often confusing emotions. Children are likely to have lots of questions, some of them perhaps uncomfortable; parents should do their best to answer honestly and with a minimum of embarrassment.

Adolescent sexuality

As boys and girls enter adolescence, their interest in sex typically intensifies and seeks expression. This makes it essential that health providers give adolescents the necessary knowledge and skills to enter this time in their lives. For teenage boys, it is typical to experience frequent erections, and to begin having nocturnal emissions, or wet dreams. Masturbation is the most common form of sexual expression for adolescents, especially males. Adolescents may also experiment with kissing and petting, oral sex, and even sexual intercourse. At this point, as many as a quarter of all people will experience a same-sex attraction, though this does not predict any future homosexuality. Though American teens are not known to be any more sexually active than teens elsewhere in the world, they do have a higher rate of pregnancy, indicating that adequate birth control information and supplies are not being provided.

Intercourse

When someone refers to sexual intercourse, they are typically referring to vaginal intercourse or coitus, in which the penis penetrates the vagina. This is the most common expression of sexuality for heterosexual couples. Vaginal intercourse can be performed in a number of different positions. Human beings are unusual among species in that women can have intercourse at any time during their menstrual cycle. Some women, however, may prefer to refrain from intercourse during menstruation. Vaginal intercourse always carries the risk of transmitting bodily fluids, which can cause pregnancy or sexually-transmitted disease. In many countries, vaginal intercourse is the most common culprit for the spread of the HIV virus.

Stages of sexual response
Researchers into sexual response have determined that there are four distinct stages of sexual response: excitement, plateau, orgasm, and resolution. Excitement is always the first stage in the process of sexual response. It can be initiated by any sort of sexual stimulus: a thought, a picture, or any direct stimulation of the senses. For men, sexual arousal triggers a rush of blood to the genitals, causing the testicles to lift and the penis to become erect. For women, sexual stimulation starts to enlarge the clitoris and the vaginal lips. The breasts may also become more sensitive. At this point, the vagina increases in length and width. The uterus also lifts, which creates even more space in the vagina.

During the plateau period of sexual response, the physiological changes that were begun in the excitement stage intensify. The penis continues to expand, and the vagina swells and becomes more sensitive. When orgasm arrives, it is actually quite similar for both males and females. Orgasms typically involve between three and twelve pelvic muscle contractions, each lasting about a second. For males, ejaculation begins when the vas deferens, seminal vesicles, and upper urethra contract. Then, muscle contractions force semen out of the penis. The female orgasm is more varied: it may either be felt as a series of small orgasms, or as a prolonged orgasm after extensive excitement and plateau. The clitoris is almost always involved in the female orgasm; once it has been adequately stimulated, the vagina will undergo a series of contractions.

In the final, post-orgasmic state of sexual response, the male and female sexual organs return to their normal and non-excited state. For men, the period after orgasm is typically a refractory period, in which they are incapable of reaching another orgasm. If resolution begins without one partner having had an orgasm, it may be slower and a bit uncomfortable. In order to improve a sexual relationship, the participants need to maintain good communication. It may be a good idea for couples to set aside a specific time to discuss their sex life, so that neither partner feels inhibited from speaking his or her mind. It is always a good idea to make any complaints or requests gently, as most people can be quite sensitive on the subject of their sexual performance.

Pregnancy

First trimester
Within forty hours of being fertilized, the egg begins dividing. This process will continue for a while, until the cluster of egg cells drifts down the oviduct. At this point, cells begin to assume special tasks and characteristics. By the fourth day after fertilization, the cell arrives in the uterus and is referred to as a blastocyst. The blastocyst attaches to the wall of the uterus and is nourished b the uterine lining (endometrium). About two weeks after fertilization, the blastocyst becomes an embryo, with different layers that will eventually become the organ systems, hair, and skin. Part of the blastocyst will become the placenta, amniotic sac, and umbilical cord. By the end of the second month of development, the embryo is a fetus, a recognizable human being with various working parts.

Second trimester
During the second trimester (that is, the fourth, fifth, and sixth months of pregnancy), the fetus will require a great amount of nourishment from the placenta because it will

be growing to a length of about 14 inches and a weight of about two pounds. The placenta must be able to supply the growing fetus with a large amount of food, oxygen, and water. By this point, all of the systems of the body will be in action, and a heartbeat will be audible with a stethoscope. In the fifth or sixth month of pregnancy, the mother will be able to feel some movements of the fetus. Although it is highly unlikely, it is possible for a fetus born in the fifth or sixth month of pregnancy to survive.

Third trimester
The fetus will gain most of its weight during the third trimester (the seventh, eighth, and ninth months of pregnancy). A good bit of this weight is fatty tissue beneath the fetal skin which helps to keep the developing fetus well nourished. At this point, a baby needs a great amount of calcium, nitrogen, and iron to develop blood and bone. During this period, the fetus relies on the immunities that have been developed by the blood of the mother to keep it from contracting any infectious diseases. These immunities will unfortunately wear off during the first six months of life, though they may be replenished if the child is breastfed early in life. Though a fetus should be able to survive if it is born in the third trimester, it will not have had enough time for its organs to develop to the point where they are relatively free from vulnerabilities.

Childbirth

First stage of labor
In the first stage of labor, the contractions of the uterus are about thirty seconds in duration and arrive every fifteen or twenty minutes. For some women, the amniotic sac may break during this period, expelling the fluid from the body. There may be a bit of bleeding also during this period, as the coagulated blood that was blocking the cervix falls away. The last part of this first stage in labor is called the transition period: during this period the contractions become much longer (up to ninety seconds) and more

intense. They may also begin arriving every three minutes. During the transition period, the cervix opens all the way, to a diameter of about 10 centimeters. This is wide enough for the head of the fetus to pass through.

Second stage of labor
In the second stage of labor, the baby is born. This stage begins with the head of the baby moving into the birth canal. As the contractions of the uterus continue to mount in intensity, the mother helps push the baby out through the cervix, into the vagina, and then out into the world. When the head of the baby appears at the opening of the vagina, it is said to be crowning. As the baby emerges from the vagina, someone will wipe any blood or mucus off of the baby's face and make sure that the umbilical cord is not fastened around the baby's neck. A great deal of fluid is expelled from the mother's body along with the baby. Once the umbilical cord stops pulsating, it will be severed from the baby.

Third stage of labor
In the third stage of childbirth, the baby has been born but the uterus continues to contract until the placenta is expelled. In cases where the placenta has a hard time exiting the mother's body, someone may exert some light pressure on the mother's abdomen to speed the process. It is important that the entire placenta be removed from the body, as it can become infected. Interestingly, breastfeeding soon after childbirth helps control internal bleeding for the mother, because it causes the secretion of a hormone that makes the uterus contract. As the mother is recovering, the health of the baby will quickly be assessed and it will be wrapped in clean, dry blankets. Once the baby is returned to the mother, she may immediately begin to nurse it.

Relationships

Nuclear and extended families
A nuclear family is a family group consisting of one adult couple (one male and one female) and their children. The strong bond

- 73 -

among the members of a nuclear family is a consistent feature of almost every society, with one notable exception being the Israeli kibbutz, in which children are raised by the entire community without any particular parents. An extended family consists of more than one adult couple, often the parents, brothers and sisters of a particular heterosexual couple. In many human societies, people live among their extended families, rather than just in a nuclear family unit. This is especially typical in societies where people do not have to move particularly quickly (that is, in agrarian or industrial rather than hunting and gathering societies).

Self-image
One of the most important determinants of how an individual forms relationships with others may be how that individual perceives him or herself. If an individual feels unlovable, it may be impossible for him or her to seek affection from others. If a person has confidence in him or herself, he or she should be able to develop honest and open relationships with others. Though the phrase is a bit clichéd, it is nevertheless true that a person cannot love another without loving him or herself. Sadly, studies have shown that individuals who have a negative opinion of themselves tend to establish relationships with people who treat them poorly, and thus reinforce their negative self-image.

Friendship
Friendship, with its bonds of loyalty, affection, and respect, is one of the great joys of life. Unfortunately, it is not available to people who are not ready to work for it. Friendship requires constant cultivation in order to prosper. Most people find that the friendships formed during childhood and adolescence are the deepest and most enduring, perhaps because the formation of strong friendships helps to ease the individual out of the family domain during this period. There is no documented society in human history that has not demonstrated admiration for the institution of friendship.

In order to develop strong friendships, individuals should be willing to listen, to express themselves honestly, to tolerate the faults of their friends, and to value trust and loyalty.

Psychosocial development

Self-actualization
In order to reach your highest potential, you have to satisfy a number of basic needs. To illustrate this, health professionals have set up a pyramid of psychological health, so that individuals can see what conditions must be met before they can excel. Before anything else is accomplished, your physiological needs for food, water, shelter, and sleep must be met. Then, if these needs are satisfied, you can work on achieving safety for yourself and your loved ones. When this is accomplished, you are free to develop loving relationships and fit into a society. These relationships are a necessary foundation for self-esteem and a healthy respect for other people. The person who has satisfied all of these needs is said to be ready for self-actualization, the fulfillment of his or her potential.

Individual values
Every individual has a set of values, criteria by which they understand and judge the world. Sometimes, though, individuals may claim to have a certain set of values even though they appear to act on another. In order to clarify your values, it is a good idea to consider carefully the consequences of your choices and ensure that they are moral and positive. Health professionals define individual values as being either instrumental or terminal: instrumental values are ways of thinking that a person holds important, for instance being loyal or loving; terminal values are goals or ideals that a person works towards, for instance happiness. The values of an individual and even of a society are constantly changing, so you have to be sensitive to the values that you are promoting with your choices.

- 74 -

Self-esteem

Self-esteem is the way that you think about yourself. Every person wants to feel as if they are important and valued in society, and as if they are living up to their potential. Having healthy self-esteem is not only derived from these feelings, but it makes it possible for you to do the things necessary to make yourself happy and content. Most health professionals agree that an individual's self-esteem is largely determined during childhood. Low self-esteem often haunts those who have been abused in the past, and can unfortunately lead people to seek out relationships in which they are treated poorly. One technique that many health professionals recommend for boosting self-esteem is positive thinking and talking. Even if it feels forced, studies have shown that encouraging the mind to take an optimistic viewpoint can eventually make good self-esteem a habit.

Emotional intelligence

In recent years, health professionals have determined that what is known as emotional intelligence may be just as important as an individual's IQ. According to the psychologist Daniel Goleman, there are five areas of emotional intelligence: self-awareness, altruism, personal motivation, empathy, and the ability to love and be loved. Studies have shown that individuals with a high level of emotional intelligence will succeed at work and in developing positive personal relationships. An individual's emotional intelligence is not the same throughout his or her life, and many businesses have begun taking active steps to develop the emotional intelligence of their employees. Essentially, developing one's emotional intelligence requires listening to one's feelings and respecting them.

Managing moods

Moods are emotional states lasting for a few hours or days. Though every individual will have bad moods from time to time, some are better at managing their moods than others. Researchers have demonstrated that the most effective ways to solve a problem, and hence emerge from a bad mood, are to take immediate action, think about other successes, resolve to try harder, or reward oneself. Individuals who try to distract themselves, perhaps through socializing, will find that this only partly improves their mood. The worst things to do when you are in a bad mood are to vent at another person, isolate yourself, or give up. Using alcohol or drugs to escape a bad mood is also an ineffective way to feel better.

Assertiveness

Although assertiveness is often confused with pushiness, it simply means acknowledging one's own feelings and making one's desires known to other people. Being assertive does not necessarily mean that one is always going to get what one wants. Oftentimes, though, the simple act of expressing one's opinion is enough to destroy any feelings of frustration or impotence. Many individuals remain passive for most of their lives, and then occasionally explode out of frustration: this is generally a result of not being consistently and politely assertive. Studies have consistently shown that assertive individuals have less stress in their lives, probably because they feel they are in control.

Refusal skills

Students should be equipped with some good ways to say "no" to any behavior in which they do not want to participate. First, students should not let the person pressuring them continue talking for a long time; it is always best to quickly decline and change the subject. Refusal skills are especially useful when teens are trying to say "no" to sex. If another person pressures a student to have sex and threatens to remove his or her love, the student should acknowledge the superficiality of the other person's love and be unmoved. It is always best to avoid engaging in a debate with any person who is trying to pressure you into a negative health behavior; simply repeating your refusal until the conversation stops is a very effective way to be assertive without being aggressive.

Communicating emotions

In academic and business relationships, the majority of communication will involve facts. However, individuals who are adept at communicating facts may struggle to communicate their feelings to each other, and this can be the most important kind of communication in achieving happiness. It is essential to realize that openly and honestly sharing feelings is the only way to develop a personal relationship. In order to do this, people should work on asking questions and honestly answering questions about themselves. Being a good listener, by asking the right questions and respecting the other person's answer, is part of establishing good emotional communication. Sometimes, though, this may mean putting aside one's own opinions to fully engage and try to understand another person's point of view.

"I" message
When health educators refer to "I" messages, they mean the process wherein a person acknowledges his or her own feelings and accepts responsibility for them. An "I" message generally consists of the way you feel and the conditions under which you feel that way; for example, "I feel sad because you are ignoring my feelings." The philosophy behind the "I" message is that you control your response to a given situation, even if it seems as if external influences are causing you to feel a certain way. Forcing yourself to acknowledge the way you feel is a good way to take control of your behavior and not allow others to influence you to do things that are unhealthy. Moreover, most individuals find that they just feel better when they are open about their feelings.

Gender differences
Extensive research has indicated that there are distinct, but not universal differences between the ways that men and women express themselves. There are various

hypotheses for why this is so: some suggest that men need to disclose facts and assert their status with language more often, while women are more schooled in intimate conversations between friends and kin. Many studies have shown that women are more adept at reading the body language and underlying meaning of verbal communication, while men are better at discerning the factual content of verbal communication. Women seem to be better able to determine the emotional state of the speaker, and often may respond to this rather than to the particular words that are spoken. These differences do not hold true for every man or woman, but acknowledging their existence might help to defuse potential conflicts between the sexes.

Nonverbal communication
Even though we normally think of communication as something we do through spoken or written language, we are constantly sending messages to one another with our bodies and tines of voice. Oftentimes, physical messages are sent and interpreted without either party being aware. The particular signals that are used are sometimes consistent for all of humanity, and sometimes are unique to a particular culture. For instance, slumped shoulders generally mean passivity and submission in every society; however, some cultures may see eye contact as a sign of respect and others may see it as a sign of hostility. One should try to be aware of the messages one is sending with one's posture and gestures, so that one can avoid sending messages that are insulting or self-defeating.

Dating

Though the word dating has come to assume a romantic connotation in American society, dating is really any time that is set aside to spend exclusively with another person. Friends are dating if they make a point to see one another. Unfortunately, the tendency to confuse dating with casual sex and drinking has led to a decrease in the amount of casual

- 76 -

dating in the United States. Many people assume that dating is strictly for finding a mate, whereas dating has a host of other benefits, from teaching one to make good conversation to introducing them to various kinds of people and ways of life. Dating, in its ideal form, is a great way to explore oneself by getting to know a wide variety of people.

Sexual attraction

Sexual attraction is just one of the many factors that contribute to the formation and maintenance of long-term relationships. In most studies, individuals are found to be most sexually attracted to people who share their age, race, ethnicity, and socioeconomic background. Many sociologists speculate that this is because individuals have more access to people that are similar to themselves, and because they intuitively understand that they are more likely to be approved by similar people. In general, men put more emphasis on looks in determining sexual partners, whereas women may value other qualities like dependability and affluence. This may be due in part to the historical need for men to find women who can reproduce easily, while women have sought a man who can provide for them during their period of pregnancy and childrearing.

Love

Anthropological view
Almost every society has some form of romantic love, if romantic love is defined as an intense attraction in which the other person is idealized and relationships are maintained for a long period of time. Many anthropologists speculate that romantic love evolved as means to induce men and women to form the partnerships in which children can thrive. That is, they view romantic love as a way to propagate the human species. Indeed, many studies have shown that romantic love tends to wane after about four years, about the length of time required to raise a child through infancy.
Anthropological studies of many different societies have confirmed that couples tend to break up and desire new partners after about four years together.

Biochemical view
A great deal of research has been performed to isolate and study the chemicals that act in the brain during the experience of romantic love. Scientists have taken a close look at neurotransmitters (the chemicals that send messages throughout the brain) and determined that dopamine, norepinephrine, and phenylethylamine all contribute to the physical feelings of love: sweaty palms, racing heart, deep and rapid breathing. These brain chemicals all have a marked similarity to amphetamines, and the brain can eventually become desensitized to them. On the other hand, partners who develop long-term, stable relationships may gradually increase the brain's release of endorphins, which produce a feeling of well-being and peace.

Mature love relationships
Scientists have marked a difference between passionate love, in which the partners are sexually charged and ecstatic, and companionate love, in which partners are friendly and deeply affectionate. In many cases, relationships that begin with passionate love eventually evolve into companionate love. On the other hand, everyone has experienced or heard of cases in which a long-term friendship suddenly becomes a passionate affair. A healthy and mature love is one in which each partner breaks down the barriers between themselves and the other, while retaining their individuality. Mature partners respect one another's differences, are not threatened by each other's independence, and constantly communicate with one another.

Failed love relationships
Although people traditionally assume that being abandoned by a romantic partner is worse than leaving a partner, many studies have discovered that the partner who ends a relationship is often more subject to psychological traumas like guilt, uncertainty,

and awkwardness. The only real help for the pain of a breakup of time, but the process can be eased if both parties treat one another with respect and kindness. During a breakup, it is important to remind oneself of one's own value as an individual, and not to take the other person's decision as a definitive statement about oneself. Also, it is important to remain engaged with other people despite any feelings of fear you may experience; it is easy to allow feelings of insecurity caused by a breakup to contaminate all the other relationships in your life.

The single life

It is becoming increasingly common in American society for men and women to go their entire lives without marrying. Single people are no longer looked down upon as somehow defective by the rest of society, and so more and more people feel comfortable remaining single for their entire lives. The most commonly-given reason for staying single is not being able to find the right person. Most studies show that few people intend to remain single forever, but they are willing to wait until their expectations are met. Some singles still claim that they are discriminated against by insurance companies, credit organizations, and medical care providers. Despite the claims of some that giving equal rights in these areas will erode the institution of marriage, there is growing support for single's rights.

Cohabitation

Couples who live together without being married are said to be cohabitating. Many people view cohabitation as a way to get to know a potential marriage partner, though studies have not conclusively shown that couples who cohabitate before marriage are less likely to get divorced. The increasing frequency of this arrangement has led some states to create "domestic partnership" legislation that grants the insurance and medical rights given to married couples to cohabitating couples. Although most married

couples have cohabitated before their nuptials, many people complain that cohabitation undermines the public respect for marriage and is damaging to relationships.

Marriage

Despite claims that the institution of marriage is eroding in recent years, over 90% of Americans will marry in their lifetime. In the past, marriage was as much a business deal as a romantic union; parents often arranged the marriages of their children to advance in society. Though this is still common in some countries, in the United States people are more likely to wed because of a romantic affection for one another. People are increasingly likely to marry someone with whom they share a background and have similar values. Even today, many couples marry because the woman is pregnant, or as a way to escape the authority of their parents. Typically, males are slightly older than females at the age of marriage.

Finding a marriage partner
For the most part, people marry someone from the same geographical area and culture as themselves. However, interracial and intercultural marriages are becoming more common and socially accepted. Most studies have revealed that individuals desire a partner with whom they share values and can communicate effectively, and for whom they are willing to make adjustments and tolerate flaws. Many couples undergo premarital assessments to determine if they are truly right for one another. These assessments typically try to measure how compatible the interests, values, and behavior of the two people are. In any case, most couples benefit from some form of counseling before marriage.

Sociological types of marriage
According to sociologists, there are two kinds of marriages: traditional and companion-oriented. In a traditional marriage, the two people conform to the prescribed marital

roles of their society; for instance, the man becomes the provider and the woman the childrearer. In a companion-oriented marriage, the partnership and the rewards of romantic love are more important than the marital roles. Some sociologists add to this distinction different categories for romantic marriages, in which the sexual passion that originally sparked the union remains present for an abnormally long time, and rescue marriages, in which one partner sees marriage as a way to escape some traumatic event in his or her past.

Benefits of marriage

Even though many people claim that the institution of marriage is under assault these days, there are still plenty of documented reasons to suggest that married people lead better lives than singles. Strong, healthy marriages seem to make people healthy and happy. In general, married people have been shown to have more money, better health, and better sex lives than singles. In particular, marriage seems to benefit men. Married men exhibit lower rates of alcohol and drug abuse, depression, and self-destructive behavior. Married men have sex twice as often as singles, and are more likely to be satisfied with their sex lives. Married women, on the other hand, see their average wages go down, though this may be due in large part to the large proportion of married women who work less in order to raise children.

Parenting

Before having a child, every individual should consider the awesome responsibility and massive effect it will have on his or her life. Many people idealize childbirth and don't acknowledge that many parents may feel a bit resentful of the changes they are forced to make. A man may feel jealous of the attention the mother gives to the new baby, and then he may feel guilty for having this jealousy. A new mother may feel overwhelmed by her new role, especially given her weakened physical condition. Indeed, studies have consistently shown that marital satisfaction generally declines after the birth of a child. The number of separations and divorces tends to rise after a child enters the family.

Raising children

At the most basic level, young children have needs for food, shelter, and protection that have to be met. Children also have psychological and emotional needs, though, and sometimes these are more difficult for a new parent to understand. In order to have strong and meaningful relationships later in life, a child must have a model. In order to enter a certain social role later in life, children need to be socialized effectively, and this happens first in the family unit. Parents are the first to set rules and social norms, and so children get their idea of what constitutes acceptable behavior from their parents. As children grow older, there will begin to be a tension between their need for independence and their ties to the family; parents will also need to be sensitive to their children on this issue.

Conflict resolution

It is inevitable in life that you will come into conflict with some difficult individuals. Many people persistently spar with others because they have a personality disorder based on low self-esteem or illness. For the most part, you will not be close enough to an individual to try and change them in any permanent way. Therefore, in most cases of conflict health professionals recommend acknowledging the other person's viewpoint, and then finding a way to either avoid or circumvent that person. If confrontation is necessary, you should state your feelings honestly and politely. If at all possible, try to avoid making confrontations unnecessarily personal. Sometimes it helps to have a third party mediate an especially contentious dispute.

Aggression

Biological causes

Oftentimes, individuals who have suffered some traumatic brain injury are more likely to display aggressive behavior. The abuse of alcohol or drugs will also increase an individual's tendency towards explosive rage. Scientific evidence has shown that many prescription medications, especially painkillers, anti-anxiety drugs, anti-depressants, steroids, and over-the-counter sedatives, may increase the risk of violent behavior. Males who commit violent crimes appear to have lower levels of serotonin in their brains, and males with a high level of testosterone are thought to be more prone to violence. As one would expect, individuals who suffer from psychological problems like schizophrenia are more likely to become violent.

Developmental causes

Children of abusive parents are much more likely to engage in violent behavior as they grow older. Although scientists believe that this is in part because such children fail to learn other coping mechanisms, there is also speculation that aggressive tendencies may be inherited. However, even if a child grows up in a nonabusive home, if they live in a violent community they are more likely to become overly aggressive. Children who perform poorly at school or are ostracized by their peers are also more likely to become violent. Individuals who display violent behavior at a young age are often rejected by their community, which only exaggerates the problem.

Other causes of violence

There is a great deal of research to suggest that the portrayal of violence in television, films, and music can incite impressionable individuals to commit similar acts. According to some statistics, the average American child will be exposed to about 40,000 deaths and countless more acts of violence during his or her childhood and adolescence. It has also been clearly illustrated that poverty, unemployment, and gang involvement often lead to violent acts. The risk of violence seems to be inversely proportionate to the chances that an individual has for success in society. It should be noted that violence seems to be tied to economics rather than to race; no racial or ethnic group has been shown to have a greater predisposition to violence.

Partner abuse

Sadly, about one in five women will be abused by a romantic partner during her life. Indeed, domestic violence is the largest cause of injury among women. Women are considered to be battered if they are the victims of repeated and persistent physical abuse. This is usually accompanied by a tremendous amount of psychological stress. Battered women are often unwilling to admit that they have been abused, and so the health care professionals who treat them are unaware of the abuse. Alcohol and stress are the reasons most often given by men to explain why they abuse their partners. Many of these men are not violent anywhere but in the home. Partner abuse seems to become more common the poorer a family becomes, and the more crowded their home becomes.

Child abuse

Although statistics have shown that impoverished parents seem to abuse their children more often, child abuse remains a problem among every socioeconomic group. Child abuse can be physical, psychological, or sexual. Sexual abuse includes virtually any sexual contact between an adult and child, whether it is kissing, fondling, oral sex, sexual intercourse, or just suggestive conversation. Pedophilia is the clinical term for any sexual abuse of a child that is perpetrated by an individual other than the child's parents. Incest, on the other hand, refers to sexual contact among members of the same family. Oftentimes, children that are psychologically or sexually abuse may develop physical symptoms, or begin to act out in society.

- 80 -

Sexual violence

Although sexual violence must ultimately be blamed on the offending individual, there are a few social factors that contribute to its prevalence. First, there is an unhealthy tendency for individuals to accept male aggression as natural, and to suggest that women should be receptive to all male advances. It is also a myth that the male sex drive is somehow unstoppable. Too often, our society seems to blame the victims of violence as if they had somehow provoked others to act out against them. Similarly, many aggressive tendencies of feelings are condoned if they are part of a "joke" or "prank." This only serves to trivialize behavior that can be very painful to the victim. Finally, the prevalence of media in which sexual violence is condoned or even glorified sends the wrong message to would-be offenders.

Sexual harassment

EOEC standards

The issue of sexual harassment in the workplace has been explicitly treated by the Equal Opportunity Employment Commission. According to this body, sexual harassment may take one of two forms. In quid pro quo harassment, an individual in a position of authority makes unwanted advances on an employee and indicates that these are a condition of receiving a promotion, raise, or of simply remaining employed. The other type of abuse is harassment by a hostile or offensive environment, in which those in positions of authority are persistently inappropriate or offensive in their dealings with employees. Sexual harassment can range from uncomfortable remarks to unwanted physical contact. Employees who feel they are being sexually harassed on the job should make detailed notes of the situation, and seek help elsewhere.

Sexual coercion

There are a number or unacceptable behaviors that fall into the category of sexual coercion. Strictly speaking, sexual coercion is any sex that takes place when one of the partners does not consent. Although women are far more likely to be coerced sexually, it is also possible for a woman to exert psychological or even physical pressure on a man to have sex. Sexual coercion can be unwanted groping, date rape, intoxicating a partner in order to lower their resistance to sex, or just talking someone into a sexual act they do not want to commit. People who are sexually coerced may want to avoid making the aggressor anger, or avoid getting a reputation as a "tease." Many men will sexually coerce women because they feel a man should have sex at every possible chance.

Rape

Rape is sexual intercourse involving one nonconsenting, unwilling, and possibly forcibly restrained partner. There is also what is known as statutory rape, which is sex between a person over the age of 16 and a person below the age of consent (which varies from state to state). Rapists are often individuals who have a difficult time establishing relationships with other people, have been sexually abused themselves, or are heavily involved with alcohol and drugs. Although many rapists blame their victims for provoking their heinous acts, studies have shown that women are raped because they encounter sexually aggressive men, not because of any particular quality in their dress or behavior.

Categories of rape

There are a few different categories of rape, depending on the motive of the rapist. An anger rape is an unplanned, random attack, usually motivated by some personal crisis in the rapist's life. A power rape is premeditated, and is committed in order to exert total control over some other person. Power rapists are often beset by a feeling of powerlessness in their own lives. Sadistic rape is usually premeditated, and involves bondage, humiliation and torture. The people

- 81 -

who commit this kind of rape are aroused by their own anger and the fear of their victim. In a gang rape, two or more men participate in a sexual assault on a single victim. The motive for this kind of rape may be more camaraderie among the males than sexual gratification for each person.

Date and acquaintance rape
Most rapes are committed by someone who is acquainted with the victim. Many acts that can be considered rape are not considered as such by the victims, who blame themselves for not being assertive or for putting themselves in a bad situation. However, any situation in which one partner has sex against their will is rape. There are a few variables that increase the risk of date and acquaintance rape. Men who are hostile to women or antisocial are more likely to commit acquaintance rape. Men who initiate a date and pay for all the expenses are more likely to be sexually aggressive. There are some social groups, fraternities for instance, that seem to be more accepting of sexual aggression. Alcohol and other drugs also increase an individual's chances of becoming sexually aggressive.

Recovery
Sadly, only a small percentage of the young women who are raped will report the crime to the police. This is especially unfortunate as studies have shown that women recover from being raped more quickly when they know that their assailant has been caught and punished. Rape can have both physical and psychological side effects; in order to recover, a woman should seek immediate medical attention after the crime. Also, a rape victim should not wash or change clothes before reporting the crime, as there may be valuable evidence there that the police can use to catch the rapist. The most important thing many rape victims can remember is that they are not to blame for what has happened to them.

Incest

One of the most traumatic forms of sexual abuse is incest, which is defined as sexual contact between any two people who are too closely related to marry. The most common incestuous pairings are father-daughter, brother-sister, and uncle-niece. Incest is particularly common when one of the parties is very young and unable to defend him or herself. The damages done by incest are not only physical it is also extremely painful for a young person to be taken advantage of by an older figure close to them. Adults who force children into incestuous relations are not always strictly pedophiles; they may simply be domineering and sexually opportunistic predators.

Teenage pregnancy

There are a number of problems that are common when teenagers become pregnant. First of all, many girls are not physically ready to bear children; their bodies may not have the right amount of folic acid to guard against birth defects. Moreover, there is a strong social stigma surrounding teenage pregnancy in most societies. Research consistently shows that women who become pregnant before the age of twenty will earn less money over the course of their lives, and are more likely to develop alcoholism, depression, and other mental illnesses. Finally, many teenagers are not ready for the responsibility of raising a child, and so the children of teenage parents are often at an immediate disadvantage.

Marital difficulties

Unrealistic expectations
However ideal the beginning of a marriage may be, eventually there will be some conflict. One of the major causes of marital discord is the harboring of unrealistic expectation by one or more of the parties. Sometimes, people assume that their partner will always be just the same, physically and mentally, as they were during the period of courtship.

Sometimes they assume that in order to truly be meant for one another, they should always automatically agree on every subject. Of course, both of these assumptions are dangerous for a relationship. In a truly healthy relationship, both parties have room to grow and change without alienating the other, and both feel empowered to speak their minds and to disagree without endangering the union.

Money and sex

Many marriages or committed relationships go askew because the individuals disagree about money. Interestingly, fights about money are rarely about how much money the couple has; instead, couples tend to fight about how the money will be spent, and who will keep track of their collective finances. Another subject about which partners often fight is sex. As a relationship matures, one party may lose interest in sex, to the consternation of the other. Marries couples often fight if one party feels they always initiate sex, or if one party feels hurt by the other's indifference. The sex life of a couple will likely change many times throughout the course of a long relationship; the best way to ensure mutual satisfaction is to always be compassionate and communicative.

Other common causes

Extra-marital affairs are about the most devastating thing that can happen to a marriage. If one partner is discovered to be cheating, the other partner is likely to feel abandoned, inadequate, unloved, and angry. When extra-marital affairs are a problem, the parties need to ask themselves whether they really love one another and feel any commitment. In a different sort of way, marriages in which both members work can be difficult. It may be necessary for one party to move for work, or for one to stay home and raise children. When one person's career seems to be more important than the other's, conflicts can often develop. In order to avoid the problems caused by dual-career marriages, individuals should understand their partner's ambitions before deciding whether that person is right for them.

Couples therapy

It is becoming increasingly common for couples to seek counseling when they have problems. According to both the couples and to objective measures, about two-thirds of those who receive counseling see improvement on their relationship. Counseling works best when both parties enter with a willingness to hear constructive criticism, and to express their own views respectfully. A good counselor is able to provide an objective and impartial perspective to problems. In order to get the most out of counseling, individuals should try and catalog all of their complaints, as well as the ways both parties could change to improve the relationship. Counselors have observed that every relationship in which both parties want to continue can be saved.

Divorce

Although divorce is becoming more popular all over the world, the United States still perennially has one of the highest rates. Divorce, which is seem by some as a way out of a bad marriage, is not without profound consequences itself. Individuals who have been divorced frequently report depression, anxiety, and feelings of hopelessness as a result. Interestingly, divorced individuals seem to be much more likely to marry again than are singles to marry a first time. Moreover, with each successive divorce, and individual becomes more and more likely to remarry! This suggests to many researchers that marriage creates the pattern of companionate living in the minds of the participants, and that this pattern is very hard to break.

Effects on children

The breakup of a marriage has enormous, indeed incalculable effects on the children of that marriage. If children are very young when the marriage dissolves, they often remain babyish and emotionally immature for an abnormally long period. Young children may blame themselves for the end of a marriage. Slightly older children may exhibit these effects, and may also have a hard time forming relationships outside of the family. Teenagers from divorced families tend to have a hard time establishing independence. Interestingly, though, divorce has not been shown to adversely affect a child's performance in school. The negative consequences seem to be exclusively psychological and social.

Helping children
In the event that a divorce becomes necessary, there are a few things that parents can do to minimize the damage to their children. First of all, even though it may be tempting, it is inappropriate to indulge children because you feel sorry for them. Spoiling a child so that he will prefer you is not good for the child. It is important to be honest with your children, but without divulging any unnecessarily painful information. Parents should never fight in front of their children. Parents undergoing a divorce should make sure their children know that it is alright for them to love both parents, and that they do not have to choose sides. If parents spend quality time with their kids, and constantly reaffirm their love, their transition through divorce can be eased.

Motor Learning, Motor Development, and Movement Concepts

Manipulative movements

Throwing

Throwing is a basic motor pattern used by an individual to propel an object away from his or her body. In order to throw, one must first grasp the object with one or both hands. It is a good idea to have one's legs shoulder-width apart, with one foot slightly in front of the other. The foot is out front should be opposite to the arm that is throwing in a one-handed throw; in other words, when throwing with the right hand the left foot should be slightly out front. Next, one should slowly bring back one's arm and take a small step with the foot that is out front. As the throwing arm swings forward, release the object. Even after the object has been released, one should continue the follow-through with the throwing arm in order to maintain proper form.

Kicking

Kicking is a simple motor pattern in which a foot is used to strike and propel an object in any direction. When kicking, the arms should be held sideways to maintain balance. As one approaches the ball, the support foot (the foot that is not striking the object) should be placed next to the object to be kicked. The kicking leg will be brought back and then will swing forward in an arc from the hip. As the foot makes contact with the object, the knee will be fully extended and the body will be leaning slightly back for balance. After contact, the kicking foot will continue its progress in the same direction as the object. While kicking, one should keep one's eyes on the object being kicked at all times.

Dribbling a basketball

Dribbling a basketball, or bouncing any other kind of ball off of the ground repeatedly, is a simple motor pattern that relies heavily on hand-eye coordination. When dribbling, one should have one's feet place in a slightly off-set, stride position. One's knees, hips, and waists will all be slightly bent, to improve balance and to make them more capable of quick adjustments. The ball should be pushed against the ground with the fingertips making contact, and the force coming from the extension of the elbow. In basketball, it is always a good idea to maintain the dribble at waist level. The eyes should for the most part be looking straight ahead, although it will be necessary to occasionally look at the ball.

Striking objects

One of the basic manipulative movements that is used in sports is striking an object with either a paddle or a racket. In this case, one is propelling some object forward with a hand-held implement. In order to do this, one should be holding the racket in the dominant hand; that is, the hand with which one feels most comfortable. When the object is at the height of the shoulder or above, an over-arm motion will be used: the racket will be drawn back, and rotated forward from the shoulder, with the follow-through drawing the implement away from the body. When striking an object below the shoulder, the racket will be brought back behind the hips and then swung forward in an arc from the shoulder: the follow-through on this type of strike is typically more brief. During this movement, the trunk will stay still, though it may be bent forward slightly.

Catching

Catching is a basic manipulative skill that entails stopping the momentum of some object that is approaching the body and controlling it with the hands. When one is catching, one should be standing still, with eyes focused on the incoming object. One's arms will be slightly bent in front of one's body, and one's hands should be the first thing to make contact with the object. Sometimes, though, it will be necessary to trap the object against one's body with the hands or arms. Establishing the proper timing for a catch is one of the more difficult motor patterns to learn. Many individuals benefit from starting off by catching a large ball.

Locomotor movements

Walking
Walking is one of the most basic motor patterns. Many people are surprised to learn that walking is essentially just a process of losing and regaining balance: the individual shifts his or her center of gravity off of the base of support briefly, and then extends a leg to catch him or herself. This makes more sense, perhaps, when one remembers what a baby's first steps resemble. During walking, one's body should not shift dramatically from one side to another, or bob up and down violently. The most natural way to walk is with the arms and legs working in opposition. That is, the right arm will swing forward as the left leg strides forth, and the right arm will swing back as the right leg strides.

Running
The locomotor pattern of running takes a few years to fully develop. When it is mature, a running pattern will involve the trunk leaning slightly forward, and both arms swinging in wide arcs and in opposition to the motion of the legs (as in walking). The supporting leg will make contact with the ground almost directly under the center of gravity. The knee of the supporting leg will bend forward slightly as the foot makes contact, and then the extension of this leg will propel the body forward. Meanwhile, the other knee will be swinging forward to create forward momentum. The swinging of the arms will create vertical momentum, which as an individual grows older will allow the stride to lengthen.

Crawling
One of the first locomotor movements that anyone learns is crawling. The motor pattern associated with crawling is quite simple. First, the individual must be able to support him or herself on hands and knees. This

requires a bit of upper-body strength. Then, as the right hand moves forward, momentarily shifting the center of gravity, the left leg will also move forward to stabilize. Similarly, as the left hand moves forward the right knee will slide forward so that balance is maintained. Using this simple pattern of movement, one is able to propel him or herself forward. It is interesting to not that crawling, just like walking and running, relies on momentarily falling out of balance and then restoring that balance to propel the individual.

Leaping
The locomotor pattern for leaping is based on the pattern for running. This is evidenced by the fact that a leap takes off from one foot and lands on the other. The position of the arms is also the same in a leap as they are in a run: that is, the left arm will swing forward with the right leg, and vice versa. The swing of the arms will be more exaggerated in a leap, in order to generate more momentum and distance. Once the individual touches down, he or she will bend the supporting leg in order to absorb the force of the body. The knee of the supporting leg will often bend considerably more than it does during the run pattern. During a leap, the trunk of the body will be a bit behind the center of gravity, in order to maintain the balance upon landing.

Hopping and galloping
A hap is a basic locomotor pattern in which one springs off of one foot, in any direction, and lands on the same foot. During a hop, the knee will not straighten all the way. Most of the propulsion of the hop and absorption of the force of landing is achieved by the ankle joint. Galloping is a more complex movement. When galloping, one lifts the lead leg, bends it, and then advances it forward to receive the weight. While this is going on, the back foot will advance to replace the supporting leg, perhaps hopping a bit forward once it has fully taken the place of the supporting leg. The rhythm of a gallop is generally uneven.

- 86 -

Skipping and jumping

The locomotor pattern for skipping is a combination of a step and a hop, accomplished first with one foot and then the other. Like a gallop, the skip has a somewhat uneven rhythm: there is the same alternation of feet and opposing motion of the arms that accompanies walking, but also a same-sided hop that throws the motion off-kilter. Jumping, on the other hand, is a fairly simple motor pattern in which one propels oneself off of the ground for a moment. To jump, one begins with feet parallel and shoulder-width apart. It helps to swing one's arms back, and then forward as the knees are bent and extended, lifting the body off of the ground. The momentum generated by the upward progress of the arms increases the height of the jump.

Traveling

The National Standard for Physical Education has defined traveling as possessing a basic level of competency in many different movement forms and demonstrating proficiency in a few specific areas. A person who can travel in this sense is able to combine different movement patterns, and to use motor patterns in a variety of different environments. He or she should be able t move forwards or sideways using a number of different patterns, and be able to change directions quickly when necessary. A person who can travel will also be able to set locomotor patterns to music, develop dance sequences to accompany music, and perform dance and gymnastic movements. Finally, an individual who has achieved this level of competency will have mature patterns of walking and running.

Chasing, fleeing, dodging

The locomotor patterns for chasing, fleeing, and dodging all depend on the presence of some other moving thing. Chasing is the attempt to overtake something or someone that is fleeing. In order to chase effectively, a person needs to be able to quickly reach top speed but also make sudden changes in direction. When fleeing, a person is traveling away from someone or thing that pursuing him or her. Again, this pattern of movement requires being able to reach top speed quickly, change directions, and dodge. Dodging is the ability to rapidly move the body in some other direction than is indicated by the original line of movement. Effective dodging may include faking a move and executing another, twisting the body, or stretching on a certain direction.

Nonlocomotor movements

Turning

Turning is one of the basic nonlocomotor movements; that is, it does not attempt to change the location of the body, but rather to alter its position. A turn is simply a smaller part of a full rotation, and like a larger rotation is created by a shift in the support base. To turn, one begins by placing one foot in front of the other. The speed of the turn will be aided by holding the arms straight out from the shoulders, such that they are parallel to the ground. The body will then be rotated to the right or left by a twisting of the hips. The feet should be set slightly apart to widen the base of support, as this twisting motion will cause the weight to be shifted so that it rests primarily on one the leg on the side one is turning towards.

Rolling

Rolling is one of the easiest non-locomotor movements, and is usually mastered within the first few months of human life. To roll, one simply lies down on the floor with the arms either pressed to one's sides or raised above one's head. Rolling usually begins by lying on one's back. Then by flexing the abdominal muscles, one is able to shift the trunk off of the center of gravity such that the body rolls over. Once a half-turn has been accomplished it is usually easier to continue a roll. Sometimes a roll is accelerated by bending the knees and swinging the legs in the direction of the roll when one is on one's sides and stomach.

- 87 -

Twisting and transferring weight

In the study of nonlocomotor patterns, twisting is considered to be identical to turning, with the only exception being that the feet are set shoulder-width apart, with toes pointing forward, during the entire movement. This tends to increase stability as the upper body rotates. Most individuals are able to twist their bodies a little more than ninety degrees to each side. Transferring weight is a component of many of the locomotor movements, like walking, jumping, or leaping. It simply means leaning in one direction, or shifting the pelvis such that more of the body weight is on one of the legs.

Stretching and balancing weight

The nonlocomotor pattern for stretching involves extending (or, in some cases, hyper-extending) any of the joints in basketball so that they are as long or as straight as possible. Although stretching normally entails a bit of discomfort, it should not be performed if it causes serious pain. Any stretching action should be performed slowly and smoothly, without bobbing or jerking. Most of the time, it is best to allow the body to gradually accustom itself to a given stretch. When balancing, the body is attempting to maintain a stationary position or adjust to the force of gravity while performing certain movements. A good practice for balance is to stand on one foot and attempt different motions with the head, arms, opposing leg, and trunk.

Jumping and landing

When it is discussed as a nonlocomotor movement, jumping is merely the transfer of weight from one foot to another. The motor pattern through which an individual regains his or her balance and reestablishes a standing position is known as landing. During a jump, the individual's arms will have been flung up, so they should be extended at the sides during landing to aid in maintaining the balance. In order to best absorb the shock of landing, the individual should have his or her knees, hips, and ankles slightly bent. It is a good idea to land on the balls of the feet, so that compensatory movements can shift the weight forward to the toes or backward to the heel as necessary.

Planes of movement

Median

Fitness professionals have a few technical terms to describe the various planes of the body in which motions can be made. The median (or midsagittal) plane extends from the top of the head down and divides the body into two symmetrical halves, right and left. Any other plane of the body that runs parallel to the median plane is known as a sagittal plane. Any kind of movement which takes the body forward from its standing position is known as flexion. Raising the leg in front of oneself, for instance, is referred to as flexion of the hip. Any movement that takes the body backwards and occurs in a sagittal plane is known as an extension; tilting the head back, for example, is called extension of the neck.

Frontal

The frontal plane, also called the coronal plane, is any plane that runs perpendicular to the median plane (that which divides the body into right and left halves. The frontal plane divides the body into a front and back, clinically referred to as an anterior and posterior. Any movement in a frontal plane that moves a part of the body towards the median plane is called an adduction. Crossing the legs, for instance, can be referred to as an adduction of the hip. A movement that takes any part of the body away from the median plane is referred to as an abduction; extending the arm away from the body, for instance, is an abduction of the shoulder. For the torso and neck, a movement in the lateral plane away from the median plane is called lateral flexion or side-bending; in the case of fingers and toes, the reference is the middle finger or toe, and adduction and abduction are considered as they refer to this axis rather than to the median plane.

Transverse

The transverse (or horizontal) plane of movement divides the body into upper and lower halves, known professionally as the superior and inferior halves. Any movement that takes place in the transverse plane and moves the body outward is called a lateral rotation; twisting the leg so that the toes point outwards, for instance, would be called a lateral rotation of the hip. A movement that brings a part of the body inward is called a medial rotation. There are a couple special terms that refer to the rotation of the forearm: when the palm of the hand faces backward, this known as pronation, while a movement in which the palm is pointed forward is called supination.

Body movements

Movements of the trunk

The mobile vertebral column allows a person to move his or her torso in a number of different directions. Anterior flexion is when the person leans his or head forward and thus stretches the back ahead. Leaning back is called posterior extension. Bending to either side is clinically referred to as lateral flexion or side-bending. The trunk can also be twisted on the pelvis, a motion called right or left rotation. The range of movement varies within the back depending on the shape of the vertebrae (lower vertebrae are largest and least mobile), the thickness of the intervertebral discs, and the degree to which the thoracic vertebrae are inhibited by the ribs. The movements of the trunk should not be confused with those in which the back stays straight while the hips move.

Movements of the scapula

The scapula is set just behind the back of the rib cage, though it is not connected to it. Instead, the scapula is suspended by a complex network of ligaments and muscles, and can therefore move in a number of different ways. When the scapula (and thus the shoulder) is raised, this is called moving superiorly, or elevation. Inferior movement of the scapula, also called depression, occurs when the shoulder moves downward. When the shoulder moves forward, this is called moving laterally. Lateral movement of the shoulder can also be called protraction or abduction. When the shoulder is moved back, it is known as medial movement, retraction, or adduction. The shoulder can also be rotated such that the inferior or bottom side moves toward the midline or away from the midline.

Movements of the arm with scapula

The excellent mobility of the scapula and the versatility of the arm muscles combine to allow a variety of movements. When the arm is raised so that it is perpendicular to the ground in front of the person, it is called anterior flexion. Raising an arm parallel to the ground on the side is called lateral abduction. Moving the arm back from its position resting at the side is called posterior extension; this movement has a much smaller range than most arm movements. Bringing the arm from a raised position closer to the body is known as medial adduction. When the arm is then moved behind the body, it is a combination of adduction and extension. The rotation of the humerus on its axis, for instance with the elbow bent and held to the person's side, can be called either medial or lateral rotation, depending on the direction of rotation.

Movements of the elbow

The elbow is capable of four distinct movements. A movement that decreases the angle between the upper arm and forearm is known as flexion. When flexion is active (that is, when the muscles are contracted), the movement is limited by the contact made between the muscles. Passive flexion has a greater range of motion. Extension of the elbow is any movement that increases the angle between the arm and forearm; the upper limit of this angle is 180 degrees. When the lower arm is rotated such that the palm faces down, and the radius crosses over the ulna, it is known as probation. When the radius and ulna are parallel, and the palm faces up or forward, it is known as supination of the elbow.

Movements of the wrist
The wrist is capable of a variety of movements. When the wrist is bent so that it is closer the anterior surface of the forearm, this is known as flexion of the wrist. The posterior surface of the hand and forearm approach one another in extension of the wrist. The wrist can also be used to tilt the hand from side to side. When the hand is moved such that the thumb approaches the radius, it is known as abduction; when the hand is moved such that the little finger is closer to the ulna, it is called adduction. The range of motion for adduction is greater than that for abduction. Because of the combinations of muscles involved, adduction is usually combined with flexion and abduction with extension.

Movements of the fingers
The fingers, because of their multiple joints, are capable of some complex movements. Still, all of these motions can be arranged in a few basic categories. When any part of a finger is raised so that it is above the palm when the palm is facing up, it is known as flexion of the finger. When the finger is stretched back so that the angle between finger and palm is increased, this is known as extension. Of course, the hand is not capable of extending fingers at much more than 180 degrees to the hand. When a finger is extended away from the medial line (in the case of the hand the medial line is considered to be an imaginary line running from the base of the hand through the middle finger) this is known as abduction; movement towards the medial line is known as adduction.

Movements of the hip
When the upper leg is raised in front of the body, this is known as hip flexion. The range of motion for hip flexion is greater if the knee is also bent. Any motion that increases the angle between the anterior surface of the upper leg and trunk is known as extension; the body has a much smaller range of motion

for extension than for flexion. The ballet move known as the grande arabesque combines leg extension with lateral rotation of the hip, in which the toes point away from the medial plane. Medial rotation of the hip entails moving the leg such that the toes inward towards the medial plane. In adduction of the hip, the thigh is brought towards or past the medial plane; in abduction of the hip, the thigh travels away from the medial plane.

Movements of the pelvis
The descriptions of the various movements that can be achieved by the pelvis assume that the femur remains in a fixed location. When the pelvis is titled forward, such that the lower back is curved and the abdomen protrudes, it is known as anteversion of the pelvis. The opposite move, in which the pelvis tilts back and the lower back straightens, is called retroversion. The pelvis can also shift so that it channels all of a person's weight to one femur, as in when a person stands on one leg: on the side bearing the weight the movement is called inferolateral, while on the other side movement is considered to be superomedial. Finally, the pelvis is able to perform a limited medial or lateral rotation, a motion incorporated by hula dancing.

Movements of the knee
The movements of which the knee joint is capable are fairly limited. Knee flexion is said to occur when the angle formed by the posterior thigh and leg decrease. When the muscles of the leg are contracted, in what is called active flexion, the range of motion is considerably smaller than when they are relaxed, as during passive flexion. Also, the knee's range of motion is greater when the hip joint is flexed. Extension of the knee is simply movement that increases the angle made by the posterior leg and thigh, and hyperextension is any movement that increases this angle above 180 degrees. The knee is capable of a very slight bit of rotation: in medial rotation, the front of the knee

moves counter-clockwise, and in lateral rotation it moves clockwise.

Movements of the foot

The movements of the foot can be described generally though, although often the terms will be used to refer to movement involving only a particular part. Dorsiflexion is a tilting of the foot upward, such that the angle between the superior surface of the foot and the anterior surface of the leg is decreased. Plantar flexion, also known as extension, is the opposite motion, in which the toes are pointed down. In abduction of the foot, the toes are pointed away from the medial plane; in adduction of the foot, toes point toward the medial plane. Finally, eversion of the foot is said to occur when the sole of the foot is directed away from the medial plane, an inversion of the foot to occur when the sole is directed toward the medial plane.

Spatial environment

In order to effectively develop, select, or administer a pattern of motor behavior, an individual has to know a few things about his or her spatial environment. Most of these determinations occur unconsciously. First, an individual must have some idea of the space that his or her body is taking up; that is, the location and position of his or her body at the beginning of the movement. The person must also have a reasonable idea of the general space in which the movement is to occur. Once these things are known, the person can determine in which direction the movement should occur: backwards, forwards, diagonally, sideways, up, or down. Finally, the person can make a more long-term assessment of the appropriate path, and of what speed of motion should be affected.

Body awareness

In order to successfully develop and implement basic motor patterns, the human body has to have an awareness of its own dimensions and potentials. For instance, the body must be aware of its current

orientation: not only its location and position, but also the range of motions that are possible from its current position. For instance, one develops an intuitive understanding that it is difficult to jump from a sitting position. The body, as it matures, will also develop a sense of balance in its various parts, so that wild movements can be made with the limbs without throwing the entire trunk off balance. In a similar line, the body will develop the ability to automatically transfer weight to best perform a given movement.

Sense of effort

As a growing human being develops, he or she will learn how to gauge the degree of effort or force that is required to perform a given task. Anyone who has ever been swatted in the nose by an infant will recognize that children are not always aware of the effort necessary to get someone's attention. So, as this sense of required effort develops, one will be able to determine whether a given movement requires fast or slow performance, and whether the force behind it must be strong or weak. Tied up with these determinations is the slightly more complicated case that arises when an individual is somehow constrained. Free movements, in which the only resistance is air and the limitations of the human body, will always require the same scale of effort; constrained motion, however, requires an accurate assessment of the strength of the constraint.

Relationships with others or objects

The full development of motor skills requires the ability to assess and adjust to the various relationships that affect motion. These can be classified as either relationships with people or with objects. In the case of relationships with people, an individual will need to be able to determine whether their motion is to be matching or contrasting; for example, a child on a see-saw will have to determine that he cannot make the same pushing motion at the

- 91 -

same time as his partner. One also has to determine whether one is leading or following another, and adjust movements accordingly. As for the relationships with objects, it is essential to be able to know the orientation of the object in relation to oneself, as well as to be able to determine whether one will need to go around, through, over, or under the object.

Perception

Perception is constantly affected by an individual's level of physical activity and training. Indeed, the information gained through participation in sports can help perception in other areas of life. For instance, baseball players will become better at determining the speed with which an object is approaching, and whether it is curving towards or away from their body. One thing that sports do to enhance perception is train the brain to separate important stimuli from the rest, so that reactions may be more rapid and efficient. People in stressful situations often have a tendency to develop a sort of tunnel vision; studies of athletes, however, reveal that the enhanced ability to process information from the visual field make it possible for them to take in a much larger field of vision.

Exteroception is the perception of things in the environment. For humans, visual perception is considered to be the most important form of exteroception affecting motor control. Indeed, many anthropologists have suggested that the survival of the human race depended on the development of an especially keen sense of vision, which could be used to distinguish prey and to hit targets from a long distance. The importance of vision for motor control is indicated by the extensive network of connections between the eye and the brain. Everything from the right side of the visual field is sent to the left side of the brain, and vice versa. The place where the two optic nerves cross is called the optic chiasma.

Vision

Human vision can be considered as either focal or ambient. Focal vision is concerned with those objects in the eye's immediate focus, is used to determine the identity of objects in the outside world, and can be easily diminished by low light. Focal vision is dependent on the perceptive ability of the cones within the retina, which are concentrated in the middle and can determine detail because they each have a bipolar cell attached. Ambient vision, on the other hand, incorporates the entire retina, is used to determine the location of objects, and is not terribly affected by poor light. Ambient vision relies on the receptivity of both rods and cones, and so is able to discern both detail and spatial relations.

Hearing

Human beings have developed an excellent sense of hearing, in part because early man needed to be able to hear the approach of potential predators or prey. Human beings are not only able to hear a sound and determine what it is, but they are also able to determine where it is coming from. This is done by comparing the sounds heard by the right and left ear. When a sound comes from straight ahead, it reaches both ears at the same time; if it is off to one side, however, it will be heard first by the ear on that side. The brain is able to take this minute difference in timing and wave quality and determine the location from which the sound has come. This information is then used by the brain to determine how the head is to be moved and how the body should be positioned.

Cutaneous senses

The cutaneous senses are those that are localized in the skin, and include the sensations of temperature, pain, and pressure. Some areas of the body are naturally more sensitive to pain and pressure than others. A variety of nerve endings, end bulbs, and corpuscles are the sensory apparatus of the skin. Each of these is especially sensitive to a particular sensation, though some receptors may be able register more than one sensation at a time. The cutaneous senses are capable of great sensitivity, as evidenced by the ability of many people to read Braille. Other experiments have discovered that areas of the body considered to be less sensitive than the fingertips (the back, for instance) are also capable of making fine distinctions.

Proprioception

Proprioception is an individual's perception of the arrangement of his or her own body parts. It may be applied to individual parts or to the body as a whole, and to the body while stationary or while in motion. Kinesthesis is a related term which refers to the sensations of body position, tension, and movement. Although kinesthesis was formerly only concerned with moving body parts, its definition has been broadened to the point where it is almost synonymous with proprioception. An individual's proprioception is mainly achieved by the vestibular system (a complex in the inner ear that controls balance), joints, tendons, and muscles. The varying tension and pressure on the various muscles of the body are transmitted to the brain.

Sensorimotor control

The control of muscles is mainly accomplished through the combined efforts of the muscle spindles and Golgi tendon organs. Muscle spindles are tiny receptors which in the muscle fiber which send and receive information to and from the central nervous system. These spindles stretch along with the muscle. Golgi tendon organs are located in the tendons that attach to muscles. They are usually concerned with slowing down any violently fast contractions by inhibiting the actions of the motor neurons in the spinal cord. Both the muscle spindles and the Golgi tendon organs work to respond to external stimuli with the appropriate

muscular responses, and to keep those reactions from becoming too violent.

Perceptual uncertainty

Individuals will often have trouble reacting to external stimuli or determining a course of motor activity if they are troubled by perceptual uncertainty. Perceptual uncertainty is any doubt in the validity of one's perceptions; it increases in proportion to the number of stimuli or events in the perceptual field. Many studies have shown that reaction time is increased as distracting stimuli are eliminated. Indeed, in many cases an absence of distraction allows the individual to begin processing a motor response before the stimuli even presents itself. This aspect of motor control is often taken advantage of by sports teams, who seek to slow down opponents by creating distractions in the visual field.

Motor control

Mechanical factors
Obviously, the human body has certain limitations within which the motor system must work. The forces that the body generates in movement are the result either of the contraction of the muscles or the elasticity of the tendons. These forces are often referred to as being active and passive, respectively. Muscles have the most potential for active force when they are extended; at this point, the muscle fibers are all lined up and capable of contracting. As for the elasticity of the tendons, this may be considered in two different ways. The tendons that extend off the ends of the muscles are said to be serial elastic components, while the tendons that run alongside the muscles are referred to as parallel elastic components.

Neurological-reflexive factors
There are a number of neurological-reflexive factors that affect motor control. All of these seem to reduce the number of commands the individual must obey in order to execute a

particular motor program. For instance, reciprocal inhibition is a feature of human reflexes that prevents the reflex from being stimulated while the extensors in the joint are activated; in other words, the doctor will get no response with his rubber mallet when you hold your leg in certain positions. The body has also got what is called a central pattern generator: that is, a sort of kinesthetic memory of common movements. In some experiments, scientists have been able to stimulate the body of an animal to perform a certain movement even if the connections between the animal's brain and body have been severed.

Abilities and skills

When considering the individual differences in the performances of motor skills, scientists are careful to make the distinction between abilities and skills. An ability is a stable, enduring trait that allows a person to perform a task at a certain level of competency. Abilities are thought to be genetic, and will stay with a person throughout his or her life. Skills, on the other hand, are developed after practice. A person who is skilled at a certain task is capable of performing it consistently at a high level. Many tasks require a mixture of ability and skill, so it is important for scientists to make this distinction. In music, for instance, some individuals may be born with the ability to hear proper pitch and intuitively understand musical structures, but they will still have to develop the skills to play a certain instrument.

Skeletal muscle

Skeletal muscle is the striated tissue that is attached to the skeleton and, through contractions, causes all of the movements of the body. Muscle tissue is made up of long molecules of protein, mainly actin and myosin. The various strands are combined in dozens of different forms to create the various muscles of the body. Whenever one of these muscle fibers is stimulated by a neuron, it contracts as much as it can.

Therefore, muscles that need to perform precise and delicate operations will have a much larger ratio of neurons to muscle fibers, because they will need to more closely regulate the amount of force created by the contraction. The muscles of the calf, for instance, have far fewer neurons per muscle fiber than do the muscles controlling the fingers.

Motor units

When health professionals refer to a motor unit, they are referring to a single motor neuron and all of the muscle fibers it can cause to contract. Every muscle is composed of a number of motor units that are somewhat independent, yet harmonious. There is a distinct hierarchy among motor units: some are used every time a muscle does anything, while others are only called upon for tasks of the most extreme difficulty. Commonly-used motor units are said to be low threshold, while less frequently-used motor units are referred to as high threshold. The amount of stimulus required to activate a motor unit is consistent, meaning that the motor unit will activate and deactivate at about the same level every time.

Muscular movements

When discussing muscular movement, health professionals use a few different terms. An agonist is any muscle that is responsible for the action being discussed. For instance, the against responsible for the bending of the elbow is the biceps. An antagonist is any muscle that opposes the movement of the agonist. A fixator is any movement that locks the body in certain position, thus giving the other muscles a steady foundation on which to work. A prime mover is a muscle or group of muscles that is primarily responsible for the movement of a joint. Finally, a synergist is a muscle besides the prime mover that supports, enhances, or guides the actions of the prime mover.

Brain

The motivation, coordination, and direction for physical activity all come from the brain. The cerebrum is the portion of the brain that deals with all conscious functions. This area of the brain contains many things crucial for movement: sensations, voluntary movement, skills, judgment of distance, and the appropriate level of force needed for a particular activity. The thalamus is the area of the brain that receives sensory messages and coordinates reflex movements. The hypothalamus, on the other hand, coordinates the autonomic functions of the body, like processes of sweating, shivering, and the dilation or constriction of the blood vessels in response to external stimuli.

The cerebellum is the area of the brain that refines skilled movements. Besides enabling the body to move efficiently and swiftly, this part of the brain coordinates the skeletal muscles for the purposes of maintaining balance. The medulla oblongata mediates the reflexes that result in the raising or lowering of the heart rate, blood pressure, and rate of breathing. The brain also contains a complex network of neurons known as the reticular activating system. This system alerts the brain whenever important sensory information is gathered by the outlying sensory nerves.

Motor development in childhood

In early infancy, a child's motor patterns will be confined to basic reflexes, like sucking and grasping. The first motor skills to develop are called the gross motor skills, and include the movements of the head, body, legs and arms. Most infants will be able to walk by the time they reach ten months of age. Fine motor skills (those accomplished with precise movements, especially of the hands) develop between the ages of one and five. By the time a child reaches the age of six, he or she can usually draw basic shapes, button a shirt, tie shoes, and write legibly. More complex manipulative skills (like throwing, catching, and striking) will not be fully developed until about the age of ten. Most of the differences observed between motor skills among children are the result of differences in socialization; that is, children who are given equal chance to develop motor skills usually do so at approximately the same rate.

Basic motor patterns

For the most part, children learn and develop their basic motor patterns through play. For this reason, children below the age of about seven should have daily activities emphasizing the use of large muscle groups, so that they may develop muscular coordination. Also, children should be working on their fine motor skills from a very young age. Especially in their early years, children require careful supervision during play, as they will not have yet refined their sense of force or coordination and may be liable to hurt another child or themselves. Activities like puzzles are excellent ways to develop both motor skills and spatial intelligence. Simple games involving a soft ball are also a good way to develop a young child's basic motor patterns.

After-contraction phenomenon

The after-contraction phenomenon is the increase in force of movement that seems to occur when the neuromuscular system becomes excited. In other words, the body's tendency to perform a certain movement lingers after that movement has been performed for a long time or with a great deal of effort. One way to experience this phenomenon is to press against a wall with one arm for a minute. After the minute is up, you should feel some tendency within the arm to rise up again. Many scientists believe that the after-contraction phenomenon occurs in many areas of daily life, and indicates the body's ability to quickly accustom itself to changes in the outside world and new motor patterns.

Tonic neck response

Over a series of studies, scientists were able to demonstrate a clear link between movement in the neck and seemingly unrelated movement in the limbs. Specifically, when the head is turned to one side the arm on that side will tend to extend, while the opposite arm will tend to flex. This phenomenon was long observed in infants, but scientists had not until recently noticed that it continues to occur in a somewhat more infrequent form among adults. Subsequent studies have shown that people are able to produce more force when they turn their head towards the limb that they are using. This runs somewhat contrary to the former idea that maximum force could only be generated in another part of the body when the head was facing forward.

Coordinative structures

The concept of coordinative structures suggests that some motor programs can group together seemingly-independent parts of the body for the easier performance of certain tasks. Formerly, theorists assumed that there must be particular commands for each independent muscle group when an action is to be performed. Though this feature of the motor system may relieve the body of some administrative stress, it can be problematic as well, as anyone knows who has tried to pat their head and rub their stomach at the same time. Scientific research has shown, however, that individuals can with practice develop the ability to uncouple their coordinated structures and restore independent control.

Gender effects

Research has consistently shown that there are basic differences in the motor performance of males and females. However, these differences have been discovered to be based on differences in conditioning and body structure rather than on any innate difference in ability. For one thing, females tend to have far fewer opportunities to develop motor skills than do males. This phenomenon is blamed on a number of different factors, from sexism in society that keeps girls from playing sports to a natural disposition to more sedentary activities. In any case, females and males that have the same number of motoric experiences are found to develop at much the same rate. This information is especially valuable for physical educators who may have to confront the false assumption that girls are not meant to play sports.

Research into the differences in motor performance between males and females has revealed that most of the advantages claimed by either gender are the result of differences in body structure. Males, for instance, tend to have more muscle mass in their upper body, and so are likely to develop superior performance in skills like throwing or striking. Females, on the other hand, are noted for having a lower center of gravity and therefore balance, and so they may be better than males at the performance of certain movements. Both sexes are limited in motor performance by their flexibility, skeletal size, body composition, and overall level of fitness. It has been frequently observed that the difference in motor performance between the best male and the worst male is much greater than the difference between the average male and female

Skilled movement

Sheridan asserted that there are four characteristics of skilled movement. These four things must be accounted for by any theory that professes to describe motor control. First, a skilled movement will display some flexibility of movement. In other words, there must be the ability to accomplish the same task with a variety of different muscles and bones. Second, a skilled movement must have a degree of uniqueness, because it is physically impossible for any two movements to be exactly alike. Third, a skilled movement must display some sort of consistency: that is,

- 96 -

the individual will be able to perform it in a similar way in a variety of situations. Finally, a skilled movement will have some degree of mutability, meaning that the individual will be able to make small adjustments during its performance.

Theories of motor control

Reflex theory
The reflex theory of motor control declared that movements are the result of a rapid, automatic responses to stimuli in the individual's environment. According to this model, the reflexes in the spinal cord are stimulated by the sensory receptors in the various parts of the body, at which point they process the information and stimulate a muscular response. Over time, an individual becomes conditioned to respond in a similar way to common stimuli, and reactions will become faster and more precise. This theory of motor control accounts for the consistency of movement, but it does not seem to make room for voluntary control of movement. Also, it does not allow for the minute adjustments that individuals seem to be able to make during the performance of a movement.

Dynamic systems theory
The dynamic systems theory of motor control is also referred to as the ecological theory or action systems theory. It posits that there is a dynamic (constantly changing) relationship between the individual and his or her environment. Within this relationship, the individual perceives various things and reacts to them either reflexively or voluntarily. Movements are the result of the integrated interaction of many smaller systems of biological, muscular, skeletal, neurological, and cardiorespiratory agents. This integration is known in dynamic systems theory as self-organization. This theory would seem to allow for the fact that minute adjustments are constantly made during the performance of a movement.

Ecological theory
The ecological theory of motor learning is based in the dynamic systems theory of motor control. It asserts that movement is the result of an interaction between the individual and his or her environment. This interaction is in large part based on the perception of the individual, as he or she is only capable of response to the environment which he or she can sense. According to the ecological theory of motor learning, individuals are constantly scanning the environment, looking for ways to improve his or her performance of movements. Over time, individuals become better able to isolate the important information in the immediate environment and respond precisely and appropriately to it.

Closed-loop theory
There are competing theories regarding the use of feedback (sensory information transmitted from various outlying parts of the body to the brain) in motor control. The closed-loop theory of motor control asserts that feedback not only can be used to initiate and plan movements, but can also help to make adjustments once movement plans have begun. According to this theory, the body doesn't need much of a plan when it begins a movement, because it is able to determine the best course during the movement. There is a great deal of evidence to suggest that individuals use closed-loop control to complete many tasks, especially those that are unfamiliar or take a long time. However, this type of motor control tends to make large demands on the attention and can be much less efficient than moves that are planned in advance.

The closed-loop theory of motor control requires that there be two different states of memory in order for a body to be able to correct its mistakes. One of these is a program of movement that has been remembered by the body and is called a memory trace. This memory trace is responsible for initiating a particular movement. The state of memory which

- 97 -

carries more responsibility for learning and controlling movement is called the perceptual trace. The perceptual trace is basically a standard of correctness: if the feedback resulting from a motion initiated by the memory trace indicates a departure from the perceptual trace, a change in the movement is ordered. In this model, the quality of a movement is only as high as the quality of the perceptual trace.

Criticisms of closed-loop motor control theory

There are three general criticism that have been made of the closed-loop theory of motor control. First, some scientists suggest that if a perceptual trace must be developed for every possible movement of which a human is capable, then the volume of these perceptual traces would quickly grow larger than the space available for their storage. Another criticism of the theory is that it has no formula for how movements will be performed for the first time; indeed, closed-loop theory really only applies to movements for which the individual has already developed a perceptual trace. Finally, some scientists insist that many movements are too brief for feedback to play a significant role in their execution, and therefore these would seem to be performed without the assistance of any perceptual trace.

Schema theory

The schema theory was developed in part as a reaction to the closed-loop theory's inability to describe how new actions are performed, how motor programs are stored, and how feedback can be a part of even the shortest movements. As with closed-loop theory, there are two distinct memory states in schemata theory. These are called schemata (the plural of schema), and are abstract versions of commonly-performed movements. According to the schema theory, the body takes common actions and develops a motor program of the general features of that action. Then, the body is able to use that abstracted program to perform any similar action. Also, the body will call up an

appropriate program when it is called upon to perform a new action.

4 sources of information

In schema theory, the body has four sources from which it can gain information about how best to perform movements. The first source of information is called the initial conditions, and is the current status of the individual: his or her posture, position of limbs, etc. The response specifications announce the unique requirements of the response, for instance which direction it will take, which limbs will be involved, etc. During the performance of this response, the body will receive the sensory consequences, giving it an idea of the status of the movement. Finally, the response outcome will give the individual a sense of the end result of the movement. All of these sources of information are used by the two schemata: the recall schema, which organizes the specific programs needed for a response; and the recognition schema, which evaluates the outcome and makes any adjustments.

Schema theory motor programs

According to schema theory, performance of a given movement enables the body to make an abstract motor program of that movement so that it will be able to perform similar movements in the future. This is known as a generalizable motor program, and will be composed of the invariant features of the movement: that is, the aspects of force and timing which will not vary in other performances of the motion. These features will be scaled (or, in scientific terms, parameterized) so that they can be applied to different cases. These specific requirements will be covered in the motor program as variant features: things, like the muscles to be used, which may vary from case to case.

Open-loop theory

The theory of motor control known as open-loop control asserts that movements are made according to a preexisting motor program, a set of muscle commands laid out for the movement is begun. These movements are performed without any

- 98 -

adjustment based on feedback, the sensory information transmitted to the brain. Open-loop motor control theory seems to explain many of the common movements that individuals make unconsciously, and there is excellent research evidence to suggest that animals often perform tasks in a way similar to the open-loop model. However, many scientists have complained that open-loop theory is only accurate in situations where the movement is too short for there to be any meaningful feedback.

Hierarchical model

One theoretical model that scientists use to explain motor control is the hierarchical model. According to this model, there is a higher level in the motor system that adjusts according to feedback, and a lower level that performs the commands of the higher. The lower level, like a low-ranking soldier in battle, will continue to execute a set of directions until the upper level gives a different order. This model is a hybrid of open-loop and closed-loop theory, in that it allows for movements that are both automatic and capable of alteration. Some studies have indicated that when learning a new task individuals will begin by using a closed-loop motor control, and will gradually move to a more hierarchical style.

Information-processing theory

According to the information-processing theory of motor learning, an individual receives information in the form of stimuli from the outside world, selects a response, and then executes that response. During the reception of information, the individual must determine the nature of the stimulus. This will be more or less difficult depending on the familiarity of the stimulus, the number of competing stimuli, and the individual's personal characteristics. In the next phase, the individual determines what response if any is required. Then, he or she organizes the appropriate motor response. The resulting movement is known as the output. One of the criticisms of the information-processing theory is that it fails to account for the role of

memory or anticipation in motor performance.

Reaction time

An individual's reaction time (RT) is how long it takes before he or she responds to a particular stimulus. RT is especially important for the information-processing school of motor learning, because it provides a direct measure of the time taken by a complete processing and response event. There are a few of common factors that influence RT. One is the number of stimuli: the more stimuli are present, the longer the RT is likely to be. RT will also tend to be shorter if there is good compatibility between stimulus and response; that is, if the desired response makes clear sense and doesn't require any consideration. Finally, RT is generally much shorter if the desired response is one which has been practiced and performed many times in the past.

Inverted-U principle

Researchers have spent a great deal of time trying to determine how arousal and anxiety affect motor performance. One of the principles that has emerged from this research is known as the inverted –U principle. It asserts that performance will increase along with arousal level for a while, but if arousal continues to increase then performance will begin to decline. The principle gets its name from the shape it makes when represented on a graph. The range of arousal in which an individual performs best is known as the zone of optimal functioning. Individuals will have different zones of optimal functioning depending on their trait anxiety: that is, their disposition to consider situations dangerous or threatening.

Hick's Law

Hick's Law was developed during the study of choice reaction time: that is, the amount of time it takes an individual to respond to an unanticipated stimulus. Basically, Hick's Law declares that choice reaction time will increase in proportion to the number of choices made available. This law, which seems a bit obvious on the surface, has become a fundamental principle of the study of motor performance because it has been able to establish such a clear predictive measure for reaction time. In fact, subsequent studies have shown that reaction time seems to increase by the same amount every time the number of choices is doubled. This law has found applications in everything from basketball to military tactics.

Spatial and temporal anticipation

Researchers into motor performance have classified anticipation as being either spatial or temporal. When a person can predict what is likely to happen in a given situation, it is known as spatial anticipation. For instance, if you are driving and the car in front of you brakes in advance of an intersection, you may suspect that the driver is going to turn. This is spatial anticipation. Temporal anticipation, on the other hand, occurs when an individual can predict when something is going to happen, or the length of time that something will take to happen. This kind of information is useful in all kinds of settings, from gauging the speed of an oncoming object to anticipating the appearance of a certain stimulus. Most researchers, however, think that motor reaction is more dramatically improved by spatial anticipation than temporal.

Mechanical strain on bones

There are several kinds of mechanical stress routinely exerted on bones. First, bones must endure the gravitational stress of holding up the rest of the body. The bones of the back, feet, and legs are particularly taxed by this effort. Next, bones are subjected to stress when they move against resistance, as for instance when a heavy object is lifted. In these cases, the bones are serving as levers and points of attachment for the muscles.

There are also cases in which bones receive stress from the effort of holding up a heavy object, as for instance when you are holding on to a heavy suitcase. This gravitational pressure from an external object is known as traction.

Individual differences research

A whole field of motor learning research, known as individual differences research, is concerned with charting the various behavioral abilities of different people. In this field, individual differences are defined as stable, enduring differences among people that contribute to permanent differences in performance. Identifying advantages in motor learning requires not only observing repeated superiority in the performance of a task, but in the researcher determining what particular ability accounts for the disparity in performance. For instance, it is not enough for a scientist to watch one person consistently make more free throws than other; in order to conclude that one person has superior motor skill, the scientist must isolate the particular ability that is superior and collect data in support of his or her hypothesis.

Motor performance

General motor ability
In the early days of research into motor ability, it was thought that the abilities to perform any task all were part of the same ability, known as the general motor ability. This idea became popular at the same time as the notion of intelligence quotient, which claimed to be able to give a universal assessment of cognitive ability. Besides being convenient, this idea seemed to be born out in most cases. Unfortunately, subsequent research has indicated that the motor abilities of an individual may vary widely between tasks. For instance, individuals with great muscular strength are often inflexible and incapable of performing precise tasks quickly. Indeed, recent tests have shown that there is

- 100 -

a great degree of variability even within the category of balance.

Ability patterns

As research has mounted suggesting that individuals may have an immensely detailed repertoire of abilities, it has become necessary for physical educators to refine their position on individual performance. Educators should expect that individuals will display somewhat consistent patterns of performance: that is, their ability in a certain task will probably be consistent with their abilities in similar tasks. However, patterns of ability are not the only factor that contributes to performance. Skill, motivation, and practice will also contribute to the performance of motor tasks in physical education class. Indeed, the most recent research in the filed suggests that mood can be one of the prime determinants of success or failure in athletic competition.

Perceptual differences

Studies have shown that differences in the quality of perception may directly affect the quality of performance of certain tasks. For instance, one study tested four kinds of visual perception in subjects: static visual acuity (perception of stationary objects, dynamic visual acuity (perception of moving objects), size constancy (perception of objects of different sizes), and depth perception. For basketball players, the study determined, the only relevant quality of vision for shooting free throws was static visual acuity. For shooting a field goal at any other time, however, the only relevant ability was dynamic visual acuity. Moreover, it is quite normal for an individual to have inequalities in his or her perceptual abilities. For this reason, researchers have concluded that differences in perceptual ability may underlie inconsistencies in the performance of seemingly-similar tasks.

Educator adjustments

It is important for physical educators to be aware that students will have different levels of ability for different tasks, and to make allowances so that students can make the most progress. It is not suitable to set the same performance goals for every student. However, neither does this mean that individuals should be allowed to focus solely on those activities in which they excel. Rather, physical educators should strive to help students become self-aware and to work conscientiously on those areas of performance in which they have less natural ability. By maintaining a positive attitude, physical educators can encourage students to improve their all-around performance rather than just stick to areas in which they are already proficient.

Other factors affecting motor performance

It is the job of a physical educator to remind students that natural ability is only one of the factors that contribute to motor performance. For instance, some individuals will improve their performance because they have had many opportunities in life to do so; this is just another way of saying that active individuals tend to have better motor performance. A child that is raised in a family or community that supports athletic endeavor will be more likely to develop good motor skills. Body type will also contribute to motor performance: healthy, flexible people are more able to take advantage of their natural abilities. Finally, motivation, competitiveness, and vigor cannot be underestimated as factors affecting motor performance. No individual can be successful at the highest level of competition simply by relying on his or her natural ability.

Assessments of motor ability

It has been difficult for scientists to create tests of motor ability that are general enough to measure something other than the performance of the specific activity of the test. The vertical jump test measures leg power by requiring the subject to jump straight into the air from a stationary position. The individual's score is measured as the difference between his or her standing reach and the highest point touched during three trial jumps. In the bar snap exercise, the subject stands holding a horizontal bar, then lifts his or her legs and swings forward as far as possible. This test measures agility, power, and coordination, and is considered to be quite challenging. It is therefore not appropriate for all people.

In the assessment of motor ability known as the figure eight run, the subject runs around a small course in which he or she is required to make several quick turns. This test is timed to determine the individual's degree of speed and agility. In a balance beam test, individuals are required to perform a few different movements (for instance standing on one foot, raising arms above the head, or standing on the toes) while traversing a beam two inches wide and twelve feet long. There are a few other clinical tests designed to measure balance, but most of these require expensive equipment and are unsuitable for the classroom. In the balance beam test, students are timed and awarded points based on the number of movements they are able to perform.

Speed is one of the easier aspects of motor ability to measure. Typically, an individual's speed is tested by timing a fifty or hundred-yard sprint. Some measures of speed seek to eliminate differences caused by acceleration, and only time individuals once they have reached top speed. In order to measure reaction time, special equipment must be purchased allowing the measurement of time to the hundredth of a second. Scientists use a number of different movements as gauges of reaction time, ranging from a simple motion of the hand to a full-body response. There are extensive records of male and female motor skill norms, so that physical educators can determine how students compare to the general population.

Health-Related Fitness

Physical fitness

Physical fitness is simply the body's ability to perform all of its tasks and still have some reserve energy in case of an emergency. People who are physically fit can meet all of their daily physical needs, have a realistic and positive image of themselves, and are working to protect themselves against future health problems. Physical fitness has three main components: flexibility, cardiovascular fitness, and muscular strength or endurance. Some other factors, like agility and balance, are also often considered when assessing physical fitness. The benefits of pursuing physical fitness throughout life are not only physical but mental and emotional; regular exercise is proven to reduce the risk of disease and increase life expectancy.

Flexibility

A person's flexibility is his or her range of motion around particular joints. An individual's flexibility will vary according to their age, gender, and posture. Some individuals may be less flexible because of bone spurs, and some individuals may be less flexible because they are overweight. Typically, an individual's flexibility will increase through childhood until adolescence, at which point joint mobility slows and diminishes for the rest of the individual's life. Muscles and the connective tissue around them (tendons and ligaments) will contract and become tighter if they are not used to their potential. Lack of flexibility can lead to a buildup of tension in the muscles, and can increase the risk of injury during exercise.

Static stretching
The health benefits of proper stretching are numerous. Proper stretching before and after a workout lengthens the muscles and prevents strain. Stiff muscles can often cause an individual to move awkwardly and be susceptible to injury. Most physiologists recommend that people engage in static (or passive) stretching for several minutes before and after vigorous exercise, and at least four or five times a week. Static stretching means gradually moving into a stretched position, which is then held from between six to sixty seconds. Static stretching after a workout helps move lactic acid out of the muscles, increases the range of motion, and speeds blood, oxygen, and nutrients to the muscle tissue.

Ballistic stretching
Not all stretching is good for the body. Ballistic stretching, in which one bounces or jerks muscles around, is capable of overstretching muscle fibers, which can result in muscle contraction rather than expansion. Ballistic stretching can also tear ligaments and weaken or break tendons, the connections between muscle and bone. The best way to stretch a muscle is to gently ease it into a stretching position, and then hold that position for a prolonged period. A stretch should never be painful, though it may feel a bit uncomfortable. Rather than immediately trying to achieve the desired level of flexibility, it is better to hold the greatest stretch your body is capable of holding comfortably. Frequent and controlled stretching is the best way to pursue your flexibility goals.

Cardiovascular fitness

An individual's cardiovascular fitness is the ability of his or her heart to pump blood through the body at the necessary rate. Proper cardiovascular fitness can be achieved through aerobic exercise: that is, any activity in which the oxygen taken into the body is equal to or more than the amount the body is using. Jogging, walking, or riding a bike can all be examples of aerobic activity. The heart also gets a great workout during anaerobic exercise, in which the body takes in less oxygen than it needs to maintain the activity. Sprinting or swimming fast can be anaerobic exercises, if they leave the person breathless. Nonaerobic exercise, like bowling or golf, does not challenge the heart and lungs and therefore will not improve cardiovascular fitness.

Resting heart rate

Health professionals recommend keeping track of your heart rate during exercise to make sure that you are conditioning your heart and lungs without overexerting. Most people are able to easily gauge their pulse by pressing on the carotid artery on the side if their neck. To do this, tilt your head back slightly and use either your middle finger, index finger, or both to find the pulse. In order to determine your resting heart rate, take your pulse at a time when you have not been engaged in any physical activity. Count the number of pulses in a minute (it may be easier to count the pulses in ten seconds and multiply by six). This is your resting heart rate; if you are in good physical condition, your heart rate should vary too much from this number even after three minutes of heavy exercise.

Target heart rate

In order to get the most from a cardiovascular workout, you must be working at about 60% to 85% of your maximum heart rate. For men, the maximum heart rate is calculated as the age in years subtracted from 220. So, the maximum heart rate of a twenty year-old man is 200. The formula for women is similar, except age is subtracted from 225. The threshold of the target heart rate, then, will be found by multiplying the maximum heart rate by .60. So, for that twenty year-old man, the target heart rate begins at 120. A person shouldn't try to achieve their maximum heart rate, especially if they are just beginning an exercise program. However, unless you exercise within your target heart rate range, you will not really improve the condition of your heart and lungs.

Muscle strength and endurance

Developing healthy muscles is not simply a matter of lifting the heaviest possible object. The ability to use your muscles over and over without getting tired is also an important part of physical fitness. Developing muscular strength and endurance helps will make body tissue firmer and more resilient. Well-maintained muscles tend to work more efficiently, and can withstand more strain. Furthermore, muscular development aids in circulation, so that the whole body can more quickly absorb and make use of nutrients in the blood. Strength and endurance training has also been shown to be one of the most effective ways to lose weight, as developed muscles burn more calories than does fat.

Exercising muscles

Muscles are in a constant state of change. If they are not used, they will atrophy and weaken; if they are regularly exercised, however, they will grow stronger and possibly larger. Muscles are best exercised when they are overloaded, or asked to do more than they usually do. When you are training your muscles, you will need to gradually increase the weight or the repetitions to ensure that your muscles are always receiving a challenge. Many fitness professionals contend that a good muscular workout will be somewhat painful, because muscles can only be developed by exceeding their normal requirements. However, not every kind of pain is profitable for a muscular workout, and individuals should be careful to distinguish muscular fatigue from injury, particularly when they are lifting heavy loads.

Strategies in exercise

Individuals who are attempting to build strength will need to use a different training strategy than those who are only seeking to build muscular endurance. In order to build strength, you should be doing a low number of repetitions with a very heavy weight. As your muscles grow stronger, you should gradually increase the amount of weight they are required to move. In order to improve muscular endurance, on the other hand, you should do a large number of repetitions with a considerably lower weight. Sometimes, it is necessary to build up a minimum of strength before you can work on endurance. For instance, an individual may need to work for quite a while before he or she can do push-ups easily enough to test his or her endurance.

Muscle exercises can be either isometric, isotonic, or isokinetic. Isometric exercises are those in which the muscle tries to move an immovable object, with muscle contractions usually lasting five to eight seconds and being repeated five or ten times a day. Isometric exercise may raise blood pressure, and is not generally recommended for building strength. In isotonic exercise, the muscle moves a moderately heavy load several times. Isotonic exercise befits strength when it is done at a high weight a small number of times, and benefits flexibility and endurance when it is performed many times with a low weight. Isokinetic exercises are performed on a machine that is specially designed to overload muscles at every point in their range of motion. These machines are highly effective in developing muscles, but are typically very expensive.

Personalized muscle workout
In order to effectively exercise your muscles, you need to exercise every major muscle group. This includes the deltoids (shoulders), pectorals (chest), triceps and biceps (back and front of arm above the elbow), quadriceps and hamstrings (front and back of leg above the knee), gluteus maximus (buttocks), and abdomen (torso below the chest). As long as all of these muscle groups are treated, exercise programs can vary widely from person to person, with the only important stipulation being that each muscle is worked until it is very tired. Weight training programs will be composed of reps (short for repetitions, the number of times each motion is performed) and sets (the number of groups of reps that will be performed).

Building muscles safely and effectively
In order to properly train muscles, you should always ensure that you work each muscle group until it is very tired. You should always allow your breathing to slow down to close to normal before continuing weight training. It is considered proper to breathe in when your muscles are relaxed, and exhale as you contract them to perform the exercise. You should never hold your breath while muscle training. Muscles will need adequate time to recover after an intense training session, usually between two and four days. Muscles can actually be harmed if they are worked on consecutive days. Still, muscles will begin to atrophy after five days of rest, so you should try and perform muscle exercises at least twice a week.

Cross-training
Many fitness experts recommend cross-training as the most effective way to develop and maintain a high level of physical fitness. In cross-training, the individual alternates between two or more different kinds of physical activity. Triatheletes, who enter competitions in which they must run, swim, and ride a bicycle, are perhaps the best known example of cross-trainers. Cross-training is so effective because the different activities work different muscle groups, and therefore gives a more balanced workout. Cross-training also minimizes the strain on any one particular part of the body, which helps one avoid injury. Moreover, cross-training gives the individual some variety in his or her workout, which is likely to make it more enjoyable.

Aerobic circuit training
Fitness professionals consistently recommend aerobic circuit training as an extremely effective way to promote and maintain general health. In aerobic circuit training, aerobic and strength exercises are combined so that both cardiovascular and muscular fitness are developed. Aerobic circuit training can be done alone, but it is probably most commonly associated with gyms and health clubs, because it usually requires a variety of fitness equipment. An aerobic circuit workout might combine cardiovascular activities like jogging, stair-

climbing, or cross-country skiing with weight-training exercises like lifting weights. Those who practice aerobic circuit training report positive gains in muscular definition and cardiovascular fitness.

Moderate exercise

According to the Center for Disease Control, individuals should engage in a minimum of thirty minutes of moderate exercise at least five days of the week. By "moderate," the CDC means any level of activity in which oxygen consumption is increased to between 3 and 6 times the amount required by the resting body. Thirty minutes of moderate physical activity is roughly equivalent to a fast walk of about two miles. It is important to note that fulfilling this exercise requirement does not necessarily mean starting a planned, regimented fitness program. A person can get thirty minutes of exercise simply by playing with a child or pet, or by cleaning vigorously. Indeed, it may be better for individuals who are out of shape to get used to exercise gradually, by introducing it into their normal lives.

Vigorous exercise

If an individual not only wants to receive the health benefits of exercise, but also wants to achieve a high level of physical fitness, then he or she will need to engage in vigorous exercise. Vigorous exercise is defined as any activity that raises the metabolic rate to six or more times the resting rate. The American College of Sports Medicine recommends aerobic exercise be performed for twenty to sixty minutes three to five times a week, and that strength training be performed two or three times a week. Studies have consistently shown that individuals who engage in regular vigorous exercise outlive their peers. Exercising vigorously generally means burning about 1500-3000 calories a week during exercise.

Water

The most important thing for you to consume before, during, and after exercise is water. On an especially hot day, active people can lose up to a quart of sweat! If you become dehydrated, your heart will have a much more difficult time providing oxygen and nutrients to your muscles. Even sports drinks cannot provide the hydrating effect of cool water, because the sodium, sugar, and potassium in them delay their absorption into the body. Salt tablets should be avoided as well; they are potentially dangerous, and totally unnecessary. Although people do lose a bit of sodium when they sweat, this is more than offset by the huge amount of salt in the average American diet.

Exercise-related injuries

According to research by the American Physical Therapy Association, most exercise-related injuries are suffered in the knees, back, shoulders, and feet. These can be acute injuries, like sprains, pulled muscles, or fractures, that are caused by some sudden trauma; or they can be overuse injuries, which arise from performing the same activity too many times. Tendinitis, muscle strains, and stress fractures are all example of overuse injury. In order to guard against injury, you should always get proper training from someone with experience, and always make sure to stretch thoroughly both before and after exercise. You should always wear whatever protective equipment is appropriate for the activity, and never exercise while under the influence of alcohol or drugs.

Adjusting to temperature

If you are exercising outdoors, it is essential for you to take the appropriate steps to protect yourself against excessive heat and cold. On extremely hot days, it is more important than ever to stay hydrated. Loose-fitting, breathable fabrics are appropriate for hot days. Always remain alert for any signs of heat exhaustion, like dizziness, light-headedness, or headache. In very cold weather, cover as much of your body as possible with layers of clothing. Clothing should be dark and breathable, as waterproof clothing will keep your perspiration from evaporating. Make sure to cover your head and neck, since at least 40% of heat escapes the body from these areas. Clothes should always be loose enough to ensure that circulation is not impeded.

<u>Signs of over training</u>
Many people who are inspired to pursue physical fitness quickly burn out because they overtrain. That is, they force themselves to exercise too intensely and too often, so that they put their bodies through a great deal of strain. Some of the signs of overtraining are continual muscle soreness, frequent injury, unintended weight loss, nervousness, and the inability to relax. People who are overtraining may have a hard time completing their workout, and will definitely have a hard time recovering. If you feel like you may be guilty of overtraining, ease of your exercise program for a while, giving yourself 24-48 hours between workouts. It is also a good idea to confer with a fitness professional.

Muscle strength

Strength, put simply, is the ability of the muscles to exert force. In order to determine how much stronger one person is than another, maximal strength must be measured. Unfortunately, maximal strength can only be ascertained by determining the most amount of force a person can exert for a brief instant and, for obvious reasons, this is a difficult thing to ascertain. Also, it should be noted that strength can really only be accurately attributed to a particular muscle or group of muscles; an individual may have a strong upper body and at the same time be very weak below the waist. Indeed, the strength of one muscle group is unrelated to the strength of any other group.

Developing strong muscles not only will improve performance in most sports, it will also reduce the risk of injury. The overload principle of weight training asserts that the best way to build muscle strength is to train at the maximum level of resistance, so that muscles will have to become accustomed to

more difficult labor. The progression principle of weight training asserts that the best way to build muscle strength is to gradually increase resistance as strength increases, so that muscles can slowly become capable of handling a bigger load. Every theory of strength training insists that weight exercises should be performed throughout the entire range of motion, so that flexibility is not compromised in the interest of strength.

<u>Kinds of strength</u>
There are a few different kinds of strength. A movement in which several different muscles are involved in a series of continuous contractions would be an example of dynamic strength. Lifting a heavy object above one's head would be an example of dynamic strength. The muscle contractions involved in such a maneuver are called isotonic, meaning that while the length of the muscle changes, the amount of tension in the muscle stays approximately the same. Static strength is exhibited when force is exerted by the body without there being any movement of the object on which the force is being exerted. Trying to push a parked truck would be an example of an activity involving static strength. In such a case, the activity of the muscles is known as isometric, because the length of the muscles does not actually change.

<u>Dynamic resistance</u>
Strength improvement is most often accomplished through isotonic or isokinetic exercise. Isokinetic exercise is exercise in which resistance remains the same throughout the entire range of motion. When muscles are forced to perform repetitive resistance exercises, they are encouraged to synthesize more contractile protein, which increases strength. Exercising at close to the maximum level of resistance creates the most strength. An appropriate weight is one which can be moved between 4 to 8 times for four sets. Most individuals find that a good place to start is at 20% of body weight for upper-body exercises, and 50% of body weight for

lower body exercises. Strength can develop within a few weeks of regular training.

Isometric exercise

Isometric exercise (in which the muscle does not contract but exerts itself against a stationary object) can cause immediate gains in strength, although these advances will diminish in time. In fact, almost all of the strength gain from an isometric exercise program will come in the first six weeks. The greatest benefits are from the maximum effort held for several seconds and performed several times a day. Because isometric exercise does not entail the contraction of the muscle, it does not improve strength throughout the range of motion. For this reason, it is most commonly used by athletes who want to improve strength at one particular joint angle. Oftentimes, isometric exercises are recommended for injured individuals whose muscles have been immobilized by a cast.

Muscular endurance

Muscular endurance is closely related to strength, though it is also somewhat distinct. Muscular endurance is the ability to continue performing any muscle activity despite fatigue in that particular muscle (as opposed to general cardio-vascular fatigue). Dynamic (isotonic) endurance is a measure of the number of repetitions of a given exercise that a muscle can perform. Static (isometric) endurance, on the other hand, is a measure of the length of time that a given muscle can hold a contraction. Unsurprisingly, the force required to hold a contraction is inversely proportional to the length of time that contraction can be held. The body seems to be able to adjust naturally when it knows that a particular contraction will have to be held for a long period of time.

Extending endurance

In research studies, scientists have determined that it requires 2 hours of continuous exercise to create the maximum number of new blood vessels and aerobic enzymes. Of course, most athletes will have to gradually increase their workload before they can reach this duration. It is not necessary to perform the entire 2 hours at the same time. Running, cycling, and cross-country skiing are considered to be the best ways to increase leg endurance. Swimming is excellent for working the shoulder and chest muscles, while rowing is good for testing the endurance of the arms and back. Most of the time, athletes who are trying to increase their muscular endurance exercise for two hours or more three times a week.

An excellent way to increase muscular endurance is high-repetition, low-resistance weight training. Using small barbells and performing four to six sets of about twenty repetitions each is a great way to increase endurance in the upper body. Weights for endurance-building activities should be between 60 and 70% of maximum resistance. In order to increase muscular endurance for a particular sport, one can simply practice that activity for a long period of time. This method of improving endurance is not as quick as weight training, but it allows one to practice sport-specific skills at the same time. It should be noted that muscular endurance is confined to the muscle group that is being worked; that is, for instance, long periods of running will do little for upper body endurance.

Muscular power

When fitness experts refer to muscular power, they mean the degree of explosiveness with which a muscle can exert force. In other words, muscular power is the muscle's ability to exert force over a brief period of time. Mathematically, power is calculated as the force multiplied by the distance, divided by the time. If the distance covered by a particular action is constant (say, the distance from a box on the floor to a shelf overhead), then it should be possible to increase power simply by increasing the force used to accomplish the act or decreasing the amount of time taken to perform the act. Most athletic endeavors require a great deal of muscular power, whether for jumping, accelerating, or throwing a ball.

Speed training

Muscle speed can be substantially increased through regular training. Workouts designed to improve speed are usually very strenuous, so they should never be performed without adequate stretching and warm-up. In order to increase muscle speed, one can simply perform a regular exercise as quickly as possible. Speed training should not be confused with interval training, however: once should fully recover from each repetition before starting again. In order to develop running speed over a short distance, one should repeatedly sprint for ten to fifty yards. Any distance of a thousand yards or greater will rely on endurance and strength rather than speed, so interval training is more appropriate.

Assisted speed training
Many athletes try to improve their muscle speed by working out under circumstances in which their muscles will have to work harder than normal, and so will become used to more rapid exertion. For instance, sprinters may train by running down a moderate hill, and swimmers may train their arms to work more quickly by swimming with flippers on their feet. Serious athletes will also aim to improve muscle speed through weight training. Sprinters spend a great deal of time trying to develop strong and flexible quadriceps muscles, so that they can explode from the starting line and have a longer stride. Lifting a weight quickly tends to improve muscle speed best.

Developing explosive speed
In order to develop explosive running speed, you must perform exercises that strengthen your quadriceps. Running hills, climbing stairs, and pushing a football sled are all good ways to develop bursts of running speed. It is also a good idea to incorporate short bursts of speed into a running routine. Some athletes

will run three miles, sprinting for ten seconds of every minute. Another way to improve running speed is by a series of sprints, with plenty of time to recover in between. If you are training for a sport like soccer or football, you should incorporate a change of direction into your sprints, so that the muscles associated with changing course are also trained.

Developing speed over intermediate distances
In order to train for running distances of up to two minutes, athletes need to train the anaerobic fast-twitch muscle fibers. This is most easily done by means of interval training, in which distances of between 100 and 400 yards are run as quickly as possible, with a brief period of rest in between. In order to train for sports that require burst of speed along with cardiovascular endurance, like soccer or basketball, it is good to run continuously, occasionally breaking into a sprint. Most fitness professionals believe that training at distances slightly greater than those required for competition is the best way to prepare. Also, many athletes report positive benefits from assisted intervals, in which running is done down hill. Theoretically, this will teach the muscles to work more quickly than usual.

Developing speed over long distances
Sports that require maintaining a high speed for longer than two minutes will primarily rely on slow-twitch muscle fibers, and less on aerobic capacity. In order to train for running, swimming, or cycling long distances, one should combine over training (that is, training at distances much longer than those that will be covered in competition) and interval training (in which a number of smaller distances are traversed, with brief rest periods in between). It is important to learn to regulate effort over a long period: distance runners, for instance, must learn to reserve some strength for the important stretch run. Oftentimes, long-distance runners benefit from running sprints at a pace much faster than they would normally

run, in order to condition their muscles to a faster pace.

Aerobic fitness

A minimum of aerobic fitness has been achieved when you are able to exercise three times a week at 65% of your maximum heart rate. The easiest means of achieving this level of fitness is by running for thirty minutes three or four times a week. Moderate aerobic fitness is achieved by exercising four or more times a week for at least thirty minutes at a heart rate 75% or more of maximum. This level of aerobic fitness is appropriate for athletes who are seeking to play vigorous sports like football or tennis. Maximum aerobic fitness can only be achieved by working close to maximum heart rate several times a week, and exercising vigorously almost every day. In order to achieve this level of fitness, you must consistently work beyond your anaerobic threshold. A good way to do this is with interval training or brief, high-intensity workouts.

Muscle groups

Head, neck, and shoulders
Some of the more precise and delicate muscles in the human body are found in the head, neck, and shoulders. The human face is covered with muscles that control facial expression. Also, the circular muscle surrounding the eye controls the lifting and shutting of the eyelid. One muscle that despite its strength is frequently forgotten is the tongue. The sterno-mastoid muscle turns the head to the side. The trapezius muscle connects the collarbone (clavicle) to the neck and raises the shoulder. Finally, the deltoid muscles are found on the outside of the shoulder and control the raising and lowering of the upper arm.

Upper torso
The human torso contains a number of large muscles that control the movements the body's trunks and limbs. The pectoral muscles are found in the upper chest and contain both major and minor versions: the major pectoral muscle is responsible for moving the arm across the chest, while the minor pectoral muscle runs at a diagonal from the clavicle to the rib cage and assists the work of the major pectoral muscle. The serratus muscle runs diagonally around the side of the chest, and controls the movement of the scapula, or shoulder blade. The intercostal muscles run along the outside of the ribcage, and control the breathing. There are also a number of small muscles that surround and assist the motion of the scapula.

Lower torso
The muscles of the torso with which many people are most familiar are those that cover the stomach: the abdominal muscles. There are two sets of abdominal muscles: the oblique abdominals extend along a person's side and control the tilting or leaning of the upper torso, while the abdominal rectus muscles cover the front of the stomach and are responsible for flexing the trunk, raising the pelvis, and compressing the abdomen. All of these muscles, or course, also serve to keep the internal organs in place and protected. On the back of the lower torso, the latissimus dorsi extend from the spine around to the side, tapering to a point just under the armpit. These muscles are responsible for moving the arm backwards.

Arms
The deltoid muscle lies at the outside and top of the human arm, and controls the raising and lowering of the upper arm. If the arm is laid so that the palm is up, the biceps is the muscle running the length of the upper arm: it is responsible for bending the elbow. A large tendon connects the biceps to the arm near the elbow. There are a few muscles in the forearm, known as flexors, which help control the motions of the hands. The length of the back of the upper arm is the triceps muscle, which works in congress with the biceps to control the extension of the arm. The back of the forearm contains another set of hand flexors. The hands themselves

contain a number of tiny muscles responsible for the precise movements of the fingers.

Buttocks and legs

The buttocks are covered by two sets of muscles, the gluteus maximus and gluteus minimus. The gluteus maximus, or "greater" gluteus, are found on the outside and control the extension of the thigh and the lifting of the body from a crouching position. The "lesser" gluteus muscles are found inside the gluteus maximus, and control the rotation of the thigh. The inside of the very upper leg is covered with a set of adductor muscles, which move the legs together; on the outside of the upper leg lie the abductor muscles, which bring the legs apart. The quadriceps extend along the front of the upper leg, and extend and raise the leg. The sartorius muscle flexes the lower leg, and runs from the hip diagonally to the inside of the knee. A long muscle on the front of the lower leg flexes the ankle and raises the foot: it is called the anterior tibial. The hamstring muscles run along the back of the upper leg and control the extension of the lower leg; the gastrocnemius and soleus muscles make up the calf.

Skeletal system

The skeletal system is composed of around 200 bones which, along with the attached ligaments and tendons, create a protective and supportive network for the body's muscles and soft tissues. There are two main components of the skeletal system: the axial skeleton and the appendicular skeleton. The axial skeleton includes the skull, spine, ribs, and sternum; the appendicular skeleton includes the pelvis, shoulders, and the various arm and leg bones attached to these. There are few differences between the male and female skeleton; the bones of a male tend to be a bit larger and heavier than those of the female, who will have a wider pelvic cavity (for childbirth). The skeleton does not move, but it is pulled in various directions by the muscles.

Bones of the head

The human skull, often thought to be a single unit, is actually composed of a few different bones. The top of the skull, the bone which covers most of the brain, is called the cranium. The part of the skull covering the top of the face, down to the upper jaw, is the maxilla. The lower jaw is called the mandible On the back of the head, the bottom of the cranium is slightly thicker at the back of the head; this feature is called the occipital ridge and allows more muscles to be attached. Humans also have what is known as the mastoid process, a group of structures at the hinge of the jaw that allow the motions of the jaw to be powerful and controlled. The human cranium has two suture lines, running perpendicular to one another along the back of the head, which indicate where the cranial capacity of humans has had to make a quick adjustment to the size of the brain.

Bones of the upper torso

The bone commonly known as the collarbone is the clavicle; it extends from one shoulder to the other and is connected in the middle to the sternum, a long bone extending down the front of the torso. At the bottom of the sternum lies the xiphoid process, which helps to protect the vital organs beneath the rib cage. The bones frequently referred to as the shoulder blades are clinically known as the scapula. These are large, triangular bones that are found behind the shoulders and have a great deal of surface area for the attachment of muscles. The human rib cage is made up of twelve bones on each side, extending from the spine around the sides to the front of the body. There is no truth to the notion that males and females have a different number of ribs.

Bones of the spine

The spine is perhaps the most complex skeletal structure in the human body. It connects to the cranium at the occipital ridge, and then extends all the way down to the coccyx, a small pointed bone at the base of the pelvis. The top seven vertebrae are called the cervical vertebrae, and are found between the

- 111 -

occipital ridge and the top of the rib cage. The next twelve vertebrae are known as the thoracic vertebrae, and extend from the top to the bottom of the rib cage, which they anchor. Below these are the five lumbar vertebrae, which curve inward slightly to support the upper body. The spine connects with the pelvis at the sacro-iliac joint, below which lie the sacrum and coccyx in succession.

Bones of the arms and hands
The upper arm is connected to the clavicle by a large ball-and-socket joint. The bone that extends from this joint to the elbow is called the humerus. At the elbow, the humerus is connected to the radius and ulna by the elbow joint. If you extend your arm out so that the palm is up, the radius is the bone that runs along the right side and the ulna is the longer bone that runs along the left side. These bones connect to the complex network of bones that make up the wrist; the complicated nature of the wrist joint allows for the amazing dexterity of the hand. The carpal are those small bones at the base of the hand that connect to the wrist joint. Each hand then has five metacarpals that connect the carpals to the fingers, and can be felt through the back of the hand. The bones that make up the fingers are known as phalanges.

Bones of the hips and legs
The spine connects to the pelvis at the lumbo-sacral joint. The pelvis, which is broader on a woman so that she can bear children, creates a sort of bowl for the visceral organs of the lower torso. At its front and bottom is the pubic arch. The pelvis is connected to the upper bones of the legs, known as the femurs, by a ball-and-socket hip joint. The femurs extend down to the hinge joint at the knee, which is covered by the patella (commonly referred to as the kneecap. The lower leg, below the knee, is made up of two bones: the fibula is the narrow bone on the outside of the leg, while the tibia is slightly thicker and runs along the inside. These bones are connected at the ankle to the foot in a complex joint structure. The bones of the feet and toes, extending out from the foot, are known as the tarsals, metatarsals, and phalanges.

Pelvis
The pelvis is a large, roughly cylindrical structure of several bones. The pelvis bears all of the weight of the upper body, and passes this weight on to the femurs through a pair of ball-and-socket joints. Of course, the pelvis must also absorb the shocks that come from the lower body during running or jumping. Oftentimes, the pelvis is divided into a superior and inferior portion by a horizontal plane across the middle. The pelvis also has three hip bones: the ilium, ischium, and pubis, respectively. Once these bones are fully fused in adulthood, they interact with the top of the femur. The shape of the pelvis can vary considerably between individuals, especially in the shape of the pelvic inlet, the cavity separating the inferior and superior regions of the pelvis.

Long bones
Long bones, as for instance the femur, are composed of three parts. These sections develop independently but will become fused into one as the individual reaches adulthood. The central shaft of a bone is called the diaphysis and the two knobby ends are the epiphyses. The hollowness of bones makes them lighter and sturdier. The epiphysis contains what is called an alveolar structure, in which fibers are arranged to best handle the stress on the bone. The hollow diaphysis contains bone marrow, where blood cells are produced. On the outside of a bone is a membrane called the periosteum; this substance carries blood vessels and assists in repairing bones that have fractured.

Types of joints

The body has several different types of joint to allow for different kinds of movement.
- In a ball-and-socket joint, one of the connecting surfaces is rounded and the other concave. As with all joints, a

ball-and-socket joint is filled with fluid to allow the smooth movement of the two parts.

- In a hinge joint, the convex surface of one joint fits against the concave surface of the other, and is arranged such that motion can only occur in one plane. An elbow is an example of a hinge joint.
- In a gliding joint, both the connecting surfaces are basically flat, and so movement is very limited. The intercarpal joints connecting the mass of bones at the bas of the hand is an example of a gliding joint.
- In an ellipsoid joint, the oval-shaped section of one bone fits into an elliptical cavity in another. This connection allows for movement in two planes. The wrist is the classic example of an ellipsoid joint.
- In a pivot joint, a pointed or rounded area in one bone fits into a ring-like structure on another. In a joint like this, as for instance in the joint connecting the base of the spine and pelvis, rotation is the only possible movement.
- In a saddle joint, both of the connecting surfaces are shaped like saddles, and fit together snugly. In a joint set up in this manner, movement can occur in two planes. The best example of a saddle joint is found where the thumb connects to the hand.

Nervous system

The nervous system collects information for the body and indicates what the body should do to survive in the present conditions. For instance, it is the nervous system that administers a bad feeling when the body is cold, and then sends a more positive message when a person warms up. These important messages are sent by the nerves, which vary in size and cover the entirety of the body. The central nervous system is composed of the brain and spinal cord, and the peripheral nervous system is composed of the rest of the body, including those organs which a person does not voluntarily control. The peripheral nervous system is divided into sympathetic and parasympathetic systems, which counterbalance one another to allow for smooth function.

Somatic system
The portion of the human body's nervous system that is responsible for moving the skeletal muscles is the somatic system (the other part of the nervous system is the autonomic system, which controls involuntary muscles like the heart). The movements created by the somatic system may be acts of the will or reflex actions. Of course, such movements will require an increased blood flow to certain areas, so the somatic nervous system relies on the autonomic system to provide a proper setting in which to effect action. The motions ordered by the somatic system are the result of information gathered by the nerves of the body; the nerves most closely concerned with the somatic system are those that extend out to the extremities of the body.

Neurons
In order for the nervous system to determine what movement is appropriate, it must be able to gather accurate information from the neurons (the single cells that make up a nerve). Neurons may be very small and round, or they may extend as fibers for several feet. Sensory neurons are those that carry messages of heat, cold, pressure, smell, and so on, to the brain. The neurons that carry messages from the central nervous system to the various muscle systems are called motor neurons. The major nerves of the body contain both sensory and motor neurons. There is a third type of neuron, the internuncial, which connect and coordinate the various parts of the central nervous system. Glial cells are those that provide structure to the nervous system but do not otherwise assist in its function.

Neurons may vary considerably in size and speed, but they all operate in a similar manner. Neurons operate on an all-or-nothing basis; that is, they either fire or do not, and will not fire more intensely for a stimulus that is much stronger than that needed to cause it to fire on the first place. For this reason, neurons are said to have a threshold, a minimum amount of stimulus required for function. The basic reflex exercise conducted during a medical exam is a good example of this function: when the knee is struck with the rubber hammer, the impulse must travel up the leg to the spinal cord, where it crosses from the sensory neurons to the motor neurons (the junction is known as a synapse). The amount of time between contact and the resulting action, a slight contraction of the quadriceps, is known as the synaptic delay.

Digestive system

The digestive system is composed of organs which work to turn food into energy. This process begins with the teeth, which grind food into small particles and thereby make them easier to digest. Food is then carried through the pharynx (throat) and esophagus to the stomach. In the stomach, it is partially digested by strong acids and enzymes. From there, food will pass through the small and large intestines, the rectum, and the anus. On this journey, it will be mixed with numerous chemicals, so that it can be absorbed into the blood and lymph system. Some food will be converted into immediate energy, and some will be stored for future use; whatever cannot be used by the body will be expelled as waste.

Muscular system

The muscles of the body are attached to the skeleton by tendons and other tissues. Muscles exert their force, and move the bones of the body, by converting chemical energy into contraction. Every muscular act is the result of some muscle growing shorter. The muscles themselves are composed of millions of tiny proteins. Muscles are served by

nerves linking them to the brain and spinal cord. There are three types of muscles: cardiac muscles are found only in the heart and pump the blood through the body; smooth muscles surround or are pare of the internal organs; skeletal muscles are those which a person has voluntary control over. Skeletal muscles are the most common tissue in the body, accounting for between 25 and 40% of body weight.

Lymphatic system

The lymphatic system is connected to the cardiovascular system through a network of capillaries. The lymphatic system filters out organisms that cause disease, controls the production of disease-fighting antibodies, and produces white blood cells. The lymphatic system also prevents body tissues from swelling by draining fluids from them. Two of the most important areas in this system are the right lymphatic duct and the thoracic duct. The right lymphatic duct moves the immunity-bolstering lymph fluid through the top half of the body, while the thoracic duct moves lymph throughout the bottom. The spleen, thymus, and lymph nodes all generate and store the chemicals which form lymph and which are essential to protecting the body from disease.

Endocrine system

The endocrine system creates and secretes the hormones that accomplish a wide variety of tasks in the body. The endocrine system is made up of glands. These glands produce chemicals that regulate metabolism, growth, and sexual development. Glands release hormones directly into the bloodstream, where they are then escorted to the various organs and tissues of the body. The endocrine system is generally considered to include the pituitary, thyroid, parathyroid, and adrenal glands, as well as the pancreas, ovaries, and testes. The endocrine system regulates its level of hormone production by monitoring the activity of hormones; when it senses that a certain hormone is active, it reduces or stops production of that hormone.

Circulatory system

The circulatory system is composed of the heart, the blood vessels, and the blood. This system circulates the blood throughout the body, giving nutrients and other essential materials to the body cells, and removing waste products from the body. Arteries carry blood away from the heart, and veins carry blood back to the heart. Within body tissues, tiny capillaries distribute blood to the various body cells. The heart takes oxygenated blood from the lungs and distributes it to the body; when blood comes back bearing carbon dioxide, the heart sends it to the lungs to be expelled. Other organs not always considered to be a part of this system (for instance the kidneys and spleen) help to remove some impurities from the blood.

Anatomical reference terms

- Lateral means further to the median plane.
- Medial means closer to the median plane.
- Anterior means facing forward or found in the front.
- Posterior means facing towards the back or located there.
- Superior means facing towards the top or located there.
- Inferior means facing or located at the bottom.
- Superficial means external, or close to the outside if the body.
- Deep refers to things inside the body.
- Proximal means closer to the trunk, or to some other major joint.
- Distal means further from the trunk or some other major joint.

Cartilage

The areas of bones that are close to joints are covered in a shiny connective tissue known as cartilage. Cartilage supports the joint structure and protects the fragile bone tissue underneath. Cartilage is susceptible to injury because it is subject to gravitational pressure as well as pressure born of joint movement itself. Long-term stress to cartilage can result in rheumatoid arthritis and osteoarthritis. There are no blood vessels in cartilage; nutrients are delivered by the synovial fluid, and from nearby blood vessels. Cartilage contains a huge number of spongy fibers because it needs to absorb a great deal of shock. Especially resilient cartilage, known as fibrocartilage, is found between the vertebrae and in the knees, among other places.

Joint capsules

A joint capsule is a sort of sleeve that surrounds a joint, preventing any loss of fluid and binding together then ends of the bones in the joint. The outside of this sleeve is made of a tough material, while the inside is more soft and loose so that movement is not impeded. Joint capsules are often especially string in areas in which movement should be discouraged; for instance, there is a strong joint capsule section on the back of the knee, which in part makes it difficult for the lower leg to bend forward. The fiber of the outer joint capsule are known as ligaments, and the inside of the joint capsule is called the synovial membrane. The synovial membrane secretes a fluid that keeps the joint lubricated and removes debris.

Ligaments

Ligaments are dense bundles of fibers running parallel to one another from one bone in a joint to another. Ligaments are a part of the joint capsule, though they may also connect to other nearby bones that are not participating in the joint the ligament supports. Ligaments are not like muscles; that is, they cannot contract. Instead, ligaments passively strengthen and support the joints by absorbing some of the tension of movement. Ligaments do contain nerve cells which are sensitive to position and speed of movement, and so ligaments can hurt. One function of this pain is to alert the person to an unnatural or dangerous movement of the joint. Ligaments may also be strained or rupture if they are placed under unnecessary or violent stress.

Muscle tissue

Muscle tissue is made up of bundles of fibers which are held in position and separated by various partitions. These partitions range from large (deep fascia, epimysium) to small (perimysium, endomysium), and often extend beyond the entire length of the muscle and form tendon connecting to another bone. Each muscle cell is extremely long and has a large amount of nuclei. Every muscle cell contains a number of smaller units called sarcomeres; these contain thick filaments of the protein myosin and thin filaments of the protein actin. Muscle tissue contracts when a nerve stimulates the muscle and the thin filaments compress within the sarcomere, causing a general muscle contraction.

How muscles are attached
In most cases, a muscle is attached to two different bones. In a movement of the body, the origin bone will be fixed in some way and the other bone (known as the insertion bone) moves because of a muscle contraction. Occasionally, health professionals will refer to the origin bone as the proximal bone. Although the only voluntary motion a muscle is capable of is contraction, muscles also have a generally elastic nature, and so if they are stretched beyond their normal length they will have a tendency to return to it. This principle in part accounts for the general tendency of the body to retain a particular shape. Muscles may be attached to bones by means of tendons or muscle fibers.

Muscle shapes
The muscles of the human body come in a variety of shapes, depending on their function. In the trapezius, for instance, the muscle fibers are arranged in a broad, flat pattern, and attach at a large number of points along the scapula. The biceps, on the other hand, is a long, narrow muscle. The muscles of the deep back are very short, and appear as knotty bundles along the spinal column. Longer muscles are generally capable of producing highly visible external movements, for instance the transporting of a heavy objects, while small, deep muscles are more often responsible for precise, balancing adjustments. Muscles that only cross over one joint are called monoarticular, while those that extend across and move more than one joint are called polyarticular.

Exercise

Frequency
As you might expect, this refers to how often you will exercise. After any form of exercise is performed your body completes a process of rebuilding and repairing. So, determining the frequency of exercise is important in order to find a balance that provides just enough stress for the body to adapt and also allows enough rest time for healing.

Intensity
Defined as the amount of effort or work that must be invested in a specific exercise workout. This too requires a good balance to ensure that the intensity is hard enough to overload the body but not so difficult that it results in overtraining, injury or burnout.

Time/duration
This is rather self-explanatory. Time is simply how long each individual session should last. This will vary based on the intensity and type.

Health benefits
Maintaining physical fitness has a number of advantages besides improving personal appearance. For one thing, it has been shown time and again that habitual exercise is the best way to prevent coronary death. In fact, individuals who don't exercise as twice as likely as active individuals to die of a heart attack. Exercise also makes the lungs more efficient, as they are able to take in more oxygen and make better use of it. This provides the body with more available energy. Exercise has also been shown to

benefit the bones. Individuals who do not exercise are more likely to have weak or brittle bones, and they are more prone to osteoporosis, in which bones lose their mineral density and become dangerously soft.

The benefits of regular exercise are both physical and mental. It is well documented that frequent exercise boosts a person's mood, increases their energy, concentration, and alertness, and reduces their anxiety. In fact, long workouts are specifically shown to cause the release of mood-elevating chemicals called endorphins into the brain. Exercise is also proven to reduce the risk of disease. By aiding the proper operation of the digestive system, exercise reduces the risk of colon and rectal cancers. Studies have also indicated that women who exercise are less likely to develop breast cancer. Finally, exercise is beneficial because it helps you lose weight and keep it off. The body's metabolism is sped up for a prolonged period after exercise, meaning food is processes more quickly and efficiently. In addition, regular exercise helps suppress the appetite.

Cardiovascular system

Exercise stimulates the release of adrenaline and lactic acid into the bloodstream, increasing the heart rate. The blood pressure also increases, to ensure that enough blood is being delivered to the brain. Generally, the distribution of blood changes during exercise: less blood is delivered to organs, and more is directed to the working muscles. In particular, less blood flows to the kidneys and intestines, meaning much less urine is produced during exercise. While a normal resting lung capacity is about 5 liters of air per minute, during vigorous exercise the lungs may be able to hold close to 200 liters of air every minute. Indeed, the lungs are able to process enough oxygen to accommodate any level of exercise; the maximum level of exertion is actually determined by the output of the heart.

Exercise improves the ability of the heart to pump blood throughout the body, increasing the volume of blood distributed with each beat by 20 to 30%. This increase in volume allows the heart to slow down so that it only beats between 40 and 60 times a minute. There is no change to the maximum heart rate, however; an individual's maximum heart rate is determined at birth and decreases only with age. It is true that exercise increases the length of time one can exercise at a high percentage of maximum heart rate. As is well known, blood pressure is decreased by regular exercise, even during exercise itself. Finally, the overall cardiac output is improved by exercise; in other words, healthy muscles receive more blood.

Regular exercise strengthens the muscles associated with respiration. Though the number of alveoli (places where carbon dioxide and oxygen are exchanged) remains constant, the improved strength of the intercostals muscles between the ribs allow the lungs to hold more air. Exercise also increases the overall blood supply, making it more difficult for individual's to become dehydrated during vigorous work. Training increases the number of red blood cells, which makes it easier for blood to supply oxygen to the body. Interestingly, regular exercise not only improves the function of existing blood vessels but creates new blood vessels in working muscles. Within the muscles, individual fibers are enlarged by exercise and there is an increase in the aerobic enzymes that process oxygen.

Muscles

When the endurance of muscles is increased, there develops a greater capacity for aerobic metabolism. In fact, the aerobic enzymes that metabolize carbohydrates, fats, and proteins will double after a few weeks of endurance training. Muscle training that aims at increasing strength or speed also enlarges the individual fibers of muscle. There is some evidence that weight training causes a splitting of muscle fibers, causing new ones to be formed. Finally, regular exercise increases the amount of blood that circulates through muscles. New capillaries will form around muscle fibers.

Gender differences

Muscular endurance and body compositon
Most studies have determined that there is very little difference in muscular endurance and body composition between fit males and females. Certainly, the range of difference is much wider within each sex than it is between comparable members of different sexes. Still, there are some general biological differences that create disparities in physical performance. For one thing, since girls tend to undergo the changes of adolescence before boys, they out-perform boys for the first few teenage years. After adolescence, males tend to be taller, heavier, stronger, and faster. Increasingly, though, fitness researchers are suspecting that male advantages in fitness may stem in large part from prejudicial treatment in society. Indeed, many studies have show that males at every age tend to receive more encouragement and training in athletic endeavor than do females.

Biological advantages
After adolescence, there are a few biological advantages held by males that enable them to outperform women of similar fitness level. For one thing males usually have a larger heart and lungs than females, and so they also have a greater aerobic capacity and cardiac output. Males will also have on average a higher proportion of hemoglobin in the blood, which enables them to speed oxygen to needy muscles more quickly. The heart rate of a male is typically stronger and slower than that of a female. Males generally have more muscle mass and less fat, so the cardiorespiratory system can spend more of its energy nourishing muscle. Finally, the shoulders of a male are typically broader and the arms and legs are longer, which gives the average male a longer stride and reach than the average female.

Issues for women

Exercise and iron deficiency
There is a persistent myth that vigorous exercise can deplete the iron resources of a woman. The life of this falsity is in part due to the fact that women have slightly lower levels of hemoglobin than do men; this substance is necessary for carrying oxygen to cells, and requires iron for its formation. Women are at no risk of developing anemia or any iron-deficiency as long as they make sure to eat a diet rich in leafy vegetables, whole grains, beans, fish, and meat. If a woman does not eat enough iron, however, or loses a great deal of blood, the iron reserves may become depleted. This can seriously inhibit a fitness plan, by making it difficult for oxygen to be transported to the needy cells

Contact sports
There persists a popular assumption that contact sports are more dangerous to women than to men. This is untrue: repeated studies have shown that the rate of injury among females who participate in such sports (for instance soccer, rugby, and basketball) is roughly the same as for males. Furthermore, the kind of injuries most commonly suffered by females are by and large the same suffered by men: sprained ankles and knee injuries. Assuming that women are given the same level of training, supervision, and protective equipment as males, there is no reason to suspect that they are any more vulnerable to injury.

Menstruation
There is no danger in exercising vigorously while menstruating. Though some women may feel hindered by the cramping and soreness they feel during this period, these symptoms are in no way an indication that the body needs to rest. Moreover, many women find that vigorous exercise actually eases the symptoms of menstruation. Women exercise for whatever length of time and at whatever level of intensity they prefer. Specifically, there is no truth to the notion that women should avoid swimming during

- 118 -

menstruation. Studies have shown that there is no danger to health posed by the physical exertion of swimming, nor is there any risk in being submerged in hot or cold water.

Pregnancy
There is no evidence to suggest that women should not continue to exercise during pregnancy. It is impossible for exercise to deprive a fetus of nourishment, and vigorous activity will not harm a fetus, which is safely guarded by the amniotic fluid. Moreover, pregnant women can receive many health benefits from exercise. A fitness plan that emphasizes body composition can help offset the weight gain associated with pregnancy. Exercises that develop strength in the abdomen, lower back, and pelvic floor can be helpful for minimizing back pain and the discomfort of carrying a child. Exercises that aim at increasing flexibility can help reduce muscle soreness during the last trimester. Finally, regular exercise can reduce the insomnia, fatigue, and constipation that often affect pregnant women.

After giving birth
Though women are likely to receive major health benefits from resuming an exercise program soon after giving birth, they should not immediately resume vigorous or contact sports for at least four weeks. Oftentimes, women can benefit from immediately resuming a program designed to strengthen the abdominal muscles, which may have been distended during pregnancy. Women should gradually increase the intensity of their exercise programs as they recover from labor. Most women find that after six months they are back at their peak level of performance. In a related note, there is no reason to suspect that exercise can interfere with lactation, so women who are breastfeeding may participate in any vigorous activity for which their body is otherwise ready.

Biomechanics

Mass
The mass of an object is simply the quantity of matter in it. Every object has a mass, which remains constant even if other masses are added to it. Mass should not be confused with weight, which is dependent on the amount of gravitational pressure that is exerted on the object. An object will have the same mass on earth as it would have on the moon or floating in outer space. The mass of an object will indicate the amount of force needed to move it: the greater the object's mass, the more force will be needed to overcome its stationary inertia. Mass is measured in either kilograms (SI) or slugs (English units).

Weight should never be confused with mass. Though weight is proportional to mass, it will vary depending on the gravitational force in which the object is located. Therefore, weight can be found by multiplying the mass by the gravitational constant. On the surface of the earth, the gravitational constant is 9.8 meters per second, or 32 feet per second (this is the rate at which objects will accelerate if dropped). Weight is measured in either Newtons (SI) or pounds (English units). Weight is a vector, and so when it is used in science it must have both a magnitude and a direction, though this direction will almost always be straight down, towards the center of the earth.

Force
Force is simply the push or pull that is exerted on an object. Force is reported as a vector; that is, it has both a magnitude and a direction. The effect of force will be in part dependent on the point of the application of the force and the line of action of the force. The point of application is the precise location where the force was exerted on the object. The line of action is an imaginary line running from the point where the force is exerted out in the direction of the force. Force is calculated by multiplying mass and acceleration. Force is typically measured in Newtons (SI) or pounds (English).

- 119 -

The amount of force a body can produce is closely related to the stability of that body. The more stable the individual's foundation, the more force he or she will be able to exert. In order to maximize force, one should try to allow the strongest muscles to do the most work; this is one of the reasons health professionals recommends lifting heavy objects with the legs rather than the back. More generally, it is recommended that one always channel lines of force along the spinal column and major bones of the body, rather than at an angle to these structures. In other words, avoid exerting unnecessary pressure on the spinal column by lifting things at an angle. Heavy objects should be carried as close to the body as possible, and the base of support should always be broad.

Friction

Friction is the force created by an object's contact with the ground as it moves. Specifically, friction is the force exerted by the ground which tends to slow down the movement of the object. If there were no friction, objects on which a force has been exerted would move forever at the same speed. The force of the friction depends on the weight of the moving object and the surface of the ground. Very smooth ground surfaces are not likely to create much friction, whereas rough, uneven surfaces will quickly bring an object to a halt.

Stability

In order to reach maximum effectiveness in movement, one needs to understand some of the basic principles of body mechanics. One of these basic principles is stability. In general, an individual will be more or less stable depending on the area of his or her supporting base. This is why, for instance, linemen in football prepare for contact by lowering themselves and placing at least one and on the ground. A very stable stance, however, may inhibit sudden movement. In the case of the lineman, this is not a problem as he knows in which direction he will have to move first; in other sports, however, it may be necessary to sacrifice a bit of stability for

mobility. A wrestler, for instance, must stand a bit more upright in order to be prepared for an attack from any side.

Center of gravity

The stability of an individual can be greatly improved if he or she simply lowers his or her center of gravity. The center of gravity, otherwise known as the center of mass, should be perpendicular to the ground along the same line as the geometric center of the base if the individual wants to have maximum stability. That is, an individual will be less stable as he or she moves the center of gravity away from the midpoint of his or her stance. In some cases, this is a good idea: runners, for instance, often lean in the direction they will be running in order to gain an advantage. Indeed, the process of walking is nothing more than continuously moving he center of gravity forward and "catching" oneself with an alternate leg.

Principles of movement

Torque

Torque is the force that causes something to rotate. Torque is calculated as the product of the force applied and the distance of the force from the axis of rotation. In other words, torque will be greater the farther away it is from the axis, if the same amount of force is applied. As an example, consider a door: it will be easier to rotate on its axis (hinge) if it is pushed from the side away from its connection to the door frame. The same principle applies to many other things, among them automobile engines and the human body. Torque is generally measured in either Newton-meters (SI) or foot-pounds (English units).

Centripetal force and acceleration

Centripetal force is any force exerted on an object that is moving in a circle. A centripetal force will create centripetal acceleration: any change in velocity that occurs during circular motion. Velocity is normally calculated as a vector (that is, it has both magnitude and direction), but in the case of circular motion the direction of the object is constantly changing. Contrary to intuition, when an object is in circular motion the centripetal force is towards the center of the circle. This becomes evident if you remember what it was like to be swung in a circle as a child: the faster you are swung, the more pull (centripetal force) you feel.

Inertia

Inertia is the term used in physics to describe any object's resistance to a change in velocity. The greater the inertia, the greater is the object's resistance to an increase or decrease in velocity. This simply means that more force will be required to change the velocity of an object that has greater inertia. The moment of inertia (also called rotational inertia) is an object's resistance to a change in its velocity of rotation. The particular rotational inertia of an object will depend on its mass, shape, and how the mass is distributed through the object. A football, for instance, is much more resistant to rotating end-over-end than it is to spinning laterally.

Velocity

Velocity is simply the measure of the speed and direction of an object. It is calculated by dividing distance by time. A simple equation for velocity indicates that the final distance should be subtracted from the initial distance, and the difference divided by the length of time taken to cover that distance. So, if an individual runs from the ten yard-line to the fifty yard-line on a football filed in five seconds, we would say he has run at a velocity of eight yards per second. Velocity s typically measured in either meters per second (SI) or feet per second (English units), though it can be expressed in any units of length and time.

Acceleration

Acceleration is the measure of the rate of change in velocity over a certain period of time. Since acceleration is a vector, it can be caused by a change in speed, direction, or both. When acceleration is negative (that is, when an object loses velocity) it is often referred to as deceleration. Acceleration is typically calculated by finding the difference between the starting and ending velocities and then dividing by the length of time in which this change was made. Typically, acceleration is measured in meters per second squared (SI) or feet per second squared (English units).

Momentum

Momentum is the tendency that any object has to continue moving. Momentum is calculated as a vector, meaning that it has both a magnitude and a direction. Momentum is calculated by multiplying mass and velocity, so two objects traveling at the same speed will have a different momentum if they have different masses, and two objects of the same mass will have a different momentum if they are traveling at different velocities. It will require more force to stop an object that is traveling with a greater momentum.

Sports and Lifetime Activities

Dance

Folk dance

A folk dance is any primitive, tribal, or ethnic form of dance. Many folk dances originated as a component of some ritual or ceremony. Folk dances ay entail some sort of special costume, though many (for instance the square dance) are performed in a variety of settings. Folk dances are a great way for children to learn about foreign cultures while improving their coordination, timing, and cardiovascular health. Some of the more common folk dances include English Morris dancing, the Spanish fandango, the Irish jig, The Hawaiian hula, the Maypole dance, and the Bohemian polka. These dances are generally associated with a certain song or certain style of music.

Aerobic dance

A basic session of aerobic dance will last from thirty to sixty minutes and will entail running, hopping, jumping, skipping, bending, stretching, and sliding. These sessions are typically led by an instructor, who guides participants through periods of warm-up, vigorous, and cool-down exercises. Aerobic dance provides an excellent cardiovascular workout, and is very good for burning fat, building muscular endurance, and increasing flexibility. Perhaps best of all, aerobic dance provides a total-body workout. It can also be performed just about anywhere. Individuals with a low level of fitness or with health concerns can begin at a low level of movement and gradually make their workout more difficult.

Square dancing

A square dance is a basic folk dance in which four couples are arranged in a square formation, and execute a series of commands given by a caller. In a square dance, the caller does not actually participate in the dance.

Most of the steps used in square dance are based on the traditional dances of American immigrants; dances from which the American square dance has borrowed include the quadrille, Morris dance, and English country dance. At present, there are two common types of square dance: traditional square dance and modern Western square dance.

Body contact style of dance

One of the forms of closed position (a form of dance in which partners face one another) used in partner dance is called body contact. In this form, the direction given by the lead partner to the other is made through more extensive contact than just the arms. Different dances may entail contact with the thighs, hips, chest, cheek, or forehead. In ballroom dance, couples often touch at the thighs and hips. In many forms of body contact dancing, couples connect at the thigh and then are standing slightly to the side of one another. Most of the more provocative forms of dancing, including the tango and the lambada, make extensive use of the body contact style.

Closed position of partner dancing

Closed position is a form of partner dancing in which two dancers hold and face one another. Closed positions of dance entail that partners contact one another with more than just the hands; typically, partners either touch with their legs, hips, or shoulders, and one partner may be at times supported by the other. In the most common type of closed position, derived from the waltz, the right hand of the leader is on the back of the follower, while the left hand of the follower rests on the right shoulder of the leader. The other hands of each dancer are clasped together. Many kinds of folk dance involve different forms of closed position, as for instance the Scandinavian dances in which the leader holds the waist of the follower.

Connection

Any kind of partner dance relies on connection between two people. Though partners may have to rely on other forms of communication, such as hand signals, the most graceful dance is led using entirely physical connection. In a partner dance, one person leads the other by gently guiding him or her. The physical connection through which the leader guides the follower is called the frame. In tension (or leverage) connection, dancers pull apart from one another with an equal but opposite that is generated by the trunk or by momentum rather than by the arms. In compression connection, the dancers are pressed together. Although tension and compression may be sustained in swing dancing, in most dances they are used to indicate upcoming movements.

Contra body movement
Contra body movement (sometimes abbreviated as CBM) is a dance used to describe a certain way of coordinating the movements of two dancers. Specifically, contra body movement involves that during a dance step, the dancer turns his or her body towards whichever foot is moving. For example, if the left foot is moving forward, the torso should swivel to the left; when the left foot moves back, the torso will swivel to the right. Contra body movement is a common feature of ballroom dances like the waltz, foxtrot, and tango. The point of contra body movement is to make a smooth transition from movement that is straight ahead or behind to movement to one of the sides.

Teaching direction of movement
When dance instructors direct the movements of their dancers, they can do so either in relation to body position or in relation to the room. When instructors give directions in relation to the room, they are said to be giving directions of progressive movement. IN this case, directions can indicate that a dancer should move along the line of dance (a large circle extending around the room), against the line of dance, to the center, or to one of the walls. Directions may also be given with respect to body position; this is done by using either the points of the compass or of the clock (as in, "take a step to five o'clock"). Dance instructors may also indicate turns by specifying right or left, clockwise or counter-clockwise, or inside or outside.

Open position of partner dancing
In partner dancing, open position means that the two people are connected only by the hands, rather than by other body parts as in closed position. The open position is used in swing dancing and Latin dancing. In these dances, much of the direction for movement is expressed in the tension and compression of the partners' arms. In order to successfully dance in open position, the leader must be able to guide the follower using only a basic frame. Only with a great deal of practice can communication between partners become so easy as to allow for fluidity on the dance floor. For most beginning dancers, open position dancers will look rigid and forced.

Gymnastics

Rhythmic gymnastics
In rhythmic gymnastics, participants develop routines in which they deftly manipulate one of five types of apparatus: balls, clubs, hoops, ribbons, or ropes. Performances in rhythmic gymnastics are made either individually or in five-person groups. In competitive rhythmic gymnastics, judges award points to the participants based on leaping ability, balance, pivot, flexibility, handling of the apparatus, and artistic merit. There is a bit of tumbling skill involved in advanced rhythmic gymnastics, though the main skills incorporated are hand-eye coordination and flexibility. Rhythmic gymnastics is considered to be an excellent way to develop body control, achieve good cardio-vascular health, and improve flexibility.

Artistic gymnastics
In artistic gymnastics, individuals perform various short routines in a number of different areas. The events that comprise artistic gymnastics are the vault, uneven bars, balance beam, floor exercises, pommel horse, still rings, parallel bars, and high bar. Most of

- 123 -

the time, a routine on each apparatus lasts for about a minute. Although gymnastics at the highest level requires incredible coordination, flexibility, and strength, any person can benefit from learning to do some basic gymnastic maneuvers. The events typically performed by men and women are slightly different: men perform more activities designed to test strength, while the events in women's artistic gymnastics showcase artistry, balance, and agility.

Tumbling

Gymnastics, cheerleading, and dance often entail some of the self-propelled acrobatic maneuvers known as tumbling movements. In tumbling, an aerial is a cartwheel executed without the hands touching the ground. In some cases, a round off that does not involve the hands will be known as an aerial. A handspring is when you spring from your feet forward so that you are being supported by your hands, and then bounce back onto your feet. A back handspring, as one might expect, is simply a handspring executed by flipping backwards onto the hands and then onto the feet. Novice gymnasts should definitely be supervised as they learn to execute aerials, handsprings, and back handsprings.

Tumbling is any individual gymnastic maneuver in which the hips are at some point above the head. Tumbling maneuvers are used not only in gymnastics but also in cheerleading and dance. In tumbling, a handstand is executed when you support your entire body weight with your hands and your body is perpendicular to the ground. A cartwheel is when you rotate your body laterally with your hips as an axis, such that your hands support your weight briefly until your feet come back around to provide support. A round off is a fast cartwheel in which the feet are brought together as the hands touch the ground. Then, the body is pushed up into the air, and you land on your feet.

Vaulting horse

The vaulting horse is an apparatus used in artistic gymnastics. In competition, the vaulting horse is used by both male and female gymnasts. Though the material used in vaulting horses has changed over the years, the basic vaulting horse is upholstered and measures about four feet long and sixteen inches across. Gymnasts get a running start, hit a trampoline, and then use the upholstered surface of the vaulting horse to propel themselves into the air. Then, they execute a series of saltos, or somersaults, and twists, rotations around an imaginary an imaginary axis drawn from the top of the head to between the feet. Gymnasts will try to perform the trick as gracefully as possible while still being able to land safely and firmly.

Uneven bars

The uneven bars are an apparatus used in gymnastics, especially by females. It consists of two bars set beside one another at different heights; in competition, the upper bar will be set at a height of 246 cm and the lower at a height of 166 cm. The bars are usually made of either wood or plastic. When performing routines on the uneven bars, gymnasts try to keep their body as straight as possible, and move easily between the bars. During a routine, a gymnast is required to move from each bar to the other, and perform a move in which the center of gravity is brought close to the bar while spinning around it. It is also important to land cleanly and safely when finishing an uneven bars routine by letting go of the bar and sailing onto the mat.

Balance beam

The balance beam is an apparatus used in artistic gymnastics. In competition it is used exclusively by females. The balance beam is a metal or steel frame supporting a wooden beam on which a leather cover is placed. It is typically about 125 cm high, 5 meters long, and 10 cm wide. When performing on the balance beam, gymnasts attempt to execute a number of cartwheels, somersaults, and dance maneuvers while maintaining balance, demonstrating ease and confidence, and moving smoothly between maneuvers. Obviously, it is important to avoid wobbling on the beam, losing balance, or hesitating. At the end of a balance beam routine, gymnasts will have to make a leap off the beam, attempting to keep feet together and land without stumbling.

Floor exercises
Floor exercises are performed by both male and female gymnasts during an artistic gymnastics program. The floor is typically about 12 meters across and twelve meters long. Most floors contain some sort of spring or foam underneath to aid the jumps and tumbling maneuvers that make a routine. Floor exercises typically consist of a combination gymnastic, dance, and acrobatic elements, including somersaults, cartwheels, and splits. At high levels of competition, gymnasts are required to complete a jump of at least two saltos (somersaults). A successful tumble in floor exercises will include a "stuck" landing, in which both feet touch the mat simultaneously and there is no sliding or stumbling.

Pommel horse
The pommel horse is an apparatus used in artistic gymnastics. A typical pommel horse is a wooden beam atop a metal frame, with a leather cover on top. Exercises on top of the pommel horse will be designed both for both a single leg and both legs. Moves performed with single legs usually involve scissoring the legs apart and spinning. For the most part, a pommel horse routine consists of spinning the legs in a circular motion and turning around. These turns, executed with the elbows locked and the arms supporting the entire body weight, are called moores and spindles. At then end of a pommel horse routine, the gymnast will dismount by swinging his or her body onto the mat, or going into a handstand and pushing off.

Rings
The rings are an apparatus used in artistic gymnastics. In competition, the rings are used exclusively by men. Rings are usually made of are wood or metal, covered with leather, and are suspended at the same height by ropes. In competition, rings are suspended 280 cm above the ground and about 50 cm apart. Rings are usually 18 cm in diameter. A routine on the rings must have components that test the swing, strength, and hold of the gymnast. One famous move associated with the rings is "iron cross," in which the gymnast suspends him or herself so that his or her arms are parallel to the ground. At the end of a routine on the rings, the gymnast will attempt to perform a combination of saltos and land with his or her feet together and without stumbling or falling.

Parallel bars
The parallel bars are a gymnastics apparatus used exclusively by male gymnasts. They are composed of two wooden or plastic bars suspended at the same height, usually about 200 cm, and set about 50 cm apart. Gymnasts grasp the two bars with their hands and perform a series of flips and holds. A routine on the parallel bars usually lasts about a minute, and is required to contain certain elements, for instance a handstand-type hold. At the end of a routine on the parallel bars, the gymnast will thrust him or herself upward off the bars, execute sequence of flips and twists, and attempt to land with his or her feet together and without stumbling or falling.

Horizontal bar
The horizontal bar, otherwise known as the high bar, is a gymnastics apparatus used exclusively in competition by male gymnasts. Typically, the bar is suspended 280 cm above the ground. A routine on the horizontal bar involves a number of flips and reversals of hand position. In fact, in upper levels of competition it is mandatory for the gymnast to perform a maneuver in which he brings his center of gravity close to the bar while swinging around it, and another maneuver in which he throws himself high into the air above the bar and then catches back onto it on the way down. The climax of a horizontal

bar routine occurs when the gymnast spins around the bar several times, then lets go and executes a series of somersaults, landing firmly with feet together.

Educational gymnastics

When teaching gymnastics, teachers should begin by introducing students to some basic concepts relating to the body, space, and time. First, students should be encouraged to focus on basic locomotor movements (walking, for instance), weight transference, and alert stillness. Students should also spend some time thinking about the body's potential for movement, and developing an awareness of the movements that are possible from any given position. Finally, teacher should give students some basic instruction on timing, so that they can begin to consider the rhythmic elements of gymnastic. Many professionals suggest the gymnastics teachers should spend some time developing timing by leading simple activities that involve the regulation and synchronization of movement.

One of the most important things that students can acquire from training in gymnastics is a sense of measured, continuous movement. In order to encourage this, teachers should help students to work on their timing, and on economizing movement. One way to help students develop a sense of flow is to break maneuvers down into small parts and allow students to see the components of a complex movement. As students advance, it is proper to show how various gymnastic movements can be linked together so that transitions appear natural. Finally, students should be able to create a basic routine that incorporates a number of disparate elements into one seamless movement.

As part of an effective study of gymnastics, students should be encouraged to consider their movements in relation to the movements of other students. To this end, teachers should have students develop basic gymnastic routines for pairs and small groups. These groups should have a defined leader to whom the others look for guidance, though this leader may change throughout the routine. Many of these routines will be set to music, and so it is important that students also work to develop a sense of rhythm. Teachers should start by having students perform very basic movements to a regular beat, and allow the routines to become more complex as the sense of rhythm dictates. Students should also get a basic understanding of how movement can respond to and interpret music.

Invasion games

Invasion games are any team games in which players have to penetrate the territory of an opponent, and either enter a goal themselves or put a ball of some kind into a goal. Invasion games are a good way for students to get an appreciation for different strategies of attack and defense, to develop teamwork skills, and to improve whatever particular skills are required by the game. Some examples of invasion games are soccer, football, basketball, hockey, lacrosse, and Ultimate Frisbee. Invasion games force students to use both their mind and body, to outwit and outmaneuver their opponent. For this reason, invasion games have been cited as beneficial to coordination, reflexes, and problem-solving skills.

Developing technical skills

One of the objectives of teaching an invasion game is to improve certain skills, like passing, receiving, or shooting a ball. In order to accomplish this objective, teachers should give direct instruction to students on the techniques used in the game in question (for instance, teaching the bounce and chest passes in basketball), including the demonstration of how to position the body to best advantage. Students should also learn how to shield the ball from defenders, and how to quickly change speed or direction while maintaining control of a ball. In the end, students will have successfully met the skills objective if they can perform with accuracy, understand the basic skills for each game, and know how to keep score in each game.

Developing basic tactics

When teaching students to participate in invasion-style games, it is important to ensure that they understand the basic rules, strategies, and tactics of the given game. To this end, students should be taught when to pass and when to maintain control of the ball (passing, of course, should be done when one is defended). Also, students should begin to consider which places on the field make are the easiest from which to score, and which places are the easiest from which an opponent can score. In most games that have a small goal at one end of the field, it is easiest to score from the middle of the filed at that end. Students should also learn about different attack and defense formations, and the various merits of each. Finally, students should learn about the different roles of the members of the team (for example, midfielders' responsibility to distribute the ball).

Evaluating student progress

When students have learned and understood the basic strategies of an invasion game, they should be capable of playing the game in a number of different formations and with teams of various sizes. They should also be able to determine the appropriate strategy for a given game situation (for instance, pursuing a risky attack when losing towards the end of a game). Students should also demonstrate the basic principles of defense, by marking opponents closely and keeping the ball away from dangerous areas. Advanced students will be able to look at a game and determine which areas need improvement, and what strategies might be more effective. These students will be able to describe the particular advantages of good players and will know the best tactics to take advantage of their team's talents.

Cooperative games

Many teachers find that cooperative games are a positive way to build teamwork among students while still developing motor skills and strategy concepts. There are six basic components that are emphasized by a cooperative game: fun, cooperation, equality, participation, and trust. A good cooperative game must be enjoyable, or else students will not want to continue. It must also require students to have faith in one another, and for all students to participate. The goal of a cooperative game is to generate enthusiasm for physical activity even among students who are normally reticent about joining in.

Competitive games

A competitive game is any one in which players or teams vie to defeat one another. Competitive games can be a great motivator in physical education class, as long as the competition is seem as a chance for everyone to test their skills and improve, rather than as a chance for superior athletes to embarrass others. In order to keep the games fun for all students, teachers should make a point of assessing student abilities and ensuring that no unfair matchups arise. Also, teachers should stress that competition is a way to find the areas in which you need to improve

Ropes courses

Over the past couple of decades, many physical education classes have incorporated adventure skills training because of the excitement they provide and the teamwork they necessitate. Ropes courses consist of a series of obstacles that students will need to overcome individually or as a team. Because many of these activities contain an element of risk, they should only be performed under close supervision and with the appropriate training. One of the wonderful things about ropes courses is that the different obstacles will require different sets of skills, so students may have varying areas of expertise. Some activities may require strength and muscular endurance, whereas others may require balance and coordination.

Commando crawl

In the ropes course activity known as the commando crawl, students will crawl a distance of four or five feet across the top of a 2-inch rope. This is done by lying on top of the rope and hooking one foot beneath while the other leg hangs down for balance. The student will then crawl across using his or her arms and leg. The rope should not be set very high above the ground, in case of a fall.

Tire swing

In the tire swing obstacle, students will have to move across a series of tires with rope to a horizontal beam. The lengths of rope will vary, so it will be difficult for students to move from high to low tires and vice versa. The tires should be set three or four feet apart, and none should be higher than four feet above the ground.

Kitten crawl

In the ropes course activity known as the kitten crawl, students will crawl across two parallel, incline ropes that begin at about five feet high and descend to a height of about two feet. In order to perform this task, students should be on all fours and slowly crawl down the rope. Spotters should be aware that students can fall between the ropes as well as off to either side.

Two-rope bridge

In the two-rope bridge activity, two ropes about five feet apart are attached to two trees or post. Students are to walk along one of the ropes while holding onto the other with their hands above their head. The bottom rope should not be more than four feet off the ground, unless some sort of safety equipment is being used.

Three-rope bridge

In the ropes course activity known as the tension traverse, three ropes are tied horizontally between two trees. Two of the ropes are set at waist height, and the third is to be walked upon. This sort of bridge is often used for traversing a river or canyon, but it should never be set very high unless appropriate safety measures are taken. For instance, many times a rope will be tied around the student's waist and attached to one of the waist-high ropes.

Tension traverse

In a tension traverse, the student will have to balance and move across a tight rope suspended very low between two trees. A rope may be tied at the top of one of the trees for the student to hang onto in an effort to control balance.

Balance beam

In a balance beam activity, a log is attached between two trees or posts at a height of about five feet, and students are required to walk across it. If the beam is set higher than five feet, a safety rope should be tied to the student; is the beam is lower than five feet, then a spotter will be all that is necessary.

Inclined log

In the inclined log activity, a balance beam is placed at an angle. For beginners, it is typically easier to move from up an inclined beam. Depending on the comfort level of the student, he or she may want to walk or crawl along the beam.

Swinging log

In the swinging log activity, students will have to traverse a log that is suspended by ropes from two trees, and will therefore be moving. Falls will be frequent in this activity, so the beam should not be set very high.

Cargo net jump

In the ropes course activity known as the cargo net jump, students will move up an inclined log to a jumping platform, from which they will jump into the center of a cargo net. The net should be dense enough that there is no danger of falling through, and it should not be set more than fifteen feet above the ground. A rope ladder may be the most convenient way for students to exit the net.

Giant's ladder

In the activity known as the giant's net, students will have to balance, jump, and swing up an enormous ladder made of logs. The rungs of this ladder should be a few feet apart, so students should have some kind of safety rope in case they fall through. Once the student reaches the top of the ladder, he or she can be lowered to the ground with the safety rope.

Electric fence

In the ropes course activity known as the electric fence, a group of students will have to get over a piece of rope extended above the ground at a height of about five feet. In order to do this, they will have to rely on teamwork and a small piece of wood, large enough for one person to stand on so that the others can pass him or her across. There are a number of successful strategies for completing this task.

Boardwalk

In the group activity known as the boardwalk, four long boards are attached such that a group of students can put their feet on the bottom boards and hold the top boards with their hands. In order to move the boards forward, the group will have to coordinate the lifting of their arms and legs.

Faith fall

A common group activity on a ropes course is a faith fall, in which one person falls backward into the arms of the rest of the group. In order to perform this exercise in trust and teamwork, the individual should stand on some elevated platform slightly above the outstretched arms of his fellows. The people who are going to do the catching should not grasp each other's hands, as this may result in heads smashing together when the person lands.

Stream crossing

In the activity called stream crossing, students have to move from one area to another without touching the ground. They are given squares of some material to walk on, but there are not as many squares as people, so students will have to devise some strategy to get all group members across.

Martial arts

Aikido

Aikido is a martial art hailing from Japan. It was developed using elements from jujitsu and kenjitsu, and, like these arts, attempts to use the opponent's own fight against him or herself. Aikido also places gat emphasis on grace and economy of movement. Aikido also incorporates some of the skills used in spear and sword combat, especially the body movements that have been developed in support of these forms of combat. One of the hallmarks of aikido is the use of joint locks, in which an opponent is immobilized by the application of pressure to a specific body part, and the throw, in which an opponent is made to fly forward by redirecting his or her momentum.

Capoeira

Capoeira is a Brazilian art of self-defense that has become very popular in the United States in recent years. A session of capoeira training provides both an excellent cardio-vascular workout and dance training. It aspires to be a mixture of the participants' body and soul, requiring both mental and physical awareness and agility. Capoeira is performed with a group of people standing in a circle around two combatants, who perform a stylized sequence of fake punches, blocks, and dodges. In a recreational session of capoeira no blows are actually landed. Capoeira is always accompanied by music, mostly percussive, and chanting, which gives a rhythm to the mock-fight.

Jujitsu

The Japanese word jujitsu is derived from two characters meaning flexibility or

- 129 -

suppleness and art. However, this name should not fool any would-be participants into assuming that jujitsu is a non-violent activity. Rather, jujitsu gets its name because it relies on using passivity to guide one's opponents astray using his or her own force. The techniques assembled in jujitsu allow a master to physically manipulate even a much larger and stronger opponent. Jujitsu is considered to be one of the most comprehensive martial arts in existence. Many of the techniques found in jujitsu rely on joint locks, chokes, and throws, all of which incorporate an advanced knowledge of movement and the human body.

Karate
Karate is a Japanese art of unarmed self-defense. In karate, the individual assumes a special stance and delivers specially targeted blows with his or her hands and feet while shouting. Karate is successful because it trains the individual to use a minimum of movement and violence to achieve his or her ends. As a workout, karate is exceptional: it trains all of the major muscle groups, and provides a fantastic cardiovascular workout. In order to practice karate effectively, an individual must have excellent balance and flexibility. Though karate is related to judo, its emphasis on blows rather than throws distinguishes it. Karate is the most globally popular of all the martial arts.

Kendo
Kendo is a form of fencing that was developed in Japan during the nineteenth century. Though kendo was originally created in the service of samurai warriors, today it is more commonly practiced with bamboo sticks and protective equipment. The sword used in kendo is typically about four feet long, and is grasped with both hands. In kendo competition, one must strike one's opponent with a particular side of the outer third of one's sword. In order to facilitate movement, participants usually wear a long skirt slit in the middle. It is also typical for a face mask, breastplate, gloves, and protective apron to be worn.

Kung Fu
Kung Fu is a Chinese martial art that is based on assuming low, strong stances and making powerful blocks. Because Kung Fu relies on positively resisting aggression, it requires a great deal of patience as well as muscular strength. Kung Fu has been around for many years, and has developed a number of different offshoots, many based on the movements of animals like the crane or snake. Even today, a variety of Kung Fu styles are passed down within families and communities. The styles that developed in the north emphasize kicking and punching, while the Kung Fu styles of the South are more akin to boxing. Some of the blocks in Kung Fu are powerful enough to break the arm of one's opponent.

Sumo wrestling
Sumo derives from the Japanese word meaning "struggle." Sumo was not always a sport for over-sized men in strange diapers. In fact, for a long time it was practiced in order to train soldiers for battle. In fact, all of the ceremony and ritual that accompanies modern sumo wrestling is derived from its military origins. Over time, specific rules, rankings, and the size of the ring have standardized sumo competition. In a sumo match, a combatant loses if he is forced out of the ring or touches any part of his body higher than his knee to the ground. In order to defeat an opponent, sumo wrestlers use a variety of slaps, holds, and tackles.

T'ai Chi Chuan
There are a number of different forms of the ancient Chinese art of exercise, personal growth, and meditation known as T'ai Chi Chuan. T'ai Chi can be practiced both to promote health and as a means of self-defense. Successful practice will increase awareness of the body, foster a mood of tranquility, and exercise all the major muscles. In order to practice T'ai Chi, the individual must stand such that his or her center of gravity is in his or her trunk or abdomen. His allows breathing to become deep and steady, and the various systems of

organs to become more balanced and harmonious. T'ai Chi aims to bring the individual into harmony with nature and reduce conflict with environmental stressors.

Tae Kwon Do

Though Karate may be the best-known martial art in the United States, Tae Kwon Do is the martial art which is most commonly practiced world-wide. Tae Kwon Do is a Korean martial art, though it bears a close similarity in appearance to Karate. Tae Kwon Do is not only a system of self-defense, it is also an art form and a way of life. The movements taught in Tae Kwon Do are meant to be performed smoothly and swiftly, and with the economy of motion that maximizes power. Part of training in Tae Kwon Do is striving to improve the artistic form of every maneuver. Over time, the regular practice of Tae Kwon Do will improve posture, coordination, and body control.

Basketball

Basketball is an excellent activity for physical education classes because it is a team sport incorporating skills that can easily be practiced individually. There are a number of basic games that will improve basketball skills, and by high school students should be able to work on strategy and teamwork concepts. Basketball is also a good choice for physical education classes because very little equipment is required. To play basketball, all a class will really need is a ball and a basket. One consideration is that students should have appropriate footwear; running shoes may not provide adequate ankle support and can mark up a gymnasium floor. There is infinite room for improvement in basketball skills, so students shouldn't ever get bored.

Passing

In order to pass a basketball, students should be holding it with their fingertips rather than the palms of their hands. When receiving a pass, bend elbows in to "give" with the ball and absorb the force. When passing, quickly straighten the elbows and snap the wrists. A chest pass is typical for long passes: the ball is held at chest level and thrown through the air to another player. One foot should be placed in front of the other in a striding position. A bounce pass is thrown with a similar form, except that it is designed to hit the floor and go to the other player's chest. This pass is good for connecting with closely-guarded teammates. A two-handed overhead pass is made with a short striding motion, and is particularly effective against shorter opponents.

Catching and dribbling

The most important thing to do when catching a basketball is to keep your eyes on the ball, and make sure you have caught it before moving. To catch a pass, advance towards to with hands extended: if the pass is at waist level or higher, keep the thumbs in and fingers up. Hands should move towards the body as they receive the ball, thus cushioning the impact. In order to dribble a ball successfully, keep your knees bent and move in a slight crouch. The forearm of the hand that is dribbling should be parallel to the ground, and the ball should be pushed with the fingertips rather than slapped with the palm. Most of the force in a dribble should be from the wrist.

Shooting

In every type of basketball shot, the body should be squared up to the basket if possible. The elbow of the shooting hand should be directly behind the ball. Eyes should be fixed on the rim, and the arm should be fully extended after the shot is released. A good shot will have a bit of backspin. When shooting a lay-up, the basket should be approached at about a forty-five degree angle, with the dominant hand on the outside (that is, the right hand if approaching from the right side). The body should be lifted by the left leg. In a jump shot, the ball should be placed just above the front of the head, with the elbow of the shooting hand just behind the ball. The ball should be released with a snap of the wrist when the shooter is at the peak if his or her jump.

Soccer

Soccer has long been the most popular sport in the world, and it is rapidly gaining in popularity in the United States. One of its advantages for physical education is that it is a sport that emphasizes foot-eye rather than hand-eye coordination, as in most other sports. Soccer also combines skills that can be practiced individually with team goals and strategy. It demands a great deal of body control and provides an excellent cardiovascular workout. Although regulation soccer matches are played with eleven on a side, any number of games can be played with a smaller group. All that is really required for soccer is a ball, although students may benefit from having special footwear, shin guards, and goalie gloves.

Dribbling and kicking
In soccer, dribbling is simply controlling the ball while advancing it in a certain direction. The ball is moved by gently touching it with the inside or outside of the foot. Effective dribbling entails keeping the ball close to your body, rather than kicking and running after it. Students should get practice moving in different directions while dribbling. To try a shot or pass in soccer, you need to kick the ball. A proper pass is hit off the inside of the foot, with the opposite foot planted next to the ball and pointing in the direction of the pass. Sometimes you may want to pass with the outside of your foot, though it is more difficult to pass the ball a great distance with this method. A shot is executed in the same way as a pass, with the ball making contact with the instep and the lower leg following through after the ball is struck.

Trapping and heading
Trapping the ball in soccer is the process of bringing moving ball under your control. Because the ball is often moving quite fast in a soccer match, it is a valuable skill to be able to slow it down. This can be done with any part of the body except for the hands or arms, though most trapping is done with the instep. In order to effectively trap the ball, you must give way slightly when the ball makes contact, to prevent it from rebounding violently. Heading the ball is an effective way of moving an airborne ball. It is important to strike the ball, rather than having the ball strike you, as this makes it easier to control and less painful. The head should lean back before the ball arrives, and then forcibly redirect the ball, following through in the desired direction.

Tackling and goalkeeping
In soccer, tackling is primarily concerned with taking the ball away from an opposing player, rather than necessarily bringing that player to the ground. A single-leg tackle may be used when approaching a player from behind, the side, or from straight ahead. The defender uses one leg to reach for the ball, while the other supports the body. The goal keeper on a soccer team is the only player allowed to use his or her hands. Because goal keepers may be required to dive for some balls, they often wear some protective padding. If a goalie is not close enough to a ball to catch it, he or she may want to punch it away. Once the goalie has controlled the ball, he or she may roll it, throw it, or kick it away.

Softball

Softball is a controversial game among physical educators; while some say that it is not active enough for young students, others argue that it is a good game to learn because it can be played throughout life. Softball is unlikely to be fun unless the participants have a decent skill level; therefore, activities should focus on basic skills until a sufficient level is reached. A softball field is easy to construct anywhere, but players will probably need to have gloves and helmets. Also, bats and balls will obviously be required. If students are going to require some time working on individual skills, they should each have a glove and ball. For inexperienced players, it is better to use a ball that is softer than normal.

Catching and throwing

If possible, you should always move your body into the path of a ball you are trying to catch. To catch a ball above the waist, extend both arms with fingers up and thumbs on the inside. Although the ball should be caught with the gloved hand, the other hand should be close by to catch the ball if it should pop out. To catch a ball on the ground, advance towards it while crouching forward. Always keep your eyes fixed on the ball, following it as it falls into your glove. After catching the ball, you may need to throw it: this is typically done by holding the ball with three or four fingertips. You should always step while throwing with the foot opposite to the throwing arm. Because throwing a softball is a difficult skill, students may benefit from slowing down the process to determine what feels natural.

Pitching and batting

In softball, a pitcher must start the throwing motion with both feet on the rubber rectangle on the mound. The ball is held in front of the body at first, and then the pitcher brings it back behind him, cocking the wrist. The pitcher then swings his or her throwing arm towards the plate while stepping forward with the opposite foot. The ball is released as the wrist snaps, with the arm continuing on its follow-through. The batter should be waiting with both hands gripping the bat, the dominant hand on top. As the ball arrives, the batter will step towards it with the foot closest to the pitcher. As the batter swings, he or she should keep his or her eye on the ball and try to swivel the hips as contact is made. After contact, the bat should continue with its follow-through.

Volleyball

Volleyball has long been a popular sport in physical education, because it offers a good workout, keeps an entire class involved, and improves a number of different skills. Volleyball is also a sport that is very popular with girls, so it is a nice alternative to male-dominated sports like football and baseball.

A volleyball court can be set up just about anywhere, although many schools will have gymnasiums that can be converted into excellent volleyball courts. The height of the net may be adjusted in accordance with the skill level of the players. Any athletic shoe is appropriate for volleyball, although students should be sure to wear shoes with non-marking soles if the game is being played in the gym. Volleyballs are inexpensive and can be purchased in varying degrees of lightness and softness, depending on the location of the court and the skill level of the players.

Serving

In order for every student to enjoy a game of volleyball, students need to acquire a basic repertoire of skills. It may be necessary to spend a bit of time practicing serving before playing a regular game. An underhand serve begins with the left leg slightly forward, and both knees slightly bent. The ball is held in the left hand, and the right hand swings back and then forward, striking the ball with an open or closed fist just above the waistline. Contact should be made with the heel of the hand. An overhand serve should put no spin on the ball. The left leg will also be slightly forward at the beginning of this serve. The ball should be tossed 2 or 3 feet above the right shoulder, after which the right arm should swing back and strike the ball while fully extended. Again, contact should be made with the heel of the hand.

Passing and setting

In volleyball, the ball can be passed twice on one side of the net before it must be struck onto the other side. Forearm passes are typically used to receive a serve or spike from the opposition, because they are effective at controlling a fast ball. In order to execute a forearm pass, stand with feet shoulder-width apart, one foot slightly ahead of the other. The forearms should be rolled outward to create a flat surface for the ball to hit. Depending on the speed of the ball, you may want to slightly swing your arms forward, with elbows locked, during contact with the ball. An overhand (or set) pass is executed by

- 133 -

positioning yourself so that your body is just under the ball. Your hands should be cupped so that the ball makes contact with the fingers and thumbs of both hands at the same time. The legs should bend slightly during a set pass, so that the ball can be more easily controlled.

Spiking and blocking
In volleyball, spiking is when you strike the ball from above the net into your opponent's territory, usually at a downward trajectory and with great force. Before spiking, you may want to get a bit of a running start in order to maximize your jump. With your feet together, jump straight up with both arms raised. The left arm should swing slightly in advance of the right, which will strike the ball with an open palm. A spike can be blocked by any of the three players on the front line of the opposing side. Blockers should jump a moment after the spiker, and raise both arms with fingers spread. The arms should be no farther apart than the width of the ball, as the point of the block is to forbid the passage of the ball.

Tennis

Tennis is very popular in physical education because it provides an excellent workout, yet can be played for a lifetime. Tennis is also a wonderful social game; men and women can play together in mixed doubles, and there are many breaks in the action that allow for conversation. The equipment requirements for tennis are a bit higher than for other sports; in order to play, every student will need a racket and a few balls. Tennis courts can be made on a variety of different surfaces, from concrete to grass. Students should have shoes that provide plenty of ankle support, as tennis requires stopping and starting frequently. A tennis net is usually about three feet high in the middle of the court.

Volleying and ground strokes
Many people do not understand that tennis is a game primarily played with the legs; the player who can consistently put his or her body in the best position to hit a shot will probably win. The volley is the simplest shot in tennis, and is usually the first to be learned. Volleys are any shot that is hit before it bounces on your side of the court; a volley requires no backswing and is therefore not unlike "catching" the ball in the center of the racket. Ground strokes can be either forehand or backhand, and are considered to be the foundation of tennis skill. The backhand, which is hit with the non-dominant hand, is typically a bit harder to learn, and is usually a weaker shot than the forehand.

Lob, overhead shot, and serve
A lob shot in tennis is exactly like a ground stoke, except the angle of the racket is changed so that the ball will soar. Lob shots are typically made in an effort to send the ball over an opponent who has come close to the net. The overhead shot, or smash, is similar to a serve, and is struck when an opponent's lob has not gone high enough. An effective overhead shot sends the ball onto your opponent's side so quickly that he or she has no chance to return. Serving is probably the most difficult shot to master in tennis; a serve is struck from behind the baseline. When serving with the right arm, place your left leg slightly forward and gently bend your knees. As you rise, throw the ball 2 or 3 feet above your head and strike it with your right arm fully extended. The right leg will typically stride forward during a serve.

Aquatic exercise

Aquatic exercises, also known as water calisthenics, are particularly effective for older individuals or those at a low level of fitness. They provide a low-impact workout for the entire body. The buoyant effect provided by being submerged on water is a major benefit for those plagued by muscle or joint pain. Exercises which involve moving against or through the water are isokinetic and are good for building muscular strength and endurance. Most water calisthenics program are not vigorous enough to provide a high level of cardiovascular exercise.

Interestingly, though, it is easier to stretch in water, and so flexibility can be improved markedly by aquatic exercises.

Badminton

Badminton is a popular sport in physical education classes because it requires a fairly low level of skill (much less than tennis, for instance) and can provide a good cardiovascular workout. Badminton can be played both indoors and out, singles or doubles, and the basic equipment is relatively inexpensive. The rules are similar to those of volleyball: points can only be scored by the one who is serving, a basic game is played to fifteen, etc. Instead of a ball, badminton is played with a shuttlecock, the most basic version of which consists of a piece of cork with feathers attached. Though badminton can be very strenuous when it is played at a high level, it can be enjoyed by individuals of any fitness level.

Boxing

Boxing is perhaps a bit too violent for most physical education programs, but it does provide a tremendous workout for the entire body. Besides boxing itself, most boxers spend a great deal of time jumping rope, running, and sparring. Punching a light bag is excellent for developing hand-eye coordination, muscular endurance, and cardio-vascular endurance. Punching a heavy bag is excellent for developing the muscles of the arms and back, as well as those muscles of the legs that provide a firm foundation for punching. Many individuals can gain major health benefits by incorporating some of the training used by boxers into their workouts: shadow-boxing, for instance, is excellent for cardio-vascular health and muscular endurance.

Canoeing and kayaking

Canoeing and kayaking are extremely enjoyable activities that can also enhance both cardiovascular health and muscular

endurance in the arms and trunk. In particular, the latissimus dorsi, deltoids, triceps, and biceps are exercised by rowing. In canoeing, an open, rounded, hollow craft is propelled across the water with a single, one-sided oar. A kayak, on he other hand, entirely covers the lower body of the rower and is smaller and lighter. A kayaker uses a single oar that has flat blades on both ends. If taken at a leisurely pace, canoeing and kayaking provide only a moderate workout, though they will require a bit of upper-body endurance. Paddling at a rate of 4 miles per hour for longer than thirty minutes, however, is likely to bring an individual well into his or her target heart rate.

Cross-country skiing

Cross-country skiing is one of the most comprehensive and arduous workouts available. It delivers an excellent cardio-vascular workout, as well as a tremendous challenge to muscular strength and endurance. Moreover, the long strides and reach required for cross-country skiing enhance flexibility. Research has consistently shown that cross-country skiing causes the human body to consume a larger amount of oxygen than almost any other activity. Because cross-country skiing is so arduous, however, it is really only appropriate for individuals who are already in decent shape. For a long time, cross-country skiing was only an option in places that receive a large amount of snow; in recent years, though, stationary cross-country machines have enabled individuals to get the advantages this activity indoors.

Diving

Competitive diving requires that the entire body be flexible, and that the legs be strong. While diving does not deliver much of a cardio-vascular workout, if it is done for a long period of time it can provide a fine test of muscular endurance. Many divers strive to improve their overall fitness by incorporating long periods of swimming into their workout.

Also, some diving instructors recommend that during practice divers should try to make a number of dives in rapid succession, as this will test the endurance of the leg muscles. Diving itself is excellent for flexibility, but most divers will be unable to complete more advanced maneuvers unless they undertake a determined stretching program away from the water.

Ultimate Frisbee

There are a number of vigorous games that can be played with a Frisbee, none of them more popular than Ultimate. When it is played at a high level, Ultimate provides an excellent cardiovascular workout as well as a stern test of muscular endurance. A game of ultimate is a bit like rugby: teams try to advance the Frisbee into an opponent's end zone by passing it. Individuals may run only when they are not throwing the Frisbee, which cannot be dropped if a goal is to be scored. The agility and coordination required to be a successful Ultimate player make it a popular choice among physical educators. There is a certain level of throwing and catching skill that must be acquired before a game of Ultimate can be undertaken; it may be a good idea to have students practice basic skills first.

Judo

In Japanese, the word judo means "gentle way." This is perhaps because judo is one of the more non-combative and graceful of the martial arts. When properly practiced, judo also entails a large amount of training and supervision, so injuries are infrequent. Judo is typically practiced with a partner and under the supervision of a master. Judo borrows many of the moves of jiu-jitsu, especially those in which the weight of one's opponent is used against him or her. However, not only is judo a weaponless form of combat, it also eschews any of the jiu-jitsu moves which could be dangerous in a friendly competition. After the ceremonial bow, a judo match begins with the combatants grasping one another by the jacket collar and sleeve.

Track and field

Athletics, also known as track and field or track and field athletics, is a collection of sport events. The word is derived from the Greek word "athlos" meaning "contest". It is a collection of sport events, which can roughly be divided into running, throwing, and jumping.

Important terms

Dance terminology
Backleading - In partner dance, the term backleading refers to a situation in which the follower independent of the leader, or even contrary to the leader. Essentially, backleading occurs when the follower anticipates the next move of the leader but executes it too soon. Sometimes, though backleading can be helpful if it allows the couple to avoid collision with another couple.

Center point of balance - In any form of dance, the center point of balance is the area around the solar plexus. Dance instructors focus on this area when teaching various forms of dance because it need only shift two or three inches from the area of support before a person will lose his or her balance. For this reason, a dancer needs to be conscious of his or her center point of balance at all times.

Heel lead - In dance, a heel lead is a move in which the moving foot touches the ground heel-first, as if the person were walking.

No foot rise - When the instructions for a particular dance refer to no foot rise, this means that the heel of the support foot remains in contact with the floor until the weight is transferred onto the other foot.

Replace - A replace, on the other hand, occurs when the weight is put back on the previous support foot while maintaining its position. This occurs in dances where the weight is rocked forward onto another foot and then brought back to the original foot.

Side lead - In a side lead, the body swivels as a step is taken. In this sort of lead, the swivel is made to the side that feels more natural; for instance, the body swivels right as the left foot steps forward.

Spotting - Spotting is a techniques use din dance turns. When spotting, a dancer picks a stationary reference point and trains his or her eyes on it; when the motion of the turn makes it impossible for him or her to maintain eye contact with the spot, he or she swiftly rotates his or her head and regains eye contact with the spot. This tends to prevent dizziness and makes turns more fluid.

Supporting foot - When dance instructions refer to a supporting foot, they mean the foot that bears the full weight or most of the weight at the beginning of the step. Oftentimes, this term will be used when the other foot is doing some special move.

Sway - In ballroom dancing, a sway is said to occur when the upper body gracefully moves to the side of the lower body. In advanced ballroom dancing, sways are used to elegantly lead into some moves, as well as to give dancers better control.

Toe lead - In dance, a toe lead occurs when the ball of the foot is the first thing to touch the ground.

Traveling dance - A traveling dance is one in which partners cover a significant distance on the dance floor. Waltzes, polkas, sambas, and foxtrots are all traveling dances.

Visual connection - The visual connection between partners is essential for coordinated movement. Though many dance experts contend that physical connection is the best way to maintain communication during a dance, visual connection is necessary during periods in which dancers are apart, and can be especially helpful or spotting during turns.

Round dance - A round dance is a folk dance in which couples are either arranged in a giant circle, or in which couples proceed in a general circle around the room.

A la seconde - In ballet, the phrase al la seconde indicates that particular move is to be done to the side.

Avant - The term avant means that a step is to be taken forward.

Arriere - The word arriere indicates that a step is to be taken backwards.

Assemble - The term assemble means that the first foot will swing out, and then the second foot will swing under the first, sending the dancer into a leap. This leap will conclude with feet together and landing at the same time.

Arabesque - In an arabesque, the body is supported on one leg while the opposite leg is extended behind the body with the knee kept straight. The back will be arched during an arabesque, and the back leg may either touch the ground or be raised in the air.

Attitude - In ballet, the attitude is the pose in which the dancer stands on one leg, with the other leg raised either in front (en avant) or behind (derriere). While holding an attitude, the leg bearing the weight is held with the knee bent at an angle of about 120 degrees.

Battement - A battement is a kicking of the leg. There are various kinds of battement, for instance battement glisse (a rapid, short kick) and a battement lent (a slow, long kick).

Chaines - A chaines is a series of rapid urns made while moving along an imaginary line or circle.

First position - First position, in ballet, is when the dancer stands with heels pressed together such that the feet make a straight line.

Fourth position - Fourth position is when the feet are parallel to one another and set slightly apart.

Fouette - In ballet, a fouette (meaning "to whip") is a movement on one leg that forces the dancer to change the direction of the hip and torso without changing the direction or position of the weight-bearing leg.

Grand jete - A grand jete is a long, horizontal jump, taking off from one leg and landing on the other. A grand jete usually involves doing a split in mid-air.

Pas - A pas is simply a step. There are numerous variations on this term, for instance pas de basque (a cross between a step and a leap), pas de chat (a sideways jump in which both legs are bent back to touch the buttocks), and a pas de bouree (in which the dancer takes small steps on his or her toes).

Port de bras - Port de bras is the term that refers to the movement of the arms around the body during various ballet movements.

Plie - In ballet, a plie occurs when the knees are bent, sometimes all the way until the buttocks touch the feet.

Pirouette - A pirouette is one of the more well-known moves in ballet, and occurs when the dancer spins on one leg with the other foot resting on the knee of the supporting leg.

Rond de jambe - Rond de jambe are circles made with the legs; they can be accomplished in the air, or along the ground.

Second position - A dancer is said to be in second position when his or her legs are more than shoulder width apart, with toes turned out.

Saute - The French word for jump is sauté, and there are a number of sautés used in ballet: petits sauté (small jumps in which the feet maintain their position); changements (in which the feet exchange locations), and echappes sautés (in which the feet split apart mid-jump and land in second position).

Third position - A ballet dancer is said to be in third position when the feet are brought in and slightly overlap, while the toes point out to each side. That is the left foot is perpendicular to the body and the right foot is brought in front of the left, also perpendicular to the body, such that the heel of the right foot is directly in front of the arch of the left foot.

Fifth position - Fifth position is similar to third position, except the feet are brought back even farther, such that the toes of each foot are next to the heels of the other.

Tours en l'air - Tours en l'air are jumps in which the dancer performs either a single or double rotation while in the air. This is a difficult movement generally performed by male dancers; it can finish with the dancer either in an attitude or arabesque.

Practice Test

Practice Questions

1. What is the best way for parents to convey to their children a healthy attitude toward alcohol consumption?
    a. Remind them that alcohol consumption by minors is illegal
    b. Model responsible alcohol use in the home
    c. Acknowledge that teenagers are inevitably going to experiment with alcohol, and encourage moderation
    d. Have a medical professional speak to them on the health hazards associated with alcohol consumption

2. Sexual activity increases a woman's risk of incurring:
    a. high blood pressure.
    b. type-2 diabetes.
    c. urinary tract infection.
    d. irritable bowel syndrome.

3. The best defense against the common cold is to:
    a. stay warm and dry.
    b. drink eight glasses of water daily.
    c. wash hands frequently.
    d. take daily supplements of zinc and vitamin C.

4. A high school student has just been raped. She should be advised to:
    a. take a shower and then call her parents.
    b. change her clothes and then call the police.
    c. immediately call the rape-crisis center or go directly to the nearest emergency room.
    d. take at least 48 hours to calm down before deciding what to do next.

5. Which of these facts about smoking is LEAST likely to discourage a 14-year-old boy from taking up the habit?
    a. Smokers are ten times more likely to die of lung cancer than nonsmokers.
    b. Smoking is a very expensive habit.
    c. Many girls won't date a boy who smokes.
    d. Smoking can seriously impair athletic performance.

6. Pregnancy is most reliably confirmed by:
    a. the absence of two or more periods.
    b. a positive result on a home pregnancy test.
    c. monitoring changes in daily body temperature.
    d. having a doctor test for HCG in the blood.

7. Before they can be used by the body as fuel, complex carbohydrates must be converted into
    a. glucose.
    b. amino acids.
    c. lipids.
    d. folic acid.

8. A diet that includes over 20 grams of fiber daily:
    a. may interfere with the effective absorption of essential vitamins and minerals.
    b. is likely to increase the concentration of cholesterol in the blood.
    c. helps prevent constipation and lowers the risk of digestive disorders.
    d. is useful in treating irritable bowel syndrome.

9. Which of the following is LEAST likely to trigger an asthma attack?
    a. Stress
    b. Moderate exercise
    c. Pollen
    d. Tobacco smoke

10. Adolescents with type-1 diabetes can best manage their disease by:
    a. frequent monitoring of blood sugar and the administration of insulin.
    b. eating frequent meals and sugary snacks.
    c. a rigorous exercise regimen.
    d. avoiding all nonessential physical activity.

11. Which of the following is likely to be most effective in teaching middle school students how to resolve conflicts among classmates?
    a. Viewing a film about conflict resolution
    b. Giving a reward to the best-behaved class in each grade
    c. Having the teacher arbitrate all disputes
    d. Practicing peer mediation

12. Which of the following drugs is NOT a stimulant?
    a. Methaqualone
    b. Amphetamine
    c. Ecstasy
    d. Cocaine

13. The main advantage of generic drugs over name-brand drugs is that generics:
    a. generally have fewer side effects.
    b. usually contain fewer additives.
    c. are generally more effective.
    d. are often less expensive.

14. Which of the following statements about date-rape drugs is true?
    a. GHB can be recognized by its distinctive smell and bitter taste.
    b. Ketamine, also known as "Special K," is a nervous system stimulant.
    c. The use of a controlled substance to assist in a sexual assault is a federal crime punishable by up to 20 years in prison.
    d. Rohypnol, or "roofies," are readily available by prescription in most American pharmacies.

15. The main dietary sources of saturated fat are:
    a. meat and dairy products.
    b. fish and poultry.
    c. fruits and vegetables.
    d. nuts and beans.

16. What is the best way to prevent accidental shootings in the home?
    a. Always unload guns before storing them.
    b. Keep all firearms in a locked container inside a locked drawer or closet.
    c. Store ammunition in a separate location from firearms.
    d. Do not keep any guns at home.

17. The most efficient way for young people to increase their strength and endurance is by:
    a. playing sports such as volleyball and basketball.
    b. making weight training a part of their daily exercise regimen.
    c. lifting heavy weights with few repetitions.
    d. lifting moderately heavy weights with many repetitions.

18. A contusion is:
    a. a muscle bruise usually caused by a jarring blow.
    b. a torn or stretched muscle or tendon.
    c. an injury to a ligament.
    d. a blow to the skull that alters mental functioning.

19. Which of these health professionals is qualified to diagnose mental disorders and prescribe medication?
    a. Licensed psychologists and mental health counselors
    b. Clinical social workers and family therapists
    c. Psychiatric nurses and licensed professional counselors
    d. Psychiatrists and pediatricians

20. Which of the following adolescents is LEAST at risk for suicide?
    a. A boy who takes the drug ecstasy with his friends every weekend.
    b. A girl whose best friend recently attempted suicide.
    c. A boy who has been persistently ridiculed by classmates concerning his sexual identity.
    d. A girl who is concerned that poor grades may prevent her from getting into the college of her choice.

21. Which of these is the best advice regarding the purchase of a health insurance policy?
    a. To reduce premiums, always opt for the highest available deductible.
    b. All policies are essentially the same, so choose the policy with the lowest premiums.
    c. Choose a policy that covers the cost of medical services that would otherwise be unaffordable.
    d. People who are young and healthy should not waste their money on health insurance.

22. Wild mood swings, sudden outbursts of rage, delusions of invincibility, and severe acne are most likely indicative of:
    a. marijuana smoking.
    b. alcoholism.
    c. steroid use.
    d. an eating disorder.

- 141 -

23. A slightly overweight 13-year-old boy is reluctant to participate in the school sports program. Which of the following is most likely to encourage his participation?
    a. Inform him that regular exercise reduces his future risk of diabetes.
    b. Point out that playing sports is good for cardiovascular fitness.
    c. Tell him that joining a team may help him get into college some day.
    d. Explain that exercise can help him control his weight while building lean muscle and strong bones.

24. According to most experts, how old should children be before parents consider letting them return to an empty home after school?
    a. At least 15
    b. At least 13, but only if an older friend is with them
    c. At least 11, but only during the day and for no more than three hours
    d. Any age, if the parent feels the child can be trusted to behave responsibly

25. In a poll of more than 6,500 teenagers, nearly a third of the girls and a quarter of the boys admitted to at least one occasion on which they neglected to seek professional help despite their need for medical attention. What was the number-one reason given by these young people for not contacting a physician?
    a. They were afraid their parents would find out.
    b. They had no way of getting to the doctor's office.
    c. They preferred to get medical advice from their friends.
    d. They were too embarrassed to talk to a doctor about their problem.

26. A teenager who believes that she has been denied employment due to a learning disorder should:
    a. be made to understand that not every individual is suited for every job.
    b. make her complaint public by writing a letter of complaint to the newspaper or to local government officials.
    c. return to the workplace and demand to be afforded reasonable accommodation as required by law.
    d. file a formal complaint with the federal Equal Employment Opportunity Commission or the local human rights commission.

27. Under the Protection of Children from Predators Act of 1998, it is a federal crime to use the Internet to transfer obscene materials to anyone under the age of:
    a. 19.
    b. 18.
    c. 17.
    d. 16.

28. In 2008, the American Academy of Pediatrics recommended that the Recommended Daily Allowance of vitamin D for infants, children, and adolescents be changed from 200 IU to:
    a. 100 IU.
    b. 250 IU.
    c. 400 IU.
    d. 800 IU.

29. Which of the following is a true statement about teenage gangs?
    a. Gangs are almost entirely an inner-city phenomenon.
    b. As many as one-third of urban gang members are believed to be girls.
    c. Nearly all gang members actively participate in major crimes.
    d. Gang membership has been declining in rural and suburban areas.

30. According to the American Academy of Pediatrics, how many young people experience symptoms of depression at some time during adolescence?
    a. Nearly all
    b. As many as one in thirteen
    c. About 3%
    d. About one in a hundred

31. Which of the following is NOT a classic symptom of depression?
    a. Chronic fatigue
    b. Feelings of worthlessness
    c. Obnoxious or aggressive behavior
    d. Difficulty making decisions

32. Which of the following is generally the most effective strategy for treating mental health disorders in adolescents?
    a. Encourage them to talk about their feelings with close friends, parents, or trusted family members.
    b. Reassure them that their problems are normal and will eventually be resolved with the passage of time.
    c. Refer them to a qualified professional for talk therapy and, if necessary, psychopharmaceutical medication.
    d. Advise them to keep a journal of their feelings and monitor the progress of symptoms for at least a month before deciding whether further intervention is required.

33. The underlying goal of cognitive therapy is to teach patients:
    a. the power of positive thinking.
    b. that problems are rarely as bad as they seem.
    c. not to blame other people for their problems.
    d. to exercise mental control over how they perceive potentially distressing situations.

34. Psychostimulants such as Ritalin and Adderall are most commonly prescribed for which disorder?
    a. Asperger's syndrome
    b. Attention deficit hyperactivity disorder
    c. Depression
    d. Obsessive-compulsive disorder

35. Children should not be given aspirin because:
    a. ibuprofen is a more effective analgesic.
    c. it is better to let a fever run its course.
    c. young children can choke on small tablets.
    d. aspirin has been linked to Reye's syndrome.

- 143 -

36. Which of the following statements about the Individuals with Disabilities Education Act (IDEA) is true?
    a. Every child with a learning problem is entitled to special-education services.
    b. In most cases, parents must assume the expense of transporting children with disabilities to and from school.
    c. Parents are entitled to participate as equal partners in developing an individualized education plan (IEP) for their child.
    d. A school district cannot make any decision about a child's IEP unless the student and both parents are present.

37. A complete exercise program incorporates both aerobic and anaerobic activities. Which of the following is an example of anaerobic exercise?
    a. Soccer
    b. Strength training
    c. Swimming
    d. Bicycling

38. A young woman should begin having annual Pap smears once she starts:
    a. menstruating.
    b. dating.
    c. high school.
    d. being sexually active.

39. Good sources of heart-healthy monounsaturated fat include:
    a. bread and pasta.
    b. peanuts and olive oil.
    c. beef and chicken.
    d. milk and yogurt.

40. The best way for young people to reduce their risk of osteoporosis later in life is to:
    a. exercise regularly, drink milk, and get enough vitamin D.
    b. switch to a high-fiber vegan diet.
    c. decrease their intake of polyunsaturated fats.
    d. take daily supplements of vitamins C and E.

41. Foods that are rich in fiber include:
    a. turkey and shellfish.
    b. yogurt and eggs.
    c. beans and whole-wheat bread.
    d. skim milk and orange juice.

42. An adolescent with a body-mass index (BMI) of 22 would be considered:
    a. underweight.
    b. normal.
    c. overweight.
    d. obese.

43. Shin splints and tendinitis are most likely to afflict participants in which of these sports?
   a. Football
   b. Hockey
   c. Lacrosse
   d. Running

44. Stretching and warming up before participating in strenuous physical activity is beneficial for all of the following EXCEPT:
   a. improving performance.
   b. gaining muscle mass.
   c. increasing flexibility.
   d. decreasing risk of injury.

45. A 12-year-old girl who is playing soccer on a hot summer afternoon suddenly feels nauseous and complains of painful spasms in the back of her calves. She is most likely experiencing:
   a. a sprained ligament.
   b. heat cramps.
   c. heat exhaustion.
   d. heatstroke.

46. A young man refuses to be tested for HIV because he is afraid his parents will find out. Which of the following would be the most useful advice to give him?
   a. Tell him that he is morally obligated to inform his parents.
   b. Inform him that federal law allows minors to be treated for STDs without parental consent.
   c. Advise him to wait until symptoms appear before seeking professional help.
   d. Explain that he can be tested at most clinics without revealing his real name.

47. Which statement about chlamydia is NOT true?
   a. It is a sexually transmitted disease.
   b. It rarely affects adolescents.
   c. It can be effectively treated with antibiotics.
   d. Left untreated, it can progress to pelvic inflammatory disease.

48. What is the first thing a person should do after being diagnosed with any STD?
   a. Seek psychological counseling from a qualified professional.
   b. Research the causes and treatment of the disease.
   c. Inform friends and family of the diagnosis.
   d. Inform all sex partners of the diagnosis.

49. Human Papillomaviruses (HPVs) are generally treated with:
   a. topical creams.
   b. antivirals.
   c. antibiotics.
   d. protease inhibitors.

50. Levonorgestrel tablets, also known as Plan B, is a progestin used for:
   a. emergency contraception.
   b. treating certain STDs.
   c. improving mood disorders.
   d. terminating pregnancy.

- 145 -

51. Bulimia differs from binge-eating disorder in that bulimics:
   a. display a preoccupation with food.
   b. frequently withdraw from family and friends.
   c. often show signs of depression.
   d. have a distorted image of their own bodies.

52. What is the best argument for using latex condoms?
   a. They are less expensive than any other method of birth control.
   b. They are the only kind of condom that offers protection from pregnancy.
   c. They are the only kind of birth control that provides protection from both pregnancy and STDs.
   d. They are the only kind of birth control that has proven to be 100% effective.

53. According to the Adolescent Life Change Event Scale (ALCES), the number-one cause of adolescent stress is:
   a. the divorce of parents.
   b. a best friend's death.
   c. the death of a parent.
   d. the death of a sibling.

54. A junior high school student whose mother has recently died shows no apparent signs of grief; indeed, his grades have begun to improve, and he has shown increased interest in various afterschool activities. Which of these is the most likely explanation of the boy's changed behavior?
   a. He did not have a good relationship with his mother.
   b. He may have sociopathic tendencies.
   c. He is intentionally concealing his feelings so his friends won't tease him.
   d. He is channeling his emotions into socially acceptable outlets to help him cope with his grief.

55. According to studies reviewed by the National Center for Health Statistics, which of the following statements is true?
   a. Children who live with two biological parents are less likely to abuse drugs than children who live with two adoptive parents.
   b. Children who grow up in a one-parent household are more likely to engage in substance abuse than children who grow up with a biological father and stepmother.
   c. Children in single-parent families are two to three times more likely to develop behavioral problems than children in two-parent families.
   d. There is no difference in the incidence of behavioral problems between children raised in two-parent nuclear families and those raised in blended families.

56. Which of the following weight-control tips would be more harmful than helpful to an obese adolescent?
   a. A single item of food often represents more than a single serving.
   b. Keep low-calorie snack foods in the home and enjoy them in moderation.
   c. Spend less time watching television and more time exercising.
   d. If you eat food that is labeled "fat-free," you don't have to be concerned about calorie intake.

57. Which of the following statements about female puberty is true?
    a. African-American girls generally enter puberty a year earlier than Caucasian girls.
    b. Most girls do not begin to develop breasts until they have begun menstruating.
    c. Having one breast noticeably larger than the other is usually symptomatic of a serious medical condition.
    d. Underarm hair is usually the first indication of the onset of puberty.

58. The leading cause of death from unintentional injury among boys and girls aged ten to nineteen is:
    a. poisoning.
    b. homicide.
    c. suffocation.
    d. motor vehicle accidents.

59. Which of these physiological changes is typical of a normal pregnancy?
    a. Slower hair growth
    b. Breast enlargement
    c. Decreased appetite
    d. A weight gain of no more than 15 pounds

60. The increase in reported cases of autism since the 1990s is most likely due to:
    a. use of the MMR vaccine.
    b. changes in diagnostic practices.
    c. maternal drug abuse.
    d. environmental pollution.

61. An ectopic pregnancy occurs when:
    a. a fertilized ovum implants in the uterine wall.
    b. a fertilized ovum implants anywhere other than the uterine wall.
    c. an ovarian follicle ruptures and discharges an ovum.
    d. endometrial tissue grows outside the uterus.

62. Involuntary body functions such as breathing, digestion, heart rate, and blood pressure are controlled by the:
    a. somatic nervous system.
    b. autonomic nervous system.
    c. central nervous system.
    d. cerebrum.

63. Acne can be made worse by:
    a. daily washing of infected areas.
    b. consuming large amounts of chocolate.
    c. eating greasy foods like pizza and french fries.
    d. high levels of stress.

64. An untrained person who sees an adult suddenly collapse and stop breathing should:
    a. search for someone in the immediate vicinity who is trained in cardiopulmonary resuscitation.
    b. call 911 and keep the victim warm until help arrives.
    c. tilt the victim's head back and begin breathing rhythmically into his or her mouth.
    d. immediately call 911, and then begin pushing hard and fast in the center of the victim's chest.

65. Anaphylaxis is a potentially life-threatening condition usually caused by:
    a. a bacterial infection.
    b. a vitamin deficiency.
    c. exposure to an allergen.
    d. polluted water.

66. According to the Drug Abuse Warning Network, 20 percent of emergency room visits related to illicit drugs in 2005 involved:
    a. methamphetamine.
    b. prescription drugs.
    c. heroin.
    d. crack cocaine.

67. Under the Federal Assistance for Needy Families (FANF) program, unmarried teenage parents are eligible for financial assistance only if they:
    a. agree to marry within two years.
    b. live in an adult-supervised setting.
    c. are employed full time in the public sector.
    d. are living independently.

68. In theory, if a sunscreen has a Sun Protection Factor (SPF) of 30:
    a. users can stay in the sun for 30 minutes without getting a sunburn.
    b. the sunscreen filters out 30% of harmful UV rays.
    c. the sunscreen is 70% more effective than no sunscreen at all
    d. users can stay in the sun safely 30 times longer than they could without a sunscreen.

69. Medications commonly prescribed for ADHD:
    a. generally have few side effects.
    b. are often prescribed irresponsibly for purposes of performance enhancement.
    c. are frequently abused by the young people for whom they are prescribed.
    d. often stunt growth in adolescents.

70. A person with type AB blood can donate blood:
    a. only to someone with type AB blood.
    b. only to someone with type AB or type O blood.
    c. only to someone with type A or type B blood.
    d. to anyone regardless of blood type.

71. According to the U.S. Department of Justice's National Crime Victimization Survey:
    a. more than 2.5 million American women are victims of domestic violence each year.
    b. domestic violence is more often directed against men than against women.
    c. children rarely witness the domestic violence that takes place in their homes.
    d. most married men are guilty of spousal abuse at some point in their lives.

- 148 -

72. Because they are absorbed quickly into the bloodstream as sugar, refined carbohydrates:
    a. make excellent mid-morning snacks for children.
    b. are useful for treating insomnia.
    c. can cause an unhealthy spike in insulin levels.
    d. are preferable to complex carbohydrates for people with type-2 diabetes.

73. Of the following people, the one most likely to benefit from an iron supplement is:
    a. a healthy 19-year-old woman.
    b. a healthy 20-year-old man.
    c. a healthy 20-year-old woman taking birth control pills.
    d. a healthy 60-year-old woman.

74. Which of the following is most likely to present accurate and unbiased information about the relationship between walnut consumption and heart disease?
    a. An article in a popular woman's magazine
    b. A health story on a television news broadcast
    c. An article in the journal of the American Heart Association
    d. A press release from the California Walnut Commission

75. Which of these houses is least likely to have a radon problem?
    a. A new house without a basement
    b. An old house with a new heating system
    c. A house that has passed an EPA-certified radon test
    d. A house that has been carefully inspected for cracks in the foundation

76. What is generally the best emergency procedure to control bleeding?
    a. Apply a tourniquet
    b. Apply pressure to the carotid artery
    c. Cover the wound in a clean cloth and apply direct pressure
    d. Clean the wound and apply a sterile bandage

77. A high-school student is having trouble dealing with an alcoholic parent. The organization that would probably be of most help to the student is:
    a. Alcoholics Anonymous.
    b. Alateen.
    c. the National Institute on Alcohol Abuse and Alcoholism.
    d. the Center for Substance Abuse Treatment.

78. Which of the following blood pressure readings would most likely be treated with medication?
    a. 90/75
    b. 110/70
    c. 135/85
    d. 140/90

79. Which of these generally decreases in response to regular physical activity?
    a. Resting heart rate
    b. Arterial elasticity
    c. Blood volume
    d. Thyroid function

80. Which of the following statements about drinking alcohol during pregnancy is NOT true?
   a. A pregnant woman can safely drink one glass of wine a day without putting her baby at risk of fetal alcohol syndrome.
   b. Alcohol consumption during pregnancy doubles the risk of miscarriage.
   c. The birth weight of babies born to women who drink alcohol during pregnancy is often significantly lower.
   d. Children born to women who drink alcohol during pregnancy are more likely to develop severe behavioral problems.

81. Learning disabilities are usually first suspected when a child:
   a. expresses a lack of interest in family activities.
   b. fails to reach certain developmental milestones beyond the normal age.
   c. has difficulty getting along with peers.
   d. presents behavioral problems in school.

82. Children who receive the DTaP vaccine:
   a. will probably need a booster shot during their teen years.
   b. need to be vaccinated against whooping cough before starting school.
   c. are immune from hepatitis B.
   d. should receive an additional vaccination for diphtheria before traveling abroad.

83. To reduce the risk of having a child with cleft lip or cleft palate, women should:
   a. undergo amniocentesis between 15 and 17 weeks of pregnancy.
   b. avoid exposure to radiation during the first trimester of pregnancy.
   c. avoid cleaning cat litter boxes during pregnancy.
   d. take folic acid before pregnancy and during the first trimester.

84. The best source of information on recent advances in the treatment of asthma would probably be:
   a. the Centers for Disease Control and Prevention.
   b. the American Lung Association.
   c. the American Red Cross.
   d. the National Organization for Rare Disorders.

85. A student who hoped to get the lead in this year's school play discovers that she has not been cast in the production. She then announces that she really wouldn't have had time to attend rehearsals anyway. This disappointed thespian is employing a defense mechanism called:
   a. projection.
   b. repression.
   c. rationalization.
   d. regression.

86. Which statement about teenage drivers is NOT true?
   a. The risk of motor vehicle crashes is higher among 16- to 19-year-olds than any other age group.
   b. Female drivers between the ages of 16 and 19 are as likely to be involved in fatal motor vehicle accidents as males of the same age.
   c. Teenagers are less likely than adults to wear seat belts.
   d. More than half of teen deaths from motor vehicle accidents occur on Friday, Saturday, or Sunday.

87. A vegan diet is most likely to be deficient in:
    a. fiber.
    b. vitamin B12.
    c. vitamin C.
    d. folic acid.

88. Middle-school students are expected to apply critical-thinking, goal-setting, and problem-solving skills for making health-promoting decisions. These skills include:
    a. identifying types of eating disorders such as bulimia, anorexia, or overeating.
    b. examining the effects of peer pressure on decision making.
    c. distinguishing risk factors associated with communicable diseases.
    d. describing physiological and emotional changes that occur during pregnancy.

89. Competencies that are generally required of health education teachers include all of the following EXCEPT:
    a. knowledge of disease prevention and control.
    b. the ability to help children develop health knowledge and health skills.
    c. familiarity with valid and reliable sources of health information.
    d. the ability to diagnose and treat personality disorders.

90. According to the Red Cross's latest first-aid guidelines for treating cardiac arrest:
    a. rescue breaths are less important than uninterrupted chest compressions.
    b. rescuers should alternate 15 chest compressions with two rescue breaths for adults.
    c. small children should be given five chest compressions for every rescue breath.
    d. rescuers should measure three fingers' width along the rib cage before starting compressions.

91. Which statement about body modification is true?
    a. Tattoos are easily removable.
    b. Painkillers are used for most piercings.
    c. Most piercings heal in less than a week.
    d. One out of five piercings lead to serious bacterial infections.

92. Which of the following strategies is LEAST likely to promote healthy interaction among family members?
    a. Eating dinner together whenever possible
    b. Taking turns choosing movies for family viewing
    c. Giving teenagers the freedom to set their own curfews
    d. Allowing children to participate in family decisions

93. A teacher who suspects that a student is being physically abused by a parent should:
    a. talk to the student and try to discover the truth of the situation.
    b. talk to the parents before risking an unfounded accusation.
    c. consult with trusted colleagues to decide upon an appropriate course of action.
    d. immediately report suspicions to police or child protective services.

94. Professional intervention is most likely to be recommended for a 16-year-old boy who:
    a. was caught drinking beer at a friend's birthday party.
    b. repeatedly forgets to perform household chores.
    c. has lost interest in most of the activities he previously enjoyed.
    d. expresses sadness about breaking up with his girlfriend.

95. In treating cases of child abuse or neglect, the main objective is to:
    a. teach the child how to cope with living in an abusive environment.
    b. identify and punish all parties involved in the abuse.
    c. find a suitable foster home for the abused or neglected child.
    d. return the child to a safe, healthy family environment.

96. A 15-year-old girl is being pressured by her friends to attend a party at which alcohol is likely to be served. Which advice would probably be most useful to her?
    a. Tell your friends you'll go, but make up some last-minute excuse to stay home.
    b. Tell your friends that you'd love to go, but you're afraid you might get in trouble with your parents.
    c. Don't let your friends bully you. Stand up for your beliefs and do what you think is right.
    d. Attend the party, but don't drink.

97. Which pair of foods is included in two different food groups in the USDA's updated food pyramid?
    a. Chicken and eggs
    b. Soy beans and chickpeas
    c. Salmon and peanuts
    d. Sesame seeds and octopus

Answer Key and Explanations

1. **B:** Parents communicate their message about substance abuse most effectively through their own attitudes and behavior. Parents should never encourage illegal behavior, nor should they expect any lecture to their children to overshadow the influence of the personal example they set in the home.

2. **C:** Due to the length and location of the female urethra, young women are three times as likely as young men to develop urinary tract infections. During intercourse, bacteria are easily pushed into the bladder.

3. **C:** One of the main ways people catch colds is by touching their eyes, nose, or mouth after coming in contact with an infected person or object. Thorough hand washing can prevent the spread of colds and other illnesses. Most scientists dispute the value of vitamin C in preventing or treating the common cold.

4. **C:** Despite the natural instinct to clean oneself after an attack, a rape victim should not shower or change clothes before seeking immediate medical and legal assistance.

5. **A:** Young people generally feel themselves to be invincible and show little regard for the future consequences of their behavior. More immediate concerns are shortages of cash, romantic rejection, and athletic inadequacy.

6. **D:** A quantitative blood test can accurately detect the pregnancy hormone hCG (human chorionic gonadotropin) as early as a week after ovulation. Skipped periods may be symptomatic of conditions other than pregnancy, while home tests may yield false negatives.

7. **A:** The body's main fuel is the simple sugar glucose. Complex carbohydrates provide the body with sustained energy by slowly breaking down into glucose.

8. **C:** A high-fiber diet supplies the body with many essential vitamins and minerals and may help lower cholesterol levels. A high-fiber diet may be problematic for people with IBS.

9. **B:** While strenuous exercise is likely to trigger an asthma attack, moderate exercise is essential to good health and rarely represents a danger to asthma sufferers. Choices A, C, and D are common triggers for asthma.

10. **A:** People with type-1 diabetes cannot produce the insulin needed to regulate sugar levels. They need to practice moderation in their physical activities as well as in their sugar intake.

11. **D:** Peer mediation teaches kids to solve problems nonviolently without adult interference. Ultimately, it is a more effective problem-solving strategy than handing out rewards or imposing punishments to settle disputes.

12. **A:** Better known as Quaaludes, methaqualone is a sedative. Unlike the stimulants amphetamine, ecstasy, and cocaine, depressants work by slowing down the central nervous system.

13. D: Generics are generally the same as their name-brand counterparts in every respect except price.

14. C: The Drug-Induced Rape Prevention and Punishment Act of 1996 imposed strict penalties for abuse of the so-called date-rape drugs. GHB is odorless and tasteless, ketamine is a depressant, and Rohypnol is not legally available in the United States.

15. A: Saturated fat is found primarily in beef, pork, lamb, cheese, and egg yolks. It tends to raise the level of LDL, or "bad cholesterol," in the blood. Nuts and beans are generally a good source of monounsaturated fat, which tend to lower harmful cholesterol levels.

16. D: Although choices A, B, and C are all valid safety measures for gun owners, the incidence of homicide is three times greater in households where firearms are present than in homes without weapons.

17. D: While playing sports is excellent for cardiovascular fitness, weight training builds muscle strength and endurance. Resistance training for young people should be limited to three times a week. It builds strength most efficiently when less weight is lifted many times.

18. A: Contusions are often characterized by ruptured blood vessels and discoloration. Choice B describes a strain; Choice C describes a sprain; Choice D describes a concussion.

19. D: Psychiatrists and pediatricians are medical doctors who can legally prescribe drugs to their patients.

20. D: A normal concern about grades is not indicative of suicidal tendencies. Among the highest suicide risks are teenagers with substance abuse problems, those who have lost a friend or relative to suicide, and those who have been repeatedly tormented in regard to sexual preferences.

21. C: Health insurance is of no value unless it covers whichever medical services may be required. Not all policies are alike, so price is not the only factor to consider. Because no one knows when illness may strike, none but the extremely wealthy can afford to be uninsured.

22. C: Anabolic steroids are illegally used by professional athletes to increase lean muscle mass. Despite the serious side-effects, three-fourths of all steroid users are teenagers.

23. D: Weight control and body-building are likely to be of greater immediate interest to a young adolescent boy than such distant, seemingly abstract goals as avoiding disease and getting into college.

24. C: "Latchkey kids" are the norm in many communities. Experts generally concur that 11-year-olds are sufficiently mature to be left home alone for short periods of time during daylight hours.

25. A: Physicians will generally uphold the privacy rights of young patients as long as doing so does not pose a danger to themselves or others; however, federal and state guidelines concerning a minor's right to medical confidentiality are not always clear-cut.

26. D: The Americans with Disabilities Act protects individuals with specific learning problems against job discrimination. The law applies to employers of 15 or more workers. The EEOC is empowered to investigate alleged violations.

27. D: The law also toughened penalties for anyone using the Internet to entice minors to engage in criminal sexual activity.

28. C: Vitamin D supports bone development by facilitating the body's absorption of calcium. Although the human body naturally produces vitamin D as a reaction to sunlight, some nutritionists believe that supplements in excess of 1,000 IU daily could be beneficial.

29. B: Male gang members no longer vastly outnumber female members. Although gang membership has grown in both rural and suburban areas, many adolescents are more interested in the social aspect of gang membership than in engaging in criminal activities.

30. B: Girls are twice as likely as boys to experience depression during adolescence. Some depressed adolescents do not act sad at all and are consequently misdiagnosed as having ADHD or a learning disorder.

31. C: Recurrent aggressive behavior is more commonly symptomatic of the manic phase of bipolar disorder.

32. C: Mental health disorders are serious medical conditions that require prompt professional attention. Neither patients nor their parents should feel embarrassed if medication proves to be necessary for effective treatment.

33. D: Cognitive therapy teaches patients not to dwell on negative thoughts that lead to stress. Often combined with behavioral therapy, it employs techniques that are more sophisticated than those implied by the generalizations expressed in choices A, B, and C.

34. B: These psychostimulant medications allow ADHD patients to focus their attention by helping them tune out distractions. They are not the same as the antidepressants sometimes used to treat other psychiatric disorders.

35. D: Reye's syndrome is a rare but potentially fatal disease. Studies have established a causal relationship between aspirin use by children and the development of Reye's syndrome. Aspirin in any form should not be ingested by anyone under the age of 19.

36. C: At least one parent must be present in developing the IEP, but the student is not required to participate in the process. Eligibility for special education is determined by testing, and transportation to and from school is always covered under IDEA.

37. B: While aerobic exercise primarily benefits the cardiorespiratory system, anaerobic exercise, such as weight lifting or rope jumping, builds strength by using muscles at high intensity for a short period of time.

38. D: Annual Pap smears effectively screen for cervical cancer by detecting sexually transmitted HPVs.

39. B: The monounsaturated fat found in olives, nuts, and legumes help lower harmful LDL cholesterol levels in the blood.

40. A: During adolescence, bones are actively growing and absorbing calcium from the blood. A vegan diet excludes calcium-rich dairy products, and calcium from vegetable sources is generally not as well absorbed by the body as the calcium in milk, yogurt, and cheese.

41. C: Fiber-rich foods include whole grains and legumes as well as most fruits and vegetables.

42. B: According to the National Heart, Lung and Blood Institute, a normal BMI, which describes weight relative to height, is between 19 and 24.9. Obesity is defined as a BMI over 30.

43. D: Tendons are most often injured due to excessive, repeated strain. Overuse injuries are common in such repetitive motion activities as running, swimming, and dancing. Collision sports such as those in choices A, B, and C are more likely to lead to acute injuries.

44. B: Warming up properly is important for the reasons cited in choices A, C, and D, but it does not build muscles.

45. B: Heat cramps are less severe and dangerous than heat exhaustion or heatstroke. Patients can usually be treated with fluids, massage, and several hours of rest.

46. B: Any STD requires prompt diagnosis and treatment. Parental concern notwithstanding, confidentiality between doctor and patient is guaranteed by law.

47. B: Common in young people between the ages of 15 and 19, chlamydia is a potentially dangerous bacterial infection that is often asymptomatic in its early stages.

48. D: All sex partners need to be screened as soon as possible to break the chain of infection.

49. A: There are more than 100 types of HPV, which are associated with genital warts and cervical cancer. The warts can usually be managed, if not cured, with topical treatments.

50. A: Emergency contraception pills do not result in abortion; rather, they are high-dosage birth control pills that prevent fertilization from occurring. The pills must be taken within 72 hours of sexual activity.

51. D: While compulsive overeaters resemble bulimics in the ways mentioned in choices A, B, and C, they do not generally induce vomiting or exercise obsessively in an effort to change their bodies. Despite the serious health risks associated with obesity, binge-eaters face fewer immediate health consequences than do bulimics, who consistently binge and purge.

52. C: Only latex condoms offer protection from STDs. No other method of birth control is as safe and inexpensive as abstinence, and no other method is 100% effective.

53. C: Studies show that there is no more stressful event in most children's lives than the death of a parent. Choices A, B, and C closely follow on the ALCES.

54. D: Channeling negative feelings into socially-acceptable outlets, or *sublimation*, is a defense mechanism used to cope with stressful situations. Months or even years may pass before a child allows himself to fully feel and express the grief associated with a loved one's death.

55. C: Although most children effectively cope with the problems associated with growing up in a single-family household, statistics show that the traditional two-parent household is most conducive to successful child-rearing.

56. D: Fat-free food products are often laden with sugar and high in calories. For optimal health, fat-free snack items should be replaced with naturally low-fat and low-calorie foods.

57. A: African-American girls generally have a year's head start in breast development and menstruation. Breast development normally precedes menstruation, which precedes the growth of underarm hair.

58. D: More young people die each year as a result of motor vehicle accidents than from homicide, poisoning, and suffocation combined.

59. B: Breasts normally grow larger during pregnancy. Hair tends to grow faster, appetite is increased, and weight increases by approximately 15 to 40 pounds.

60. B: There is no substantiated evidence linking vaccination or environmental factors to an increased incidence of autism. It is more likely that more cases have been reported in recent years because parents and doctors have been more successful in recognizing and correctly diagnosing early indications of the disorder.

61. B: In most ectopic pregnancies, the embryo attaches to the lining of the fallopian tube instead of implanting in the uterine wall. Left untreated, an ectopic pregnancy can be fatal. Choice C describes the normal process of ovulation. Choice D describes endometriosis.

62. B: The autonomic nervous system maintains homeostasis in the body. For the most part, it is not subject to voluntary control.

63. D: While ordinary, daily stress has little effect on the skin, unusual emotional stress can stimulate the production of sebum in the sebaceous glands. Chocolate, greasy foods, and ordinary face-washing generally have no effect on acne.

64. D: When it comes to CPR, doing something is almost always better than doing nothing at all. Chest compressions alone can often save someone's life.

65. C: Anaphylaxis is a severe reaction that occurs when certain allergic individuals come into contact with even a minute quantity of the substance they are allergic to. Common allergens include insect stings, peanuts, shellfish, and penicillin.

66. C: Heroin use has grown among adolescents in recent years due to lower prices and increased availability. Because today's street heroin is much purer than the heroin commonly available in the past, it can be effectively snorted or smoked instead of injected, which increases its appeal to first-time adolescent users.

67. B: To qualify for aid, applicants must live with a responsible adult or in an adult-supervised setting. They are also required to participate in qualified educational and training activities.

68. D: The SPF rating is calculated by comparing the amount of time needed to produce a sunburn on protected skin to the amount of time needed to cause a sunburn on unprotected skin. Theoretically, a person who normally burns in 20 minutes could use a SPF 30 sunscreen to stay in the sun for 600 minutes (20 x 30) without burning. In practice, however, sunscreens are often applied too sparingly or are washed away by perspiration and thus do not provide full protection.

69. A: Although drugs like Ritalin and Adderall are often abused when obtained by young people for whom they were not prescribed, they have proved to be generally safe and efficacious when properly used by the patients who need them.

70. A: Because type AB blood carries both A and B antigens, a person with this blood type can receive blood from any blood group but can only give blood to someone whose blood carries the same antigens. Type O carries neither A nor B antigens and is therefore compatible with all blood groups.

71. A: Women are much more likely to be the victims of domestic violence than are men, and their abuse is frequently witnessed by their children. The overwhelming majority of men do not perpetrate domestic violence in their lifetimes.

72. C: Sugar causes insulin levels to spike, which contributes to weight gain and cell inflammation. Diabetics need to be extremely cautious about any sugar intake.

73. A: The recommended dietary allowance of iron for women ages 19 to 50 is 18 mg daily. While all menstruating women are at risk of being iron deficient, women on birth control pills generally experience less bleeding and thus lose less iron. Men over 19 and women over 60 require only 8 mg. of iron daily, which is readily obtainable in most non-vegetarian diets.

74. C: Unlike the California Walnut Commission, the American Heart Association does not have a commercial interest in promoting the health benefits of eating walnuts. Popular magazines and television health reports are likely to oversimplify the information they present, which, in this case, would probably be based on the Walnut Commission's press release.

75. C: Testing is the only sure way to determine whether radon is present. Radon can be a problem in a house of any age, with or without a basement or cracked foundation.

76. C: Direct pressure constricts the blood vessels and stems blood flow. Pressure on the carotid artery can cause brain damage. Tourniquets can damage nerves and blood vessels. Attempting to clean a deep wound may increase bleeding.

77. B: Alateen is dedicated to helping young people cope with alcoholic family members. Alcoholics Anonymous helps its members to achieve and maintain sobriety. The NIAAA conducts research on alcohol-related problems, while the Center for Substance Abuse Treatment offers referrals to drug and alcohol treatment programs.

78. D: A reading of 140/90 is the minimal definition of hypertension. Choices A and B represent normal blood pressure, while choice C would be characterized as high-normal, or prehypertension, and would probably be observed for a period of time before medication would be deemed appropriate.

79. A: A healthy, efficient heart pumps more blood each time it beats and can therefore beat at a slower rate. Physical activity contributes to good health by increasing arterial elasticity, blood volume, and thyroid function.

80. A: The precise amount of alcohol required to cause fetal alcohol syndrome is not known. Alcohol interferes with normal fetal growth and must be completely avoided during pregnancy.

81. B: Children are expected to reach certain mental, emotional, and behavioral milestones before they are old enough to attend school. A child who has not learned to speak in short sentences by four years of age, for example, probably needs to be evaluated by a learning specialist.

82. A: A booster shot for tetanus is recommended every 10 years. Whooping cough is the same as pertussis, which is included in the diphtheria, tetanus, and pertussis vaccine. The vaccine does not protect a child from hepatitis B, but it does give lifelong protection from diphtheria.

83. D: Folic acid deficiency can cause cleft lip and cleft palate. These conditions are not associated with radiation or cleaning litter boxes, although the latter can lead to toxoplasmosis. Amniocentesis may detect, but not prevent, these birth defects.

84. B: The American Lung Association is dedicated to improving lung health, focusing on asthma, smoking prevention, and pollution control. While choices A, C, and D all provide information on health issues, they are not focused on respiratory disorders.

85. C: Rationalization is a defense mechanism whereby people attempt to hide their true feelings by providing alternative explanations for unacceptable behavior. Rather than admit that she is disappointed, the girl pretends that she is glad not to have been cast in the play.

86. B: Young female drivers are involved in fewer accidents than males. In 2004, the rate of motor vehicle fatalities for males age 16 to 19 was one-and-a-half times that of their female counterparts.

87. B: Vitamin B12 is derived almost exclusively from animal products, which are excluded from a vegan diet. While a well-planned vegan diet can easily provide an adequate supply of fiber, vitamin C, and folic acid, it should probably include supplements of B12 or food products fortified with the vitamin.

88. B: Middle-school students are expected to acquire all of these skills, but only choice B specifically involves the application of critical-thinking and problem-solving skills.

89. D: Health teachers should know about personality disorders and be familiar with the options that exist for their diagnosis and treatment; however, they are not trained to be therapeutic or psychiatric professionals.

90. A: Current guidelines focus on maximizing circulation, and studies show that circulation must be rebuilt each time chest compression is interrupted. The goal is 100 compressions per minute. Choices B, C, and D describe previous Red Cross guidelines.

91. D: Piercings are often done improperly or are not cared for adequately during the healing process. Piercings are rarely performed using painkillers, and healing may take anywhere from a few weeks to a year. Various methods of tattoo removal exist, but scarring and skin color variations usually remain.

92. C: Healthy family interactions involve building trust, expressing affection, and setting limits. Few adolescents are mature enough to be given free rein in setting curfews. Setting reasonable curfews shows teens that parents care about their safety, and obeying family rules allows the adolescent to show that he or she can be trusted to behave responsibly.

93. D: Teachers in all 50 states are legally required to report any reasonable suspicion of child abuse to the proper authorities. Abused children often deny abuse to protect an abusive parent.

94. C: Loss of interest in pleasurable activities may be symptomatic of depression, which requires therapeutic intervention. It is not unusual for adolescents to try alcohol, forget to do chores, or be despondent over a failed romance.

95. D: The child's welfare is always of primary importance. It is often possible to take corrective measures that allow a child to be safely returned to his or her family. Punishment of the guilty parties is generally less constructive than finding and eliminating the causes of neglect or abuse.

96. C: Teenagers need to learn how to say "no" to peers who urge them to violate their core beliefs. Making up excuses is not as useful in the long run as learning how to think about consequences and then having the courage to do the right thing.

97. B: The current food pyramid includes the subgroup "dry beans and peas" as part of both the "vegetable" group and the "meat and beans" group. Choices A, C, and D are all included in the "meat and beans" group.

Secret Key #1 – Time is Your Greatest Enemy

To succeed on the GACE, you must use your time wisely. Many students do not finish at least one section. The time constraints are brutal. To succeed, you must ration your time properly.

Pace Yourself

Wear a watch. At the beginning of the test, check the time (or start a chronometer on your watch to count the minutes), and check the time after every few questions to make sure you are "on schedule."

If you are forced to speed up, do it efficiently. Usually one or more answer choices can be eliminated without too much difficulty. Above all, don't panic. Don't speed up and just begin guessing at random choices. By pacing yourself, and continually monitoring your progress against your watch, you will always know exactly how far ahead or behind you are with your available time. If you find that you are one minute behind on the test, don't skip one question without spending any time on it, just to catch back up. Take 15 fewer seconds on the next four questions, and after four questions you'll have caught back up. Once you catch back up, you can continue working each problem at your normal pace.

Furthermore, don't dwell on the problems that you were rushed on. If a problem was taking up too much time and you made a hurried guess, it must be difficult. The difficult questions are the ones you are most likely to miss anyway, so it isn't a big loss. It is better to end with more time than you need than to run out of time.

Lastly, sometimes it is beneficial to slow down if you are constantly getting ahead of time. You are always more likely to catch a careless mistake by working more slowly than quickly, and among very high-scoring test takers (those who are likely to have lots of time left over), careless errors affect the score more than mastery of material.

Secret Key #2 - Guessing is not Guesswork

You probably know that guessing is a good idea - unlike other standardized tests, there is no penalty for getting a wrong answer. Even if you have no idea about a question, you still have a 20-25% chance of getting it right.

Most test takers do not understand the impact that proper guessing can have on their score. Unless you score extremely high, guessing will significantly contribute to your final score.

Monkeys Take the Test

What most test takers don't realize is that to insure that 20-25% chance, you have to guess randomly. If you put 20 monkeys in a room to take this test, assuming they answered once per question and behaved themselves, on average they would get 20-25% of the questions correct. Put 20 test takers in the room, and the average will be much lower among guessed questions. Why?

1. The test writers intentionally writes deceptive answer choices that "look" right. A test taker has no idea about a question, so picks the "best looking" answer, which is often wrong. The monkey has no idea what looks good and what doesn't, so will consistently be lucky about 20-25% of the time.
2. Test takers will eliminate answer choices from the guessing pool based on a hunch or intuition. Simple but correct answers often get excluded, leaving a 0% chance of being correct. The monkey has no clue, and often gets lucky with the best choice.

This is why the process of elimination endorsed by most test courses is flawed and detrimental to your performance- test takers don't guess, they make an ignorant stab in the dark that is usually worse than random.

$5 Challenge

Let me introduce one of the most valuable ideas of this course- the $5 challenge:

You only mark your "best guess" if you are willing to bet $5 on it.
You only eliminate choices from guessing if you are willing to bet $5 on it.

Why $5? Five dollars is an amount of money that is small yet not insignificant, and can really add up fast (20 questions could cost you $100). Likewise, each answer choice on one question of the test will have a small impact on your overall score, but it can really add up to a lot of points in the end.

The process of elimination IS valuable.

However, if you accidentally eliminate the right answer or go on a hunch for an incorrect answer, your chances drop dramatically: to 0%. By guessing among all the answer choices, you are GUARANTEED to have a shot at the right answer.

That's why the $5 test is so valuable- if you give up the advantage and safety of a pure guess, it had better be worth the risk.

What we still haven't covered is how to be sure that whatever guess you make is truly random. Here's the easiest way:

Always pick the first answer choice among those remaining.

Such a technique means that you have decided, before you see a single test question, exactly how you are going to guess- and since the order of choices tells you nothing about

which one is correct, this guessing technique is perfectly random.

This section is not meant to scare you away from making educated guesses or eliminating choices- you just need to define when a choice is worth eliminating. The $5 test, along with a pre-defined random guessing strategy, is the best way to make sure you reap all of the benefits of guessing.

Secret Key #3 - Practice Smarter, Not Harder

Many test takers delay the test preparation process because they dread the awful amounts of practice time they think necessary to succeed on the test. We have refined an effective method that will take you only a fraction of the time.

There are a number of "obstacles" in your way to succeed. Among these are answering questions, finishing in time, and mastering test-taking strategies. All must be executed on the day of the test at peak performance, or your score will suffer. The test is a mental marathon that has a large impact on your future.

Just like a marathon runner, it is important to work your way up to the full challenge. So first you just worry about questions, and then time, and finally strategy:

Success Strategy

1. Find a good source for practice tests.
2. If you are willing to make a larger time investment, consider using more than one study guide- often the different approaches of multiple authors will help you "get" difficult concepts.
3. Take a practice test with no time constraints, with all study helps "open book." Take your time with questions

and focus on applying strategies.
4. Take a practice test with time constraints, with all guides "open book."
5. Take a final practice test with no open material and time limits

If you have time to take more practice tests, just repeat step 5. By gradually exposing yourself to the full rigors of the test environment, you will condition your mind to the stress of test day and maximize your success.

Secret Key #4 - Prepare, Don't Procrastinate

Let me state an obvious fact: if you take the test three times, you will get three different scores. This is due to the way you feel on test day, the level of preparedness you have, and, despite the test writers' claims to the contrary, some tests WILL be easier for you than others.

Since your future depends so much on your score, you should maximize your chances of success. In order to maximize the likelihood of success, you've got to prepare in advance. This means taking practice tests and spending time learning the information and test taking strategies you will need to succeed.

Never take the test as a "practice" test, expecting that you can just take it again if you need to. Feel free to take sample tests on your own, but when you go to take the official test, be prepared, be focused, and do your best the first time!

Secret Key #5 - Test Yourself

Everyone knows that time is money. There is no need to spend too much of your time or too little of your time preparing for the test.

You should only spend as much of your precious time preparing as is necessary for you to get the score you need.

Once you have taken a practice test under real conditions of time constraints, then you will know if you are ready for the test or not.

If you have scored extremely high the first time that you take the practice test, then there is not much point in spending countless hours studying. You are already there.

Benchmark your abilities by retaking practice tests and seeing how much you have improved. Once you score high enough to guarantee success, then you are ready.

If you have scored well below where you need, then knuckle down and begin studying in earnest. Check your improvement regularly through the use of practice tests under real conditions. Above all, don't worry, panic, or give up. The key is perseverance!

Then, when you go to take the test, remain confident and remember how well you did on the practice tests. If you can score high enough on a practice test, then you can do the same on the real thing.

General Strategies

The most important thing you can do is to ignore your fears and jump into the test immediately- do not be overwhelmed by any strange-sounding terms. You have to jump into the test like jumping into a pool- all at once is the easiest way.

Make Predictions

As you read and understand the question, try to guess what the answer will be. Remember that several of the answer choices are wrong, and once you begin reading them, your mind will immediately become cluttered with answer choices designed to throw you off. Your mind is typically the most focused immediately after you have read the question and digested its contents. If you can, try to predict what the correct answer will be. You may be surprised at what you can predict.

Quickly scan the choices and see if your prediction is in the listed answer choices. If it is, then you can be quite confident that you have the right answer. It still won't hurt to check the other answer choices, but most of the time, you've got it!

Answer the Question

It may seem obvious to only pick answer choices that answer the question, but the test writers can create some excellent answer choices that are wrong. Don't pick an answer just because it sounds right, or you believe it to be true. It MUST answer the question. Once you've made your selection, always go back and check it against the question and make sure that you didn't misread the question, and the answer choice does answer the question posed.

Benchmark

After you read the first answer choice, decide if you think it sounds correct or not. If it doesn't, move on to the next answer choice. If it does, mentally mark that answer choice. This doesn't mean that you've definitely selected it as your answer choice, it just means that it's the best you've seen thus far. Go ahead and read the next choice. If the next choice is worse than the one you've already selected, keep going to the next answer choice. If the next choice is better than the choice you've already selected, mentally mark the new answer choice as your best guess.

The first answer choice that you select becomes your standard. Every other answer choice must be benchmarked against that standard. That choice is correct until proven otherwise by another answer choice beating it out. Once you've decided that no other answer choice seems as good, do one final check to ensure that your answer choice answers the question posed.

Valid Information

Don't discount any of the information provided in the question. Every piece of information may be necessary to determine the correct answer. None of the information in the question is there to throw you off (while the answer choices will certainly have information to throw you off). If two seemingly unrelated topics are discussed, don't ignore either. You can be confident there is a relationship, or it wouldn't be included in the question, and you are probably going to have to determine what is that relationship to find the answer.

Avoid "Fact Traps"

Don't get distracted by a choice that is factually true. Your search is for the answer that answers the question. Stay focused and don't fall for an answer that is true but incorrect. Always go back to the question and make sure you're choosing an answer that actually answers the question and is not just a true statement. An answer can be factually correct, but it MUST answer the question asked. Additionally, two answers can both be seemingly correct, so be sure to read all of the answer choices, and make sure that you get the one that BEST answers the question.

Milk the Question

Some of the questions may throw you completely off. They might deal with a subject you have not been exposed to, or one that you haven't reviewed in years. While your lack of knowledge about the subject will be a hindrance, the question itself can give you many clues that will help you find the correct answer. Read the question carefully and look for clues. Watch particularly for adjectives and nouns describing difficult terms or words that you don't recognize. Regardless of if you completely understand a word or not, replacing it with a synonym either provided or one you more familiar with may help you to understand what the questions are asking. Rather than wracking your mind about specific detailed information

- 164 -

concerning a difficult term or word, try to use mental substitutes that are easier to understand.

The Trap of Familiarity

Don't just choose a word because you recognize it. On difficult questions, you may not recognize a number of words in the answer choices. The test writers don't put "make-believe" words on the test; so don't think that just because you only recognize all the words in one answer choice means that answer choice must be correct. If you only recognize words in one answer choice, then focus on that one. Is it correct? Try your best to determine if it is correct. If it is, that is great, but if it doesn't, eliminate it. Each word and answer choice you eliminate increases your chances of getting the question correct, even if you then have to guess among the unfamiliar choices.

Eliminate Answers

Eliminate choices as soon as you realize they are wrong. But be careful! Make sure you consider all of the possible answer choices. Just because one appears right, doesn't mean that the next one won't be even better! The test writers will usually put more than one good answer choice for every question, so read all of them. Don't worry if you are stuck between two that seem right. By getting down to just two remaining possible choices, your odds are now 50/50. Rather than wasting too much time, play the odds. You are guessing, but guessing wisely, because you've been able to knock out some of the answer choices that you know are wrong. If you are eliminating choices and realize that the last answer choice you are left with is also obviously wrong, don't panic. Start over and consider each choice again. There may easily be something that you missed the first time and will realize on the second pass.

Tough Questions

If you are stumped on a problem or it appears too hard or too difficult, don't waste time.

Move on! Remember though, if you can quickly check for obviously incorrect answer choices, your chances of guessing correctly are greatly improved. Before you completely give up, at least try to knock out a couple of possible answers. Eliminate what you can and then guess at the remaining answer choices before moving on.

Brainstorm

If you get stuck on a difficult question, spend a few seconds quickly brainstorming. Run through the complete list of possible answer choices. Look at each choice and ask yourself, "Could this answer the question satisfactorily?" Go through each answer choice and consider it independently of the other. By systematically going through all possibilities, you may find something that you would otherwise overlook. Remember that when you get stuck, it's important to try to keep moving.

Read Carefully

Understand the problem. Read the question and answer choices carefully. Don't miss the question because you misread the terms. You have plenty of time to read each question thoroughly and make sure you understand what is being asked. Yet a happy medium must be attained, so don't waste too much time. You must read carefully, but efficiently.

Face Value

When in doubt, use common sense. Always accept the situation in the problem at face value. Don't read too much into it. These problems will not require you to make huge leaps of logic. The test writers aren't trying to throw you off with a cheap trick. If you have to go beyond creativity and make a leap of logic in order to have an answer choice answer the question, then you should look at the other answer choices. Don't overcomplicate the problem by creating theoretical relationships or explanations that will warp time or space. These are normal problems rooted in reality. It's just that the applicable relationship or explanation may not be readily apparent and you have to figure things out. Use your common sense to interpret anything that isn't clear.

Prefixes

If you're having trouble with a word in the question or answer choices, try dissecting it. Take advantage of every clue that the word might include. Prefixes and suffixes can be a huge help. Usually they allow you to determine a basic meaning. Pre- means before, post- means after, pro - is positive, de- is negative. From these prefixes and suffixes, you can get an idea of the general meaning of the word and try to put it into context. Beware though of any traps. Just because con is the opposite of pro, doesn't necessarily mean congress is the opposite of progress!

Hedge Phrases

Watch out for critical "hedge" phrases, such as likely, may, can, will often, sometimes, often, almost, mostly, usually, generally, rarely, sometimes. Question writers insert these hedge phrases to cover every possibility. Often an answer choice will be wrong simply because it leaves no room for exception. Avoid answer choices that have definitive words like "exactly," and "always".

Switchback Words

Stay alert for "switchbacks". These are the words and phrases frequently used to alert you to shifts in thought. The most common switchback word is "but". Others include although, however, nevertheless, on the other hand, even though, while, in spite of, despite, regardless of.

New Information

Correct answer choices will rarely have completely new information included. Answer choices typically are straightforward reflections of the material asked about and will directly relate to the question. If a new piece of information is included in an answer choice that doesn't even seem to relate to the topic being asked about, then that answer choice is likely incorrect. All of the information needed to answer the question is usually provided for you, and so you should not have to make guesses that are unsupported or choose answer choices that require unknown information that cannot be reasoned on its own.

Time Management

On technical questions, don't get lost on the technical terms. Don't spend too much time on any one question. If you don't know what a term means, then since you don't have a dictionary, odds are you aren't going to get much further. You should immediately recognize terms as whether or not you know them. If you don't, work with the other clues that you have, the other answer choices and terms provided, but don't waste too much time trying to figure out a difficult term.

Contextual Clues

Look for contextual clues. An answer can be right but not correct. The contextual clues will help you find the answer that is most right and is correct. Understand the context in which a phrase or statement is made. This will help you make important distinctions.

Don't Panic

Panicking will not answer any questions for you. Therefore, it isn't helpful. When you first see the question, if your mind goes blank, take a deep breath. Force yourself to mechanically go through the steps of solving the problem and using the strategies you've learned.

Pace Yourself

Don't get clock fever. It's easy to be overwhelmed when you're looking at a page full of questions, your mind is full of random thoughts and feeling confused, and the clock is ticking down faster than you would like. Calm down and maintain the pace that you have set for yourself. As long as you are on track by monitoring your pace, you are guaranteed to have enough time for yourself. When you get to the last few minutes of the test, it may seem like you won't have enough time left, but if you only have as many questions as you should have left at that point, then you're right on track!

Answer Selection

The best way to pick an answer choice is to eliminate all of those that are wrong, until only one is left and confirm that is the correct answer. Sometimes though, an answer choice may immediately look right. Be careful! Take a second to make sure that the other choices are not equally obvious. Don't make a hasty mistake. There are only two times that you should stop before checking other answers. First is when you are positive that the answer choice you have selected is correct. Second is when time is almost out and you have to make a quick guess!

Check Your Work

Since you will probably not know every term listed and the answer to every question, it is important that you get credit for the ones that you do know. Don't miss any questions through careless mistakes. If at all possible, try to take a second to look back over your answer selection and make sure you've selected the correct answer choice and haven't made a costly careless mistake (such as marking an answer choice that you didn't mean to mark). This quick double check should more than pay for itself in caught mistakes for the time it costs.

Beware of Directly Quoted Answers

Sometimes an answer choice will repeat word for word a portion of the question or reference section. However, beware of such exact duplication – it may be a trap! More than likely, the correct choice will paraphrase or summarize a point, rather than being exactly the same wording.

Slang

Scientific sounding answers are better than slang ones. An answer choice that begins "To compare the outcomes…" is much more likely to be correct than one that begins "Because some people insisted…"

Extreme Statements

Avoid wild answers that throw out highly controversial ideas that are proclaimed as established fact. An answer choice that states the "process should be used in certain situations, if…" is much more likely to be correct than one that states the "process should be discontinued completely." The first is a calm rational statement and doesn't even make a definitive, uncompromising stance, using a hedge word "if" to provide wiggle room, whereas the second choice is a radical idea and far more extreme.

Answer Choice Families

When you have two or more answer choices that are direct opposites or parallels, one of them is usually the correct answer. For instance, if one answer choice states "x increases" and another answer choice states "x decreases" or "y increases," then those two or three answer choices are very similar in construction and fall into the same family of answer choices. A family of answer choices is when two or three answer choices are very similar in construction, and yet often have a directly opposite meaning. Usually the correct answer choice will be in that family of answer choices. The "odd man out" or answer choice that doesn't seem to fit the parallel construction of the other answer choices is more likely to be incorrect.

Special Report: What Your Test Score Will Tell You About Your IQ

Did you know that most standardized tests correlate very strongly with IQ? In fact, your general intelligence is a better predictor of your success than any other factor, and most tests intentionally measure this trait to some degree to ensure that those selected by the test are truly qualified for the test's purposes.

Before we can delve into the relation between your test score and IQ, I will first have to explain what exactly is IQ. Here's the formula:

Your IQ = 100 + (Number of standard deviations below or above the average)*15

Now, let's define standard deviations by using an example. If we have 5 people with 5 different heights, then first we calculate the average. Let's say the average was 65 inches. The standard deviation is the "average distance" away from the average of each of the members. It is a direct measure of variability - if the 5 people included Jackie Chan and Shaquille O'Neal, obviously there's a lot more variability in that group than a group of 5 sisters who are all within 6 inches in height of each other. The standard deviation uses a number to characterize the average range of difference within a group.

A convenient feature of most groups is that they have a "normal" distribution- makes sense that most things would be normal, right? Without getting into a bunch of statistical mumbo-jumbo, you just need to know that if you know the average of the group and the standard deviation, you can successfully predict someone's percentile rank in the group.

Confused? Let me give you an example. If instead of 5 people's heights, we had 100 people, we could figure out their rank in height JUST by knowing the average, standard deviation, and their height. We wouldn't need to know each person's height and manually rank them, we could just predict their rank based on three numbers.

What this means is that you can take your PERCENTILE rank that is often given with your test and relate this to your RELATIVE IQ of people taking the test - that is, your IQ relative to the people taking the test. Obviously, there's no way to know your actual IQ because the people taking a standardized test are usually not very good samples of the general population- many of those with extremely low IQ's never achieve a level of success or competency necessary to complete a typical standardized test. In fact, professional psychologists who measure IQ actually have to use non-written tests that can fairly measure the IQ of those not able to complete a traditional test.

The bottom line is to not take your test score too seriously, but it is fun to compute your "relative IQ" among the people who took the test with you. I've done the calculations below. Just look up your percentile rank in the left and then you'll see your "relative IQ" for your test in the right hand column-

Percentile Rank	Your Relative IQ		Percentile Rank	Your Relative IQ
99	135		59	103
98	131		58	103
97	128		57	103
96	126		56	102
95	125		55	102
94	123		54	102
93	122		53	101
92	121		52	101
91	120		51	100
90	119		50	100
89	118		49	100
88	118		48	99
87	117		47	99
86	116		46	98
85	116		45	98
84	115		44	98
83	114		43	97
82	114		42	97
81	113		41	97
80	113		40	96
79	112		39	96
78	112		38	95
77	111		37	95
76	111		36	95
75	110		35	94
74	110		34	94
73	109		33	93
72	109		32	93
71	108		31	93
70	108		30	92
69	107		29	92
68	107		28	91
67	107		27	91
66	106		26	90
65	106		25	90
64	105		24	89
63	105		23	89
62	105		22	88
61	104		21	88
60	104		20	87

Special Report: Additional Bonus Material

Due to our efforts to try to keep this book to a manageable length, we've created a link that will give you access to all of your additional bonus material.

Please visit http://www.mometrix.com/bonus948/gacehealthphed to access the information.